D0085496

# The World Is Too Much with Us

# THE MODERN MISSION ERA, 1792–1992
## AN APPRAISAL
a series edited by Wilbert R. Shenk

THE MODERN MISSION ERA, 1792–1992
AN APPRAISAL

A SERIES EDITED BY WILBERT R. SHENK

# The World
# Is Too Much with Us
## "Culture"
## in Modern Protestant Missions

*by*
## Charles R. Taber

MERCER
MUP

To a dear brother and colleague
in the gospel,
Charles R. Taber

ISBN 0-86554-388-7

*The World Is Too Much with Us*
Copyright ©1991
Mercer University Press
Macon, Georgia 31207
All rights reserved
printed in the United States of America


The paper used in this publication meets
the minimum requirements of American National Standard
for Information Sciences— Permanence of Paper
for Printed Library Materials, ANSI Z39.48-1984.
∞


*Library of Congress Cataloging-in-Publication Data*
Taber, Charles R.
The world is too much with us : ''culture'' in
modern Protestant missions / by Charles R. Taber.

xxiv + 208pp. 6″ × 9″ (15 × 23 cm.) — The modern mission era, 1792–1992: an appraisal
Includes bibliographical references and index.
ISBN 0-86554-388-7 (alk. paper)
1. Missions—Theory. 2. Christianity and culture—History—19th century. 3. Christianity and
culture—History—20th century. 4. Protestant
churches—Missions—History—19th century.
5. Protestant churches—Missions—History—20th
century. 6. Missions—Anthropological aspects.
I. Title. II. Series.
BV2063.T28      1990
266′.001—dc20                                90-26922
**CIP**

for
**BETTY,**
*my wife,*
*friend,*
*lover,*
*and partner*

# CONTENTS

# General Introduction

The modern mission movement emerged during the last years of the eighteenth century. Publication of William Carey's manifesto *An Enquiry Into the Obligations of Christians to Use Means for the Conversion of the Heathen* in 1792 has often been cited as the symbolic starting point. That same year the English Baptists, prodded by enthusiastic upstarts like Carey himself, formed the Baptist Missionary Society and the Carey family sailed for India the following year. During the next twenty-five years, groups of Christians in Great Britain, Europe, and North America, newly awakened to their missionary "obligations," founded an impressive array of mission societies.

Roman Catholic missions had suffered a major setback when Pope Clement XIV ordered dissolution of the Jesuits in 1773. After 1825 Roman Catholic missions began to recover as old missionary orders were revived and new ones were created.

The modern mission movement takes its name from the so-called modern period of world history, which began with the Enlightenment and the social, political, religious, and economic revolutions during the last third of the eighteenth century. The modern mission initiative would lead to far-reaching changes in the location and composition of the Christian church. During the final years of the twentieth century, more than half of all Christians were to be found outside the region that had been the historical heartland of Christianity for nearly fifteen hundred years. New centers of Christian strength and vitality were now to be found where missionary initiatives had been focused in widely scattered places in the Americas, Africa, and Asia. One must speak of missionary initiatives to indicate that from the beginning missionaries were joined in this endeavor by colaborers indigenous to a particular culture. Without such remarkable collaboration the enterprise would have had a quite different issue. As it was, modern missions fundamentally changed Christian identity.

The most important development in the eighteenth century was the Enlightenment—a powerful constellation of fresh ideas that released forces affecting all areas of human existence and inexorably extended to all parts of the globe. Through the core ideas it birthed, the Enlightenment redirected the course of human development. It was a European phenomenon and the Enlightenment fostered in Europeans a new spirit and outlook. In the words of Peter Gay, "In the century of the Enlightenment, educated Europeans awoke to a new sense of life. They experienced an expansive sense of power over nature and themselves."[1] This "new sense of life" was to have many ramifications. The Enlightenment Project was carried along by a dynamic Western messianism.

Before the end of the eighteenth century Enlightenment ideas had been translated into a political program—first in the formation of the United States of America, especially as enshrined in its constitution, but more radically in the French Revolution of 1789—based on liberal, democratic, and nationalist ideals. These revolutionary ideas have continued to reverberate throughout the world ever since, toppling one *ancien regime* after another.

The Enlightenment challenged religion with special intensity by its aggressive doctrine of the powers and possibilities of human reason joined with an attitude of radical skepticism. Religion increasingly was on the defensive. Some theologians sought to accommodate themselves to these new demands, fashioning a theology that conformed to the canons of the new science. Others reacted by intensifying their faith experience through movements such as Pietism and the Evangelical Revival. Where people managed to hold in tension inward piety and outward concern for the world, these renewal movements became engines of wide-ranging innovation, the modern mission movement being one of the most evident fruits.

As the end of the twentieth century approached it was increasingly agreed that the modern era had passed and the postmodern period had begun. Although it was too early to delineate fully the characteristics of the new epoch, some features were becoming evident. Intellectually, the long-dominant Enlightenment view of scientific knowledge had been superseded. Science was no longer understood to be sole arbiter of knowledge by virtue of holding the keys to inviolable "scientific" laws to which all branches of human knowledge had to answer. Science itself was now understood to be a product of culture and subject to historical conditioning.

---

[1]Peter Gay, *The Enlightenment—An Interpretation, vol. 2, The Science of Freedom* (New York: Alfred A. Knopf, 1969).

Politically, the postmodern era signaled the end of some five centuries of Western hegemony in the world. From the sixteenth century onward Western powers gradually came to dominate the world through economic, military, political, and intellectual means. The Spanish and Portuguese crowns, with the blessing of the church, were the first to take territories and create colonies in other parts of the world. Dutch, British, French, Danes, Germans, Italians, Russians, Americans, and Japanese all followed with their own colonial ventures. The American defeat in Vietnam in 1975 and rout of the Russians in Afghanistan together with the collapse of the socialist system in the 1980s signaled that a far-reaching geopolitical realignment was under way. In the postmodern world a restructuring of the international economic and political order had begun.

The advent of the postmodern period coincided with an epochal shift for the Christian church. Viewing the entire sweep of Christian history, some scholars have discerned just three periods, each defined by the geographical "center" and the sociopolitical tradition that predominated.

According to this view, the first stage of Christian expansion and development extended from the time of Jesus Christ to 70 C.E. This was the Jewish phase. The destruction of the temple in Jerusalem in 70 C.E. effectively ended Jewish influence on the Christian movement.

The Christian story then entered its second phase, the Hellenic-European, which lasted until well into the twentieth century. Europe soon became the geographical heartland. Christian expansion which endured was almost exclusively in European Christendom. World War II was a watershed in world affairs as well as for Christendom. Among conciliar Protestants, formation of the World Council of Churches in 1948 marked a new beginning. For Roman Catholics Vatican Council II, convened in 1962, represented a definitive transition. Conservative Protestants felt the impact of the approaching end of the old era as a result of major international events such as the Berlin Consultation on Evangelism in 1966 and the Lausanne Consultation on World Evangelization in 1974. For each ecclesiastical tradition the story was the same. The time of European dominance was coming to an end and church leaders from other parts of the world increasingly filled leadership roles.

This transition from the Hellenic-European phase to the postmodern was a direct result of the modern mission movement. In this respect the modern mission movement contributed in no small measure to bringing about an end to historical Christendom. The line of development from Jerusalem in

33 C.E. was from a pronounced particularity toward a global communion of diverse peoples held together by their loyalty to Jesus Christ.

Viewed in this light the nineteenth century represents one of the truly seminal periods of Christian history. The great motivating center of the modern mission movement was the vision that "the earth will be full of the knowledge of the Lord as the waters cover the sea" (Isaiah 11:9b). The basis for fulfilling that vision, as William Carey and others argued, was the final instruction given by Jesus to his motley band of followers to "go and make disciples of all nations" (Matthew 28:18-20). Carey's generation managed to impress on the Christian church that it had a present duty to continue fulfilling the apostolic mandate. The modern mission movement was led in each generation by a small coterie of people gripped by the hope of seeing all peoples of the world give their allegiance to Jesus Christ. By the nineteenth century the geographical and political implications of such an undertaking were largely known. Steady progress in technology made it appear feasible.

The task before us in this book—and its companion volumes—is to essay this movement through closer analysis of certain key themes, paying special attention to the long-term direction of its development. Critics have charged that the modern mission movement was little more than a sustained attempt to impose Euro-American culture on the peoples who came under its sway. They assert that this effort was simply the religious dimension of the wider quest for Western hegemony in the world. Closer study confirms that this unfolding story was indeed marked by ambiguity and complexity. To be sure, the missionary drama was played out on the same stage as the powerful political and economic developments of the period; missions have been stained by their association with Western imperialism. By virtue of its global reach the movement became a primary carrier of modernity and the artifacts and institutions associated with modernity early became hallmarks of missions. But there is more to be said. Missions released influences that contributed to the subversion and eventual overthrow of colonialism in its many forms.

If modern missions were themselves an expression of the culture in which they arose, by virtue of their attempt to introduce change in other cultures they found themselves up against fundamental questions for which they had no ready answers. Charles R. Taber's study of the way the concept of "culture" was slowly and painfully developed only in the nineteenth century places the discussion of missions and culture in a new perspective. Ethnocentricism was a universal characteristic—for all peoples and all cultures—until "culture" became an abstraction, thereby opening the way for the development of the disciplines of anthropology and sociology. It was precisely people who were engaged in cross-cultural contact who began to apply principles of scientific observation and analysis to cultures and languages. Missionaries were among those who participated in this movement. But as Taber demonstrates in *The World Is Too Much with Us*, the human sciences were far from value-free. Missionaries came under the influence of certain schools of thought, and at times borrowed too uncritically from the anthropologists and sociologists. In the end, the relationship between missionary and social scientist was inevitable, for both were interested in gaining an understanding of other cultures. That they did not have the same purpose in developing that understanding may account for the fact that it was long a relationship marked by a certain lack of rapport.

The authors of the volumes comprising this series geographically and culturally represent the North Atlantic. They acknowledge the limitations this imposes. There are indeed other perspectives from which the modern mission era must be studied in order to complete the picture, and the past generation has seen an impressive growth of studies by scholars from Asia, Africa, and Latin America. This series, The Modern Mission Era, 1792–1992: An Appraisal, is offered as a contribution to an enlarged and enriched understanding of what will increasingly be seen as a shared experience.

— Wilbert R. Shenk, general editor

# Introduction

The purpose of this book is to explore the interaction in recent history between the modern missionary movement, especially its Protestant expressions, and concurrent developments in the social sciences, specifically the emergence of the concept of culture. As such, it is necessary, I think, to distinguish this book from several others which deal with closely related questions, but which have quite distinct aims.

Unlike H. Richard Niebuhr's now classic *Christ and Culture*,[1] this is not an attempt to create a general typology of Christian responses to culture. Unlike Paul Tillich's *Theology of Culture*,[2] this essay does not spell out a general theological critique of culture. Nor does it aim, as does Charles H. Kraft's *Christianity in Culture*,[3] to analyze the relationship between those two realities; nor to explore the interaction between theology, anthropology, and missions, as does Harvie M. Conn's *Eternal Word and Changing Worlds*.[4] And it is certainly not a textbook in cultural anthropology, such as Paul G. Hiebert's *Cultural Anthropology*.[5] Finally, it does not cover the same ground as three recent books by Roman Catholic scholars, Louis Luzbetak's *The Church and Cultures*,[6] Aylward Shorter's *To-*

---

[1]H. Richard Niebuhr, *Christ and Culture* (New York: Harper Colophon Books, 1951).

[2]Paul Tillich, *Theology of Culture*, ed. Robert C. Kimball (New York: Oxford University Press, 1959).

[3]Charles H. Kraft, *Christianity in Culture* (Maryknoll NY: Orbis Books, 1979).

[4]Harvie M. Conn, *Eternal Word and Changing Worlds* (Grand Rapids MI: Zondervan Pub. House, Academie Books, 1984).

[5]Paul G. Hiebert, *Cultural Anthropology* (Philadelphia: J. B. Lippincott, 1976).

[6]Louis J. Luzbetak, S.V.D., *The Church and Cultures: New Perspectives in Missiological Anthropology* (Maryknoll NY: Orbis Books, 1988).

*ward a Theology of Inculturation*,[7] and Robert J. Schreiter's *Constructing Local Theologies*,[8] though it overlaps at a number of points with each.

Though the title of this book already makes the point explicit, it may be useful to underline the fact that I am concerned chiefly with Protestant missions in the nineteenth and twentieth centuries. Obviously, Roman Catholics preceded Protestants in mission by many centuries, and there is a large body of Catholic literature regarding missions and culture. This will be alluded to from time to time. But apart from the stated limits of the series of which this book is a part, the modern Protestant missionary movement has displayed some significant features that distinguish it from Catholic missions, distinctive features which have both theological and historical roots. Roman Catholics, for instance, have always in principle been open to the concept of natural revelation and even to the possibility of salvific value in other religions; Vatican II openly expressed these latent ideas, and made missionary theory consistent with what was always implicit in official doctrine. Protestants have had different ideas in this area. Furthermore, the two different traditions have had different historical experiences in entering mission fields and relating to social, cultural, and political realities. These differences merit separate treatment.

It is the major thesis of this essay that the ideas and attitudes about culture displayed by missionaries are crucially shaped by their own ambient culture, by their theological beliefs, and by their personal experiences; and that these ideas and attitudes in turn crucially affect for good or ill how they understand and do mission. This is true even when the ideas are tacit and inchoate; it is of course also true when they constitute concepts which are quite explicit and even highly self-confident.

It may be felt by some that I devote too much attention to the social provenance of missionaries and to the sweep of general world history, especially to what the powerful nations were up to in the colonial enterprise. This, some may think, is not "culture." But it is a chief emphasis of my study that ideas do not arise in a vacuum, but rather out of a matrix of specific social structures, social dynamics, and historical processes.

---

[7]Aylward Shorter, W.F., *Toward a Theology of Inculturation* (Maryknoll NY: Orbis Books, 1988).

[8]Robert J. Schreiter, C.PP.S. *Constructing Local Theologies* (Maryknoll NY: Orbis Books, 1984).

In fact, so important in my view is the role of historical processes for the genesis of ideas that I must sketch here a brief outline of these processes as they occurred during the past five centuries. In this way, I hope to help readers keep in mind the historical forest as they stroll among the trees throughout this book.

In 1450, the West was not especially dominant in the global scheme of things. It was one nexus of political, economic, and technical powers among others, but by no means the greatest one. China was almost universally recognized as the world leader in many domains. Close behind it were the Islamic Empire in the Middle East and the civilization of India. Other societies and empires in Asia, Africa, and America were recognized as at least their equals in wealth, power, and general level of "civilization" by the European nations.

But in the five centuries since then, the West has come to dominate the world, and the wealth, power, and cultural prestige of the globe have been flowing from the southern hemisphere to the northern in a constant stream. I say "northern hemisphere" because "West" is no longer adequate: Japan must be included, and in somewhat different ways the Soviet Union has been involved. And I say "southern hemisphere" because the more common "Third World" is invidious.

On the basis of initial navigational and military superiority stemming from a small number of innovations partly borrowed from others, the Western powers gradually conquered much of the rest of the world in successive waves of colonial expansion, economic exploitation, and, as both means and by-product, cultural destruction. Today the wealth and power of the world are heavily concentrated in the northern hemisphere, the major part of which is Western. The only partly successful counterprocess has been launched by OPEC on the basis of its near monopoly on petroleum. There have also been major movements of cultural and religious self-affirmation and renewal in the non-Western world, with varying results.

But what has happened is not merely that economic power and wealth have been concentrated; they have gradually but inexorably been centralized in a global system of extreme complexity and comprehensiveness.[9] In 1450, the various societies of the world, Western and non-Western, maintained trade relations, waged occasional wars, borrowed ideas and tech-

---

[9]Immanuel Wallerstein, *The Capitalist World-Economy* (Cambridge: Cambridge University Press, 1979).

niques from each other, and so on. But these were for the most part marginal to the daily lives of the vast majority of people. Societies, and even regions and communities within societies, were economically autonomous and self-sustaining as regards basic staples and resources.

The last five centuries have seen, first, the centralization of economic structures within each of the emerging colonial empires to the benefit of the mother country, which was the essence of classic mercantile colonialism; and then, especially since World War II, the integration of all earlier systems into a massive global system in which all parts are interrelated and, for better or worse, interdependent. But much of the power inside this system is vested in huge corporations, the so-called transnationals, which operate in many countries and control such vast amounts of money and resources that they cannot be effectively made accountable to any society or government. Since the death of the classical colonial system, it is these companies, based without exception in the northern hemisphere, and enjoying the enthusiastic support of their home governments, which ensure that the flow of wealth from south to north continues unabated.

Especially since World War II, it has been a chief role of the United States to exercise its economic, diplomatic, and military power to foster and expand this global system. Through the vicissitudes of the dismantling of the old colonial empires, the United States has done this by a variety of means: support of local regimes that favor the system and pressure or force against regimes that question it; successive versions of "development"; and the subsuming of all efforts to defend "free" enterprise under the ideological banners of the cold war against the communist menace. In these and other ways, the United States has systematically defended the interests of the transnational corporations against all efforts to mitigate their impact on the southern hemisphere. As an example, the United States has passionately and consistently resisted all efforts initiated in the southern hemisphere to devise a new, just economic world order.

Concurrently, the world of ideas in the West has moved through successive phases called Renaissance, Reformation, and Enlightenment. Concepts of human autonomy vis-a-vis institutions and God, of evolutionism, of relativism, and of the superiority of the West have flourished. The Industrial Revolution, urbanization, and the rise of bureaucracy continued the process of modernization in the West. The increased autonomy and specialization of institutions and the gradual but inexorable marginalization of institutional religion have led to the secularization of the Western mind. But, as we shall see in chapter 7, this has not meant that Westerners have managed without gods; it has only meant that the truly powerful gods of the West have arisen not in the religion box but in the other boxes: the economy, science and technology, and the state.

It would be beyond the scope of this book to trace in detail the intimate connections between the "external" processes of the conquest of the world and the "internal" processes in the history of ideas, especially the connection between Western dominance and the notion of Western superiority. Suffice it to say that such connections can be demonstrated. I will bring them to light from time to time as occasion arises. What is clear, however, is that in the past century or so the West has been aggressively exporting its culture as a further means of domination. Since World War II this has been done by means of a kind of commercialized deluge: books and periodicals, media and films, music, Western goods, and the list goes on. The concept of culture, in other words, did not emerge in a vacuum, but in the context of very real ideologies and power structures and relationships.

It has been shown by a number of researchers, for example, and notably by Adam Kuper,[10] that the concept of culture in general and the concept of primitive society in particular were intellectual by-products of the times and circumstances in which they arose; they had and still have clearly ideological content and intent.

For my part, I am convinced that the modern Protestant missionary movement itself would not have arisen in just the form it actually took if circumstances had been different. Moreover, it was—and in many circles still is—a basic assumption of Western modernity, including the missionary movement, that one can simply take one's own culture for granted— its worldview, its mental and emotional habits, its styles of expression and action, its values and priorities; it is other people's cultures that are problematic. But to adopt that ethnocentric stance is to blind oneself to the fallibility of one's culture, and also to fail to notice how thoroughly one is shaped by that culture. It is a matter of simple integrity to be willing to examine critically one's own culture, even before looking at anyone else's. Thus the emphasis of this book.

But ideas not only arise from a context as ideas; they find expression in styles of life and work. Consequently, the choices missionaries have

---

[10]Adam Kuper, *The Invention of Primitive Society* (London and New York: Routledge & Kegan Paul, 1988).

made as to how they should live and how they should view and approach their tasks also come under our scrutiny.

I trust the reader will not read this book as an indictment of missions or missionaries; it is certainly not intended as such. In fact, my admiration for my predecessors in the movement, especially the initial pioneers on each field, is enormous. If Christopher Columbus, Roald Amundsen, or Yury Alekseyevich Gagarin were heroic, then the missionary pioneers were more heroic. For they went into the unknown not for the duration of an expedition but for life; and they went not alone, but with families.

So if I point out that heroes and heroines are not thereby superhuman, I am saying no more than Paul did with regard to himself and his fellow apostles: "But we have only earthenware jars to hold this treasure [the gospel]," so that the "transcendent power" is God's alone (2 Corinthians 4:7). Missionaries were willingly, in fact eagerly, caught up in the sweep of God's redemptive action in history; but they did not always fully understand all that God was doing through and around them. God chose not to work without them; but what God wrought was always more than they knew.

This is the burden of Hoekendijk's masterful low-key recounting of the story of the church in Indonesia. Under both Portuguese and Dutch rule, he points out, mission was a matter of fits and starts, of wise and foolish methods; yet out of it all God brought forth a genuinely Indonesian church. He concludes:

> One might humbly surmise a few factors [in the historic process], keeping in mind that the Holy Spirit is the true factor in the story. To become humble, we should first of all remember that there are no *prima donnas* in these *Opera Dei*, either in Indonesia or in Euramerica. So this cannot be an exact chronicle of the sower. It rather has to be the story of the soils producing fruits "automatically." Whoever appropriates this story as representing the result of his or her endeavors is out.[11]

I will examine my theme in seven chapters. Chapter 1 will introduce the topic and a number of questions surrounding it that will have to be examined. Chapter 2 will trace the prehistory of the concept of culture from antiquity through the Enlightenment, up to the dawn of the modern Prot-

---

[11] J. C. Hoekendijk, "A Perspective on Indonesia," in *Christopaganism or Indigenous Christianity?*, ed. Tetsunao Yamamori and Charles R. Taber (South Pasadena: William Carey Library, 1975) 75.

estant missionary movement. Chapter 3 will describe the historical context of the nineteenth century, in terms of processes such as the industrial revolution, the abolitionist movement, and the colonial enterprise; key ideas such as evolution; and the birth of cultural anthropology. Chapter 4 will situate and describe the place and role of the modern missionary movement in that century, tracing both the ways in which it was influenced by prevalent ideas and attitudes and the ways in which it contributed to our understanding of culture and cultures. Chapter 5 will look at twentieth-century theories of culture, and chapter 6 will show which of these have influenced missiology and in what ways. Finally, chapter 7 will attempt an examination and evaluation of issues remaining unresolved.

The heart of the book is in chapters 4 through 7. It is there that I point out how decisive for missiological anthropology it was that functionalism was the vogue in anthropology when missions first became aware of the discipline in a major way during the first quarter of the twentieth century. The influence of functionalism provided for missions both a powerful set of tools which advanced understanding immensely, and a set of blinkers which prevented missions from seeing certain things which it would have been important to notice. Missions adopted anthropology with open arms as a kit of tools for the job; but the philosophical foundations and the limitations of functionalist anthropology were not sufficiently noticed.

In particular, Malinowskian functionalism pressed missions in the direction of excessive relativism, in over-reaction against the ethnocentrism and iconoclasm of earlier periods; it encouraged missions to think of cultures as closed, bounded systems, and to overlook the dynamic interconnections between cultures; and it led missions to exaggerate the stability of cultures and their resistance to change. These limitations have hindered missions from seeing and dealing adequately with cultural change, with the nature of ethical absolutes, and with the implications of the global politico-economic system. The underlying philosophical issues will be examined in chapter 7.

Since this book is an interpretive essay rather than a monograph, I have tried to keep the documentation unobtrusive. In fact, I have made no attempt to be comprehensive, let alone exhaustive, in the sources I have consulted. But I trust my selection is representative not only of the dominant strands in the story, but of the range of variation as well. This does not mean, naturally, that I imagine that the substance of the book comes entirely out of my own head! On the contrary, I have relied heavily on a number of sources, which I must acknowledge at this point. These fall into three categories.

First are those that were useful at specific points in my argument. These, of course, are cited in footnotes. For the history of the concept of culture at different historical periods, I have used a sampling of the literature: theoretically creative writings in books and journals, widely used textbooks, and ethnographic writings. I have tried to represent fairly contributions from the various countries of the West.

For the views and attitudes of missionaries and missiologists, I have again cited a sampling of the literature from various missionary-sending countries: scholarly papers and books, official documents, and popular missionary writings published for apologetic and promotional purposes. There is also, especially for the missions of the nineteenth century, a growing body of secondary critical and intepretive literature written by such scholars as John K. Fairbank, William R. Hutchison, and Andrew F. Walls.

The second major set of sources are the eight books mentioned earlier in this introduction, works of Niebuhr, Tillich, Kraft, Conn, Hiebert, Luzbetak, Shorter, and Schreiter. These provided a wealth of stimulating ideas and a conceptual matrix for the discussion of culture from specifically Christian and missiological perspectives, which cannot be adequately represented in footnotes. My debt to all of these authors is immense, as anyone can tell who has read them before reading this essay.

In the third place, a number of works were of very substantial help as documentation for major chunks of my argument, especially in two areas. For the history of missions, I have of course used Latourette's monumental *A History of the Expansion of Christianity*,[12] as well as the much shorter work by Stephen Neill, *A History of Christian Missions*.[13] Both these books are out of date, and their analyses are quite inadequate, especially for my present purpose. But they have not yet been superceded, and they provide an indispensable overall historical framework as well as the factual data— names, places, dates, events—to which ideas must always be connected in the real world.

---

[12]Kenneth Scott Latourette, *The Great Century*, vols. 5 and 6 of *A History of the Expansion of Christianity* (Repr. Grand Rapids: Zondervan Publishing Co., 1970; New York: Harper & Row, 1943, 1944).

[13]Stephen Neill, *A History of Christian Missions* (Harmondsworth, England: Penguin Books, 1964).

For the history of the concept of culture and of the discipline of anthropology, nothing matches Marvin Harris's massive *The Rise of Anthropological Theory*.[14] Harris is strongly committed to historical materialism, which I am not. But his bias is forthrightly and forcefully expressed, so that it can be allowed for, and his scholarship is unparalleled. I have also found extremely useful the work of Adam Kuper referred to above, *The Invention of Primitive Society*.[15]

One detail of format remains to be explained. In order to minimize the number of footnotes, I have in several instances cited only by title and date in the body of the text very old works which I mention for purely historical reasons but for which the present reader will probably have little use.

Sensitivity to the need for inclusive language is very recent among Western writers. Thus, many of the authors I will quote used sexist language. Rather than cluttering the text with multiple occurrences of [*sic*], I am serving notice here that (a) I have noticed and deplored the occurrence of sexist usage in the quotations; (b) I have tried to use inclusive language consistently myself; but (c) I do not feel it appropriate to beat over the head my predecessors who were not in their day sensitized regarding sexist language.

A final pleasant duty remains: to express my gratitude to a number of persons who have contributed significantly to my own development and to the emergence of this book. First of all, to my late missionary parents, Floyd W. Taber and Ada D. Taber, I owe my strong commitment to Jesus Christ and his gospel, to the truth, to scholarship, and to respect for all human beings. To my teachers at the Hartford Seminary Foundation, especially Paul Leser, I owe my initiation into the world of culture studies. My former colleagues in the United Bible Societies and the late journal *Practical Anthropology*, especially Eugene A. Nida, William A. Smalley, William D. Reyburn, and Jacob A. Loewen, helped me pursue my anthropological education in a number of directions.

Donald N. Larson, Louis J. Luzbetak, S.V.D, Aylward Shorter, W.F., Darrell L. Whiteman, and the authors of the other books in this series— Jonathon J. Bonk, Dana L. Robert, David A. Schattschneider, A. Christopher Smith, and Norman E. Thomas—made valuable suggestions at var-

---

[14]Marvin Harris, *The Rise of Anthropological Theory* (New York: Thomas Y. Crowell Co., 1968).

[15]Kuper, *The Invention of Primitive Society*.

ious stages of the project. Thomas A. Stokes and Christine Quillen of the library at my school, Emmanuel School of Religion, did yeoman duty in making available to me resources through interlibrary loan. I am deeply indebted to the personnel of the theological libraries at Emory University, Vanderbilt University, Union Theological Seminary in Virginia, and especially Yale Divinity School. Eldon and Verda Heinrich offered hospitality during a foray to Atlanta. H. McKennie Goodpasture did invaluable spadework at Union to make my brief visit there as productive as possible. The Overseas Ministries Study Center in New Haven provided the ideal context for the last stages of writing the book. Robert J. Schreiter, C.PP.S., and Mary Motte, F.M.M., provided indispensable help in tracking down the genesis of the Roman Catholic usage of the term "inculturation."

An opportunity was given me by the E. Stanley Jones School of World Mission and Evangelism at Asbury Theological Seminary to test my first efforts at analysis of the substance of chapters 5 and 6, when I was invited to lecture there in an all-school seminar and in one or two classes. The feedback from faculty and students was most encouraging.

Special thanks must go to Wilbert R. Shenk, who conceived the idea of the Bicentennial Series, has served as its general editor, and has provided constant challenge and encouragement. My son, Charles S. Taber, taught me all I know about computers and word processing, despite an almost invincible lack of talent in that direction on my part. My wife, Betty J. Taber, has been a partner and a tower of strength during my entire adult pilgrimage, and without her I would not even have been marginally qualified to write this book, much less have actually done it. Finally, four people in addition to Betty have read and commented on the entire manuscript: Alfred C. Krass, Wilbert R. Shenk, William A. Smalley, and Darrell L. Whiteman. Their criticisms and suggestions have rescued me from a number of errors, sharpened my analysis, and in every way immeasurably improved the book. Obviously, with all of this help, any errors of fact or interpretation in the final product are mine alone.

# CHAPTER 1

# What Is "Culture"?

What is culture, and what does it have to do with Christian missions? How have missionaries conceived of culture, and how have they reacted to it?

It is an interesting fact, surely not accidental, that the two centuries of the development of modern Protestant missions have largely coincided with the period during which the explicit formal concept of culture and cultures was emerging in the West from the womb of the Enlightenment, and being debated and refined in the nascent discipline of cultural anthropology. What interactions took place between missionaries who were at the cutting edge of cross-cultural contact, and anthropologists who were formulating concepts of culture? What historical and intellectual roots gave rise to the specific activities of each, and what consequences flowed from their respective understandings? It is the purpose of this essay to explore these and related questions. As the title indicates, we are not dealing with a static situation, but with a dynamically evolving one. Just as anthropologists have proposed a series of definitions of the concept which are only partly compatible with each other, so missionaries and missiologists have understood and responded to culture and cultures in a variety of ways, some more and others less informed by the theoretical debates in anthropology.

The experience of immersion and participation in a culture is universal and ubiquitous: all human beings live in culture as fish live in water. It is a quite different matter, however, to have an explicit and self-conscious concept of culture. Such a concept, in fact, is as recent as the nineteenth century. In the absence of a formal concept, people tend to take their own culture for granted and not to reflect critically on it. They tend to respond to it piecemeal, as a congeries of phenomena, not as a single more or less coherent phenomenon. But for the most part people do not reflect on their culture as such at all; it is rather the lens through which they see and reflect on everything else in their experience. People spontaneously assume that what their culture prescribes is "natural," so that other ways are by definition "unnatural," exotic, or even perverse.

A measure of self-conscious reflection can be caused by confrontation with alien people who, to our amazement, live by quite different customs from ourselves; or on occasions when our own culture quite conspicuously does not work very well to serve our needs or the needs of society; or when religious conversion leads us to wonder about a possible conflict between some aspect or aspects of our culture and our new-found faith. But the sense of unease, or anger, or frustration, or shock, or amusement, or revulsion one feels at such times is almost invariably reaction to a feature or features of the culture rather than to the culture as a whole.

If the experience of culture is so ubiquitous and universal, why did it take so long for anyone to perceive and name the phenomenon? The reason, no doubt, is that culture is an extremely abstract concept. In contrast, concepts and terms for concrete human groups—groups such as those named by the English terms family, lineage, clan, village, tribe, nation, people—are present in every human language, wherever such groups themselves exist. This is because groups are empirically available and socially important to everyone by virtue of membership and the crucial practical contrast between membership and nonmembership. Most especially in nonliterate societies, primary groups such as family and community are, in the frequent absence of larger, secondary groups, the very stuff of daily experience, the source of identity, of security, of belonging. It would be astonishing if so central a reality in every society were not named, if it were not in fact the focus of an elaborate nomenclature. Culture, on the other hand, exists only in people's heads, and they are usually not aware of that fact. Though Freud of course did not have culture in mind when he theorized the concept of the unconscious, that is where culture largely resides.

But what is this omnipresent though mostly hidden reality, culture? Several decades ago, Kroeber and Kluckhohn collected almost two hundred definitions from the literature up to their time (1952).[1] These represented a number of quite different theoretical emphases and perspectives, which

---

[1]Alfred L. Kroeber and Clyde Kluckhohn, *Culture: A Critical Review of Concepts and Definitions*, Anthropological Papers 47/1 (Cambridge, MA: Peabody Museum, 1952).

we will explore in the course of this essay. For that matter, we will need to take seriously some understandings that have emerged since 1952.

But through all of this diversity, certain constant features characterize virtually all definitions of culture. Few anthropologists would totally reject the following attempt, though many would want to shift the emphasis or to add details: *culture is a more or less coherent set of ideas* (symbols, taxonomies, definitions, explanations, values, attitudes, and rules) *which are created and shared by a group of people and transmitted to their children, and which enable them to make sense of their experience and to cope with their natural and social worlds to their collective advantage.* This definition includes an explanation of the origin of culture (created by a group); of its nature (ideas: symbols, taxonomies, definitions, explanations, values, attitudes, rules); of its perpetuation (socially transmitted); and of its functions (to make sense, to cope).

There are other ways to describe culture.[2] Various scholars have used the metaphors of maps or plans (ordered, conventional representations of reality), of rules for living, or of systems of meaning.

Culture can also be described as the specific means by which universal human requirements for survival and well-being are satisfied in particular instances. Human beings require water and nutrition, so each culture defines certain substances as beverages and food. Human beings require protection from a variety of hazards—natural, supernatural, and human—so culture offers housing and clothing, magic and medicine, army and police. Human beings require channels for the legitimate expression of their sexual impulses, so culture prescribes rules for mating and marriage. Human beings require a social matrix in which to belong and thrive, and culture defines the groups I mentioned above. Human beings require means of communication with their fellows, and culture provides them with a language and other symbol systems. Human beings require frequent opportunities for physical exercise, and culture offers work and play. Human beings require answers to their questions and the exercise of their minds, and culture offers them a worldview, a logic, a method of interpreting experience. Human beings require means for the expression of their aspirations for excellence, and culture offers them esthetic and other norms.

---

[2]For a fuller discussion of the points being made in the next several paragraphs, see Charles R. Taber, "Culture, Ideology and Christian Mission," in *Unto the Uttermost,* ed. Doug Priest, Jr. (Pasadena: William Carey Library, 1984) 155-75.

Finally, human beings require a sense of relationship with the Ultimate, and culture offers religion. Whatever human beings require to survive and to thrive does not come to them raw, directly from nature, but mediated through the meaning systems called cultures.

Most scholars today organize their treatment of culture around three foci: material culture, which is concerned with the interaction of human groups with their physical habitat, including their use of its resources to make tools, implements, clothing, and housing; social culture, which deals with how they organize their groups; and ideational culture, which includes worldview, language and other symbol systems, and religion.

Donald Jacobs offers a slightly more complex model; he describes culture as consisting of a number of concentric levels or layers. At the core are "philosophical presuppositions" regarding the nature of "the powers" and the dynamics of power. These translate at the next level into values and themes, such as the value of human effort and the theme of the worth of work. Finally, this worldview core is expressed outwardly in symbols, rituals, and other behaviors. The point of the model, according to Jacobs, is that in Christian conversion "all levels of one's life are not changed or altered to the same extent" or at the same rate of speed. Conversion, says Jacobs, begins at the outer levels and only gradually if ever does it reach the core.[3] I will raise questions about this model later in the study.

Finally, culture can also be described in terms of certain universal properties:

1. Culture is *learned,* as distinct from being genetically programmed. Other mammalian species, even our closest cousins the apes, have large areas of their behavioral repertoire, particularly those elements most crucial to survival, genetically preprogrammed. This makes for much greater security: if by accident an infant is deprived of the protection of adults, it has some chance of surviving. But the genetic mechanism is relatively inflexible, making it rather specifically adapted to one niche and one way of life. If circumstances change drastically, survival can be threatened. Human infants, on the other hand, are born helpless and vulnerable, with virtually no pre-programmed behaviors. This is very risky; the infant needs the protection, provision, example, and teaching of adults for an extended

---

[3] Donald R. Jacobs, "Culture and the Phenomena of Conversion," *Gospel in Culture* 1:2 (April 1978): 4-14.

portion of its lifespan before it can live on its own. At best, the human infant at birth has only a vast, open-ended set of potentials, which are given form and content by the learning process; and that process is centrally cultural. The human pattern offsets the risk involved by far greater flexibility in the face of changing circumstances.

2. Culture is *mental,* which means it exists in people's minds, not somewhere in the observable world. The ideas people have in their heads are often provoked or otherwise shaped by the material conditions of life; and they are often given outward expression in behaviors such as singing or running, or in the material products of behaviors, such as houses and paintings. But the outward behaviors and artifacts are not themselves culture, only cultural products. A major question in anthropology, as we shall see, is how possible or legitimate it is to infer culture from its empirical manifestations.

3. Culture is *adaptive*; it, rather than specific biological adaptations, enables humans to live successfully in diverse environments. This is closely connected with learning. Human beings as a biological species are remarkably homogeneous and undifferentiated, not specially fitted for any particular environment. The range of variation in adaptive bodily features such as skin pigmentation and body shape and size is much narrower than in other species. We are not particularly strong or fast, our teeth and nails are laughable as weapons. But we have a large, complex brain, which creates and learns cultural means to adapt to all the environments—even outer space—in which we choose to exist.

4. Culture is *shared* by a human group, and constitutes the chief ingredient of group solidarity. This means that culture is charged with meaning, or rather meanings, which can be communicated by language and other sorts of signs and symbols, as well as all other kinds of behavior. The process of cooperation, the process of teaching and learning, are crucial to culture.

5. Culture is *selective,* in that among the gamut of human possibilities it chooses some options rather than others for its bearers. In some domains, possible options are few; there are only two sides to a road, and each culture chooses whether to drive on the right or on the left. There are mathematically only four possible ways to reckon descent: through both parents alike, through both parents differently, through father, or through mother. Each culture in the world uses one of these. In other domains, acceptable choices are more numerous and individual options freer. But each

culture in each area defines some possibilities as being in bounds and some as being out of bounds.

6. Culture is *normative,* in that it rewards conformity and punishes deviance. This is connected to the selectivity of culture: once a culture has articulated its commands, permissions, and prohibitions, it enforces them. Rewards range from praise and reputation to position and power; they can also be purely symbolic. Punishments range from mocking laughter to banishment or death. The norms and criteria enforced by culture routinely are those that support existing structures and processes and existing concentrations of power and prestige.

7. Culture is more or less *integrated,* so that its different parts are generally mutually supportive. We seldom do anything that relates to only one human requirement. We eat, for example, for physical nutrition; but we often eat together as an expression of social belonging; and we present and eat the food as attractively as possible to satisfy our esthetic tastes. Marriage provides legitimate expression for the sexual needs of the partners; but it also provides a social matrix in which to rear children; and in many societies it also has economic, political, and even religious significance.

8. Culture is *heterogeneous,* since the members of a society, by virtue of significant differences between them, experience culture differently. The simple fact of standing in a different social location because of differences of age or sex, let alone differences of social class or caste, leads us to see, interpret, and evaluate reality differently. Each position in the social scheme opens some doors for knowledge and closes others; it offers more or less access to social power. And these differences translate into significant differences in worldview, even within a single culture. It is this fact that is heavily stressed by the sociology of knowledge.

9. Culture is *cumulative,* the experience of each generation enriching later generations. This is most obvious in cultures that have written records. But even in nonliterate societies, the experience and wisdom of each generation are passed on orally to the next to constitute the lore of a people.

10. Culture is *adaptable,* since it more or less readily changes in response to changing circumstances. This is really only an extension of adaptiveness to the historical dimension. As I said at the beginning of this discussion, the human way makes for great risks, but for extraordinary flexibility. Adaptation is limited only by the imagination, the courage, the abilities, and the resources of the human creators and bearers of culture. It

will be readily noticed that adaptibility stands in tension with normative-
ness, since the latter resists change. How these "forces" interact in the life
of a society determines how effectively the society's culture changes under
the pressure of changed circumstances.

It will be noticed that in specifying these properties, I am in effect an-
swering prematurely some of the questions I will be raising later in this
chapter and discussing at length throughout the book and especially in the
last chapter. But since this is not a mystery novel, perhaps it is not inappropriate to give away some of the secrets, if this helps the reader understand what we are talking about.

One of the most immediately apparent facts about different cultures is
that they are in fact different. At least, they differ in an amazing number
of ways in those features that are most visible, such as food and clothing,
art and music, manners and gestures. The significance of this needs to be
explored carefully.

The concept of culture, as we shall see, arose and was elaborated gradually during a period of time extending from the earliest dawn of the Enlightenment to the present. The term "culture" itself was applied
consciously to this emerging concept in the 1840s in German and the 1860s
in English. For eighteen centuries, from the birth of the church to the rise
of the new discipline of anthropology, Christians dealt with culture in the
piecemeal terms described above. The earlier stages of this history will be
discussed briefly in chapter 2, so as to set the stage for a more detailed
treatment of the early and recent contributions of missionaries to knowledge in the West of non-Western cultures, the development of the concept
of culture in anthropology, and the full-fledged enlistment of cultural anthropology by missions in our century.

For the two centuries of our focal concern, we will explore the development of understandings and evaluations of culture in the modern Protestant missionary movement. But in order to do so, we will need to sketch,
at least in broad strokes, the interactions between the events and processes
of world history, the appearance of concepts and the emergence of modern
science, and the missionary movement itself. These matters will in fact occupy the bulk of our attention.

It must be pointed out at the outset that missionaries and missiologists
have contributed far more to our ethnographic information than to the development of the formal concept of culture; and that they have made use
of the practical and theoretical riches of cultural anthropology in a rather

eclectic and uncritical way. In this way, as we shall see, they have learned a great deal, and have gained invaluable tools for mission. But, as we shall also see, the specific versions and theories of culture which they have borrowed have philosophical, not to say ideological, roots and entailments of which they were not always sufficiently wary. Questions arise at a deep level which need to be faced as we examine the complex interaction of missiology and anthropology. We shall discover that the use in missiology of scientific concepts with their philosophical baggage brings both blessings and curses, for which we shall need to draw up a sort of balance sheet.

Among the questions we shall have occasion to probe are the following eight.

1. I have described culture as a configuration of ideas, that is, as something that exists essentially inside people's heads. But the question now needs to be asked: Exactly what is the nature of the relationship between those ideas and the material conditions under which the group exists— habitat, resources, population density and distribution, objective power relations, and the like?

If we think cultural ideas are essentially independent of material conditions, then we have adopted an idealist position that has its modern roots in the thinking of philosphers like Kant and Hegel, and that is expressed today in the work of such anthropologists as Clifford Geertz and Victor Turner. We shall, for example, assign a powerful causative role in human affairs to religions and ideologies, as in those analyses that credit Christianity with the genesis of Western civilization.

If, on the other hand, we think that cultural ideas arise from, or are determined by, the material conditions of existence, we have adopted a materialist position with its modern roots in the thought of Baron d'Holbach and Marx, represented in contemporary anthropology by such thinkers as Leslie White and Marvin Harris. In this case, we would look for concrete power relations within a society or to conditions of habitat and technology as explanations of religion or ideology. Marx, for example, considered the Christian religion in Europe as a tool to justify and perpetuate the dominance of society by capitalists. This was a part of his systematic assignment of *all* ideas and ideologies to what he called the "superstructure," which was *always* determined by the "base," which consisted in control of the "means of production." These would be, in an agricultural society, land; and in an industrial society, factories.

If we adopt the first stance, we will find it possible to define the gospel without reference to the material conditions of life, a gospel which is primarily ideas and which we can preach without asking whether our hearers are hungry or hurting or oppressed. This would be quite compatible with much theologizing through the centuries, but it is not so clear that it is compatible with the Bible. If, on the other hand, we adopt the second stance, we will find it necessary at least to notice and do something about the fact that for many people the material conditions of life are miserable and cause suffering; we may also be led to analyze critically why this should be so and to address the systemic and structural causes of human suffering.

2. Is each culture a discrete, bounded, sui generis phenomenon, co-existing but not essentially interacting with its neighbors? Or is it part of a dynamic vortex of interaction, both creative and destructive? Are cultural boundaries relatively hermetic or relatively open? Our answer to this question will determine our view of the legitimacy or illegitimacy of bringing to bear influence from one culture on another; it will also determine whether we look for explanations of cultural phenomena exclusively inside the boundaries of a culture, or whether we look to larger matrices within which individual cultures operate and are also subject to the effects of external forces.

For example, if we feel that each culture is discrete, we will be comfortable with approaching and working with each one separately—Navajo and Pueblo in New Mexico, for instance, or Xhosa and Afrikaner in South Africa, or white American and black American. If we insist on seeing the connections, we will work at the borders between these groups, attempting to understand and cope with the dynamics of their relationships.

3. Is culture in fact fully integrated and coherent by definition, as functionalism argued, or are coherence and integration between the various aspects and domains of culture a desideratum which is empirically a matter of degree, with cultures varying along a scale from fully harmonious integration to a high degree of chaos? The older view, which prevailed until the 1920s, was that culture is an inventory of unconnected items; this can lead to the mistaken impression that one can pick and choose which elements to approve and perpetuate and which to disapprove and eliminate.

Missionaries, for instance, tended to approve agriculture and to condemn polygyny, without noticing how in many cases these were interconnected in actual practice. But to go to the opposite extreme can lead to paralysis and defeatism about needed change and a tendency to accept as inevitable things that ought not to be tolerated. A remarkably insightful essay written in 1935 by F. E. Williams steered a prudent path between extreme functionalism and helter-skelter diffusionism based on notions of the unrelatedness of cultural traits and complexes.[4]

4. Is culture essentially static, so that change is a pathology; or is it inherently dynamic, so that long-term cultural immutability is the unusual case? How one answers this question will determine in part how truly one believes in the efficacy of the gospel to bring about needed change. A view of culture as set in concrete, especially when coupled with overt or covert relativism, can lead to a debilitating pessimism about the impact of the gospel.

5. Do cultures, which as we have seen differ greatly in the most visible external levels, continue to differ as we dig deeper? As one peels away the successive layers and approaches the core of each of the cultures, does one ever come to a point where the differences vanish? Are there any genuine cultural universals—things which are true in all cultures, good in all cultures, right in all cultures, beautiful in all cultures? Are there, anywhere "under the sun," any absolutes? Or must we look for them elsewhere? Or are there none, so that we are adrift on a boundless ocean of cultural relativity, without map or compass?

6. Does culture totally determine the individual, replacing in the role of ultimate explanation earlier and mostly discredited notions of genetic determination? Or does the individual have some degree of freedom with respect to his or her culture as he or she has some freedom with respect to genes? Is the answer the same in all cultures and for all individuals? Are so-called primitive cultures, in particular, more strongly determinative of the lives of their members than so-called modern cultures? This latter question is raised specifically because popular notions derived from anthropology, and the actual practice of many anthropologists, would suggest that in modern societies, persons are relatively free vis-à-vis their cultures; whereas in "primitive" cultures, the thoughts and actions of persons are supposed to be more narrowly controlled by the collectivity and its highly homogeneous culture. Clearly these are questions with profound implications for mission in the broad sense and for evangelization in the

---

[4]F. E. Williams, *The Blending of Cultures: An Essay on the Aims of Native Education,* Anthropological Reports 16 (Territory of Papua, 1935).

narrow sense, and even for our understanding of the possibilities and limits of spiritual growth and discipline in the Christian community.

7. Is culture essentially good, or ethically neutral, or bad, or a mixture of good and evil? If the last, in what terms should one envisage the mixture? Are sin and evil lodged exclusively in the minds and hearts of fallen individuals, or can they be found entrenched in cultures and structures as well? Or is the whole question illegitimate, in that good and evil are relative to which culture one is talking about? Are some cultures good and others bad? It will become clear that one's choice among these options will profoundly affect not only how one conceives of culture, but how one will do mission.

8. Finally, what is the relationship between culture and religion? Is religion merely one chapter in the description of a culture, or does it have any sort of autonomy? Does religion pervade all of a culture, or is it compartmentalized? Is the relationship always the same, regardless of what kind of culture or what kind of religion we are dealing with? From a traditional missiological perspective, is religion the domain where idols rule and which must therefore be addressed directly by the gospel, while other domains are good or neutral? Or is it conceivable that idols could rule in domains other than the religious? Obviously, answers here have far-reaching missiological implications.

It must be emphasized that, in exposing the philosophical and ideological roots and entailments of various statements of the concept of culture, I will in no way impugn the motives of missionaries and missiologists who borrowed them; but I will at times question the wisdom of using this or that formulation without understanding its antecedents and its consequences. As I have hinted in the brief outline above, the form of a concept which we use can have subtle but decisive effects on how we define our task, its requirements, its difficulties, its opportunities, and its possibilities and impossibilities, and therefore on the end results that we achieve or that we settle for.

It should also be pointed out that the discipline of anthropology, while it can at times serve an indispensable purpose in liberating our minds from the captivity of ethnocentrism, remains a very Western endeavor, resting on entirely Western philosophical foundations; in this it is exactly like all the rest of modern science. As such, paradoxically, it can also serve to maintain our cultural captivity. We need to gain freedom not only from the naive world-taken-for-granted of our common Western civilization, but also from the equally Western if more sophisticated scientific tools of Western civilization, including cultural anthropology. For the "present age"—which powerfully shapes us but from which the gospel needs to free us by the "renewing of our minds" (Romans 12:2)—includes not only popular culture but also the various specialized and elitist domains of culture. Otherwise we may end up like the man in the parable, freed from one demon only to be possessed by seven others.

# CHAPTER 2

# The Prehistory of "Culture"

How have people who worshipped God as revealed in the Hebrew and Christian Scriptures understood and related to the reality which, in modern terms, has come to be called "culture"? And how, if they have thought about the question at all, have they conceived the relations between their "culture" and their "religion"?

## Ancient Times to the Seventeenth Century

In prehistoric societies these questions would have been meaningless. What we today call "culture" would have been, for them, something designed and bequeathed to the ethnic group by God, or the spirits, or the ancestors, or some combination of these; as such, culture was a necessary part of the identity of a group, and conformity to cultural norms *was* to do the will of the Ultimate. We must remember, of course, that these people had no self-conscious *concept* of culture, any more than a fish has a concept of water. "Religion," in turn, would have had little or no separate institutional embodiment, but would have been pervasive in all areas of culture as constituting the Ultimate legitimation of the whole; specifically it was that complex of beliefs and practices by which good relations with the Ultimate could be established and maintained.

In such a society, membership in the religion would be coterminous with the society itself, and all members of the society would participate automatically and unquestioningly in the ethnic religion as a necessary dimension of their membership. Dissent would be virtually unthinkable, especially since no alternatives would be available. The same would be true today of a truly isolated non-literate society.

The situation would change, naturally, if representatives of another, alien religion were to address evangelistic efforts to the society. Then people would have to face the issue of the possible falsification or contamination of their traditional religion. This in turn could lead to a new, self-conscious examination of the traditional religion; and whether the conclusion of the process was conversion to the new or a determined clinging to the old, the situation would never be as it was before.

In larger, technically and socially more complex societies, including those in the Mediterranean and Asian regions which developed literacy, cities, division of labor, and social stratification, it was still taken for granted that one's relations with the Ultimate would follow the prescribed patterns belonging to one's ethnic identity, so that religious membership would continue to be identical with society. But when a more fully developed sense of the transcendence of the Ultimate appeared, religion could serve as a foil and even as a judgment against the existing situation, so that prophets could bring messages of condemnation as well as comfort. But whether religion brought solace or doom, it belonged inseparably to peoplehood, and was intrinsic to a people's culture.

This was clearly the case even when complex urban societies came into contact with each other and conquered each other, as can be seen from the histories of ancient Egypt, Mesopotamia, Persia, Greece, and Rome.

But in such situations of intense contact or conquest, a different situation entirely could, and sometimes did, arise: people might spontaneously decide that someone else's religion was preferable to their own and convert to it; or a religion might as part of its very essence have universal aspirations and make universal claims. This did in fact happen with Buddhism (as contrasted with its matrix Hinduism, which is ethnic to this day); it happened in some strands of Judaism at various periods in history; it happened, of course, with Christianity; and it happened with Islam. Universal religions, whatever their official doctrine, are necessarily less bound to a particular culture than purely ethnic ones, and often serve as the basis for critiques of a particular status quo. But they usually are more: they are religions of salvation. As solutions to the flaws of the world, they offer salvation in one or more of several forms: as present escape from the present world; as a better world to be constituted here below; or as future escape into another world.

The relationship of these new, consciously adopted religions to culture and cultures was necessarily complex: since each people as it was converted already had a culture, and in most cases their former religion was an intrinsic part of that culture, it could be thought that the adoption of a new religion would entail the replacement of the old culture by the matrix culture of the new religion. This was to a high degree true of Judaism and Islam, which explicitly demanded of converts a quite total repudiation of their former "pagan" culture, though the substitution was often in fact not as complete as theory expected.

Empirically, Judaism in the last two thousand years has preserved its cultural integrity by largely forsaking its earlier episodic missionary outreach. Islam, on the other hand, has been embodied, especially at the level of folk religion, in a multitude of cultural forms, but this has happened in spite of official doctrine to the contrary.[1] Buddhism and Christianity have had a much more checkered history in this regard, both in terms of their official positions and in terms of their missionary praxis. But, as Lamin Sanneh has shown, Christianity is the only religion in history to have *both* a universal mission *and* an intentionally multicultural membership and expression,[2] as laid down at the Jerusalem Council reported in Acts 15. Almost from the beginning, and certainly ever since Paul's missionary career, Christianity has intentionally addressed the entire population of the world but has only occasionally and partially imposed a single culture upon its multi-cultural converts.

But it is time to examine the question in a more detailed historical framework.

*Ancient Israel.* The case of ancient Israel is instructive. According to its national self-image recorded in the Hebrew Scriptures, the call to Abraham, and the constituting of an incipient nation under Moses gave rise to a series of crucial processes. First, there was the avowedly *ethnic* basis of the divine election: the chosen people were understood to be physical descendants of Abraham, Isaac, and Jacob. Second, there was the direct intervention of God to deliver Israel from Egypt. Third, there was the covenant establishing this people as God's elect. Fourth, there was the Law, specifically given to define the differentness of Israel from "the nations" and Israel's peculiar status as the people of God. Fifth, there was a centuries-long struggle to achieve empirically the promise of God in the Land,

---

[1]Phil Parshall, *Bridges to Islam* (Grand Rapids MI: Baker, 1983) describes folk Islam, in contrast with "official" Islam, from a Christian perspective. See also Clifford Geertz, *Islam Observed: Religious Development in Morocco and Indonesia* (New Haven: Yale University Press, 1968).

[2]Lamin Sanneh, *Translating the Message* (Maryknoll NY: Orbis Books, 1989).

a struggle precisely between the demand for differentness expressed in the Law and spelled out in cultural minutiae controlling all of life, and the constant pressure to be "like the other nations." This struggle persisted during the entire period from the Conquest under Joshua through and beyond the Jewish Rebellion and the destruction of Jerusalem in A.D. 70.

Interestingly, two features of this centuries-long sequence make the entire history of ancient Israel culturally not nearly as much unlike that of their neighbors as one might expect. On the one hand, the intrinsic connection between ethnicity, culture, and religion was throughout unquestioned. There could be, and were, in the centuries just before and after Jesus, opportunities for Gentiles to be incorporated into Israel as proselytes. There could be, and were, intense debates about what specific cultural forms were in fact consonant with the will of God. But these were minor variations on a theme which was itself taken for granted in the official version of Israelite/Jewish identity. On the other hand, as modern Old Testament scholarship has abundantly shown, many of the very cultural forms by which Israel defined its uniqueness were in fact borrowed from the neighbors. Cultural diffusion and cultural contact were, then as now, widespread, and the chosen people participated in them like everyone else. The process was only intensified by the successive Assyrian, Babylonian, Persian, and Macedonian conquests, the Diaspora, the Hellenization of the Mediterranean world, and the expansion of the Roman Empire.

*The Early Church.* In Christian history, one needs to distinguish between what happened before Constantine and what happened after. But the Christian church almost from its beginning stood in a quite different relation to ambient cultures and to particular cultural forms than had Israel. Even during the initial period when the church was exclusively Jewish, Christians disagreed about how their new allegiance as Jews to Jesus the Messiah should be expressed within their Jewish heritage.

But as soon as Gentiles began to be included in the church on a large scale, the simple nexus between ethnicity, culture, and religion was shattered, even though it took some Christians a long time to realize the fact. While I am uneasy with the contemporary tendency in some circles to reduce the issues involved, for example, in the Jerusalem Council (Acts 15), to a mere question of culture clash, there is no doubt that cultural differences were a major factor in the difficulties the church experienced. But there is in the New Testament no overall examination or evaluation of culture or cultures, either Jewish or Hellenistic. One can only infer from various bits and pieces of Paul's corpus that he, at least, believed in and practised a degree of cultural relativism that surely shocked some of his colleagues profoundly (see especially 1 Corinthians 9:19-23).

In the second century, we are familiar with the tension between the relatively positive position adopted by Clement of Alexandria and Justin Martyr, and the more negative stance of Tertullian with respect to Greco-Roman culture. (Issues relating to Jewish culture were by this time already no longer relevant in the church.) Clement, for example, spoke in his *Miscellanies* (I.5) of Greek philosophy as "a schoolmaster" to bring the Greeks to Christ, serving in exactly the same way as the Mosaic Law had for the Hebrews, and he urged his readers to "use, but not to linger and spend time, with secular culture [*kosmiko paideia*]."

Justin Martyr, for his part, developed the well-known concept of the *logos spermatikos*, the "seed-bearing Word," which was his way of making allowances for the light of divine revelation to come to people who had no knowledge of Christ; he thought that Plato more than anyone else had been moved by that Word. Origen adopted a similar stance in a letter to Gregory Thaumaturgus (ca. A.D. 230), in which he urged Gregory to use philosophy and other cultural resources in the service of God, just as the Israelites had used the wealth of Egypt for the construction of the tabernacle; though he warned that this did pose some perils that needed to be guarded against.[3]

Tertullian, on the other hand, thundered that Jerusalem had nothing in common with Athens, though a good case could be made that he was indulging in hyperbole. He acknowledged a limited value in civilization as opposed to savagery (a well-worn contrast in his day), but he argued in *Apology* (xxi) that Christ did not come to bring "boors and savages into some civilization...; but as one who aimed to enlighten men already civilized, and under illusions from their very culture [*urbanitas*], that they might come to the knowledge of the truth."[4]

---

[3]"Letter from Origen to Gregory," in *Fathers of the Third Century*, A. Cleveland Cove, ed., vol. 6, *The Ante-Nicene Fathers* (Grand Rapids MI: Eerdmans, 1951) 393-94.

[4]The translation of Clement's *paideia* and Tertullian's *urbanitas* by "culture" should probably be questioned as anachronistic. *Paideia* usually means something like "education," and *urbanitas* might be rendered "sophistication." But in these contexts "culture" may be semilegitimate. Hans Küng calls Clement's *paideia* "a grand educational process" and says that Clement and Origen so described "the whole history of humanity." See Hans Küng, *Theology for the Third Millenium* (New York: Doubleday, 1988) 145.

These differences between the yea-sayers on the one hand and Tertullian on the other stemmed in part, no doubt, from differences of personality as well as from different experiences in conversion to Christ. But the persecuted minority status of the church in the Roman Empire forced a measure of critical reflection on culture that became much rarer after Constantine, at least in the centers of power in the church. The Eastern Church increasingly became the religious arm of the Byzantine State, thus falling into the traditional role of religion in Roman society long before the Empire. The Western Church was, as we shall see, more and more preoccupied with the task of reconstructing Western civilization after the collapse of Rome. This is particularly the point of view from which Augustine of Hippo wrote *The City of God*. Of the five stances described in Niebuhr's classic *Christ and Culture*,[5] Augustine took the position that Christ is the transformer of culture.

*The Church in the West.* When Rome and the Western Empire fell in the fifth century, the church was the only institution which could and did survive in the West with a reassuring presence and a large measure of acceptability. It is not without significance that Clovis, King of the Franks, converted and brought his domain into the church just a couple of decades after the downfall of the Western Empire. From that time on, the church was the major architect and custodian of those realities that came to be called Western Christian Civilization, Christendom, and specifically the Holy Roman Empire.[6] Thus, the church naturally came to have a proprietorially positive view of culture. From time to time, minority dissenting views were expressed, as in monasticism (considered under the aspect of flight from the evil world), in the fulminations of prophetic figures like Savonarola, or in numerous "heretical" movements.

All five attitudes described by Niebuhr were, as he showed, represented during those centuries in the Western Church; but the position officially espoused by the church was clearly the one Niebuhr labeled "the Christ of culture." The other positions, it will be recalled, were "Christ against culture," "Christ above culture," "Christ and culture in paradox," and Augustine's position, "Christ the transformer of culture." Nie-

---

[5]H. Richard Niebuhr, *Christ and Culture* (New York: Harper, 1951).

[6]Christopher Dawson, *Religion and the Rise of Western Civilization* (Repr. Garden City NY: Image Books, 1958; orig. 1950).

buhr had little to say about the Eastern churches, and nothing at all about the churches outside the European sphere.

In a sense, the efforts of the church can be seen as an attempt to revive the ancient notion of an integral connection between culture and religion. The church went at this, however, in two quite different directions. In the East, existing ethnicity, nationality, and language were simply confirmed, and the church became a major intrinsic component of each particular ethnic complex: Greek, Coptic, Armenian, or Slavic. This may have stemmed from the long-time survival of the Byzantine Empire, which seems to have partially continued the ancient Roman pattern of conquering peoples without assimilating them culturally.

It is interesting that this policy continues largely to this day in the churches of the Orthodox family. In the West, on the other hand, though missionary outreach continued unabated, every effort was made to create a new quasi-ethnicity and to use a single language (Latin) that would transcend existing ethnic and national identifications. The rise of modern nation states in western Europe showed that this effort was only partially successful. In very modern terms, the Eastern churches may be said to have contextualized uncritically, and the Western church to have largely resisted contextualization. Since the modern Protestant missionary movement arose in the West, and until very recently was almost totally ignorant of the Eastern churches, our focus from here on will be largely on the West.

*External Mission.* From the fall of the Western Empire to the eve of the Reformation, the church's main contact with cultures new to it was in Europe, as the process of Christianization continued. Elsewhere, it was tangential and occasional, except for its prolonged conflict with Islam at its eastern border. When it did meet other cultures, especially "advanced" ones, it often displayed admiration and imitation, as well as fear and hostility.

Missionary efforts directed at Christianizing those parts of western, northern, central, and eastern Europe which had not yet been converted by A.D. 500 were launched by many different agencies and took many forms. With respect to the cultures encountered in the process, a variety of positions were implemented, some relatively positive, some relatively negative; but in none was culture as such much in view, only its constituent bits and pieces. Some missionaries, however, did give consideration to the group identities and structures of their hosts. Cultural features were sometimes addressed, as in the letter of Gregory the Great to the abbot Mellitus, a member of the team of Augustine of Canterbury which was sent to evangelize Britain (A.D. 601).[7] But most of the time the prominent questions were more specifically religious, and in not a few cases matters of political power predominated. As we have seen, the Western and Eastern churches differed in their language policies: the Western church imposed Latin wherever it ruled, while the Eastern churches were readier to adopt the vernacular in accordance with what Sanneh has called the genius of the gospel.

It was in relation to the Islamic powers and cultures of the Middle East that the church displayed the most consistently and aggressively hostile stance. The Crusades represented in their intent and in their sometime effects the overwhelmingly prevalent attitude of the church towards the Muslim world, against which the more conciliatory positions of Ramon Lull and St. Francis of Assisi were distinctly in the minority. But it should be noted—in fact, it is a commonplace—that while the conflict was unrelenting at the religious and political levels, the West learned enormously from Islam in countless cultural domains, notably philosophy, science, mathematics, and arts and crafts. How could this happen? I think that the ability of Europeans to borrow cultural valuables wholesale from hated enemies stemmed in part from the very naivete of the prevalent notion of culture as a mere inventory of items. The medieval church would not have been nearly as open to Islamic culture if it had had a modern functionalist understanding of culture!

As is well known, the earliest Christian mission in the Far East was that of the Nestorian Christians of Iraq, who established a thriving work in Beijing and were well received by the imperial court and even by some Buddhist leaders in the seventh century. They were, from what evidence is available, quite accommodating in matters of culture and religious terminology. But this effort died after two centuries leaving no permanent traces.

During the Middle Ages, contact between the church and Christendom on the one hand, and the Far East on the other, was tenuous in the extreme. Very occasional voyages like those of Marco Polo, and two or three explicitly missionary expeditions a century, constituted almost the whole of the contact between the West and the Far East. But it is worthy of emphasis that on the basis of that little contact, Westerners came to have an attitude

---

[7]Bede, *Ecclesiastical History of the English Nation* I.30.

of admiration amounting to awe of almost everything Chinese, religion excepted. Again, religious arrogance and exclusiveness did not preclude cultural imitation.

*The Iberian Expansion.* The first large-scale encounter between the church and a wide range of non-Western cultures (plural, though the concept of plurality came much later) came during the age of Iberian expansion (1450-1750). It was under these circumstances, at the height of the first phase of European arrogant self-confidence, that *other people's* cultures became consciously problematical on a large scale. Actually, as has already been pointed out, until the present century few if any persons apart from cultural anthropologists thought of culture at all in an abstract and generic way. Among missionaries, who were of all Westerners the ones most intimately and continually involved in more than one culture, the commonest view was that the missionary's own culture (quite often labeled "Christian") was unproblematic, while the cultures of "heathens" were intensely problematic.

From that day to this, two basic postures have characterized missions which have gone out from self-consciously "superior" and more powerful countries to supposedly inferior and less powerful ones: for a long time, the dominant position was to despise both peoples and cultures, to condone or even to promote the conquest and enslavement of the peoples "for their own good," and to work for the radical replacement of indigenous cultures by the "Christian" model. But there was also from the beginning a minority counter-tendency. In the Iberian period, there were those like Bartolomé de las Casas who defended the rights and dignity of the indigenous peoples of the New World; and there were those, especially various Jesuits, who described cultures insightfully and sympathetically. The Jesuit *Relations*, indeed, published from 1610 to 1791, ran to 73 volumes of careful observation and description. Virtually all that we know of the cultures of many peoples from the period of conquest until relatively recent times was recorded and preserved for us in these documents. A particularly outstanding example of early ethnography was the work of Bernardo de Sahagún, who in the sixteenth century described the Aztecs. But the Jesuits did not achieve an explicit or coherent concept of culture.

The Iberian expansion presented a new feature in terms of the history of missions: for the first time on a major scale, missions were allied with secular power in a way that gave them the ability to coerce their audiences and not only to persuade them. It was not long before they also had the means to offer material inducements that often quite swamped the gospel. For all of the previous centuries, with few exceptions missionaries could be described by a paraphrase of Paul's expression: not many powerful, not many rich. The gospel had to make its own way on its own intrinsic merits. Now and henceforth, missionaries had not only the gospel, but many other valuable things as well. The confusions and distortions this fact has brought to missions have been acknowledged and addressed only superficially at best, as in the phrase from nineteenth-century China, "rice Christians."

We must pause here to recognize that some missionaries were, from our point of view, much more sophisticated than might be supposed. Francis X. Clooney,[8] for instance, has shown that Roberto de Nobili, the well-known Jesuit missionary in south India in the early seventeenth century, though he obviously did not use the vocabulary of "religion" and "culture" that was not invented until more than two centuries later, did apply the label "classical society" to India; in terms of his categories of thought, what he meant by this expression was that he found Indian institutions and customs, including caste, to be as legitimate and as compatible with Christianity as ancient Roman ones, and therefore to be confirmed and blessed by the church. But he also, as a man of his time and an intellectual heir of Thomas Aquinas, thought that "reason" was universally the same, and therefore that the role of Christian missions was not to change cultural *forms*, but to assign them from Christian sources their true *meaning*, which had to replace the false meanings assigned by pagan religion. In a sense, for Nobili evangelization was absorbed into apologetics.

I might add as an aside that the notion that reason is universally present and uniform was in the West virtually unquestioned from the time of the medieval scholastics through the nineteenth century. It has been only in the present century, as we shall see, that anyone has seriously proposed that it might not be so. It is of some interest, perhaps, that the view that reason is universally the same and that religion appeals preeminently to reason remains the official Muslim position. The corollary of such a position, as Nobili argued, was that any purported alternative reason was in fact error which must be combated.

*Reformation and Counter-Reformation.* It is a commonplace that the Reformers of the sixteenth century and their immediate followers had little

---

[8]Francis X. Clooney, "Roberto de Nobili, Adaptation and the Reasonable Interpretation of Religion," *Missiology* 18 (January 1990): 25-36.

or no interest in cross-cultural missions. Nor did any of them develop anything like a concept of culture. However, several of them had definite ideas about the relationship of Christianity and the church to society and its institutions, especially the state. They also had well-developed ideas about human nature and sin. All of these have had an important impact on the views and attitudes of their latter-day disciples toward culture. Luther developed a concept of "two kingdoms," for instance, which has led not a few of his followers to restrict the authority of the church to the "religious" sphere while granting to the state and other institutions a quite unqualified autonomy in other spheres. Among the fruits of this distinction have been at various moments in history the quasi-absolutizing of peoplehood, the divinization of the state and the economy, and the reduction of religion to the private affective life.

In contrast, Calvin, while he held very strong views about human fallenness and sinfulness ("total depravity"), held a quite high view of the institutions of society and their role in human well-being, especially insofar as these institutions were guided by an activist church. The Anabaptists, in contrast with both Lutherans and Calvinists, took a negative and separatist stance vis-à-vis human institutions, especially the state. This, it must be said, was more true of the spiritual heirs of Menno Simons than of Simons himself. Other perspectives, notably the Arminian and the Pietist, had characteristic features which could not but affect the views which their adherents had of culture as that concept later emerged.

On the Roman Catholic side, the Counter-Reformation did two things which from a modern perspective may seem to be mutually contradictory: on the one hand, the Council of Trent hardened the tendencies in the Church towards monoculturalism, as could be seen in the famous Chinese Rites controversy. This was a controversy between missionary orders, Jesuits who wanted to allow their Chinese converts to continue to practise their familial rites of ancestor veneration, and Dominicans who argued that these rites were part of pagan religion. Both sides appealed to the Vatican, which after many decades made the Dominican position official. Yet on the other hand, it was also the case that the Counter-Reformation greatly increased the zeal and energy of Roman Catholic missions around the world. The apparent contradiction is resolved if one realizes that culture was viewed as being inherent in the gospel.

## The Enlightenment

A number of historians and other scholars have described at great length the antecedents of the Enlightenment. We will content ourselves with highlighting three factors which contributed greatly to the shape which the Enlightenment took when it appeared. *First,* let us mention the relativizing effects of the Reformation itself. While this was of course no part of the intentions of the Reformers, who were typically at least as dogmatic as any pope, the de facto co-existence of a number of versions of "the truth" could not fail to evoke in some minds at least the whisper of incipient relativism. Sharp conflict of dogmas arouses in some temperaments increased combativeness; but in others it creates a weariness and a skepticism that undermines confident faith. *Second,* in the aftermath of the High Renaissance, came a renewed confidence in human beings and their innate capabilities. Human beings were discovering all kinds of fascinating facts about the universe and about themselves, as well as devising technical powers which enabled them to have an impact on their world hitherto unimaginable. *Third,* there was a rapidly increasing and diversifying contact with non-Western peoples along the African coast, in South and East Asia, and of course in the New World.

In these contacts, the negative and positive views described above persisted, though in modified and, as it were, secularized form. The negative view, which was widespread, emphasized the notion that these peoples and their cultures were barbarian or even savage, needing the civilizing influence of Westerners (missionaries tended to see themselves in this role). This view was often used to justify conquest, colonization, and slavery. The positive view was that these people were "in a state of nature," "noble savages," like Shakespeare's Caliban, in contrast with the deformed products of Western civilization. Rousseau was one exponent of this idea. Controversy about this question took the form of a debate about the relative merits of nature and civilization: were human beings naturally good but deformed by civilization, or were they naturally savage and in need of civilizing?

All three of these factors tended to create in the Western world an intellectual and social climate favorable to human autonomy, to human creativity, to human dominance of the world. These values, however, were often not applied to non-Europeans when contact occurred. This climate fostered a number of ideas which significantly shaped the concept of culture when it finally emerged in the nineteenth century. To these we now turn.[9]

1. The predominant idea, which was determinative of a number of crucial developments in the eighteenth and nineteenth centuries, notably in the sciences, was that of *natural law*. This took form first in the physics and astronomy of Galileo, Bacon, and Newton; but it had a decisive impact in all areas of Enlightenment thought, from chemistry and biology to politics, economics, and even ethics. Its ultimate effect was to banish God to the fringes of the universe, as in deism, if not to eliminate God altogether, as in atheism and materialism.

2. There was the emergence in full flower of the *empiricism* and *rationalism* earlier espoused by Bacon and Descartes respectively, this time in the works of Locke and others. Both were assertions of the autonomy of the human mind, and both became important components of modernity.

3. Since Harris, whom I have been following, says little about this next point, I turn to Tawney,[10] who has described in exhaustive and convincing detail the transformation of the European economic world over the centuries from the Middle Ages to the Enlightenment. Macchiavelli, Locke, Montesquieu, Rousseau, and others declared the autonomy of human *institutions,* especially the state, from the tutelage of the church or even of God. Human institutions, they insisted, were not divinely established or sanctioned, but were created by human beings by means of what Rousseau called "the social contract." They were thus properly subject to alteration or rejection by human beings if they ceased to serve their purposes in a satisfactory manner. Both the American and the French Revolutions in their very different ways exemplified deliberate and self-conscious efforts to replace oppressive political and economic institutions with new and liberating ones.

4. At the same time, however, a number of thinkers were arguing for a *historical determinism* which would logically call into question claims of the right and freedom of people to alter their institutions. Closely related was the position of some conservatives, who were in fact more prominent

---

[9]For my discussion of the Enlightenment and its antecedents and consequences, I have closely followed the relevant chapters of Marvin Harris, *The Rise of Anthropological Theory* (New York: Crowell, 1968).

[10]R. H. Tawney, *Religion and the Rise of Capitalism* (New York: Harcourt, Brace and Co., 1926).

in the following century, that the development of institutions followed its own inner logic and ought not to be subject to tampering by human intentionality. The Enlightenment was thus the time when the very profound issues of freedom versus determinism began to be seriously debated in Western thought.

5. Both *idealism* and *materialism* found expression in the Enlightenment and entered into the creation of the concept of culture. Idealism, in this context, means the view that the driving force in human affairs, including the events and movements of history, is to be found in ideas, including philosophical and religious ideas. Materialism, also in this specific context, means the view that the driving force of history is in material, objective realities, such as climate, terrain, material resources, technology, material and political power relations, and the like. Idealists argued that ideas shape reality, materialists that material reality shapes ideas. Though Baron d'Holbach took a strongly materialistic view that later influenced Marx, the dominant eighteenth-century perspective on human history was idealistic, in the sense that "reason" was the engine that powered the process by which history and historical change could be seen as "progress."

6. The Enlightenment saw a passionate debate between thinkers like Turgot on the one hand, who emphasized the unity and essential homogeneity of humankind and therefore pursued in one form or another what they called "universal history" (or, as regards language, "universal grammar"); and, on the other hand, those pre-romantics like Jean-Jacques Rousseau who gloried in particularities and differences. The former were the heirs of the "universal reason" people and were in turn followed by those social scientists like Harris who want to make nomothetic generalizations; the latter were the precursors of yesterday's Romantics and today's Malinowskian and Kroeberian functionalists.

7. Finally, the Enlightenment was the age when the idea of *evolution* and *progress*—which is to say that change equals improvement—became fashionable, before becoming the triumphant Zeitgeist of the nineteenth century. Montesquieu and Adam Ferguson developed concepts of evolutionary stages which anticipated some aspects of Morgan's work a century later, while Voltaire wrote of the passage from barbarism to civilization, in which the chief agency was "reason." Almost by definition, Enlightenment evolutionists were optimistic about the long-term future of the human race, but one Helvetius may have been the most optimistic of all; which

will give rise in my next chapter to a pungent remark by Harris about Spencer.

Out of these concepts and controversies, various Enlightenment thinkers developed incipient concepts of culture, some of them quite subtle and sophisticated, but they did not adopt a uniform label for their ideas. However, some of the philosophical and ideological concepts which we have described constituted points of departure for later debates.

A number of eighteenth-century thinkers foreshadowed the methodological concerns of anthropology, as distinct from its purely descriptive aspect. Of an early precursor, Olfert Dapper, who published in 1698 a *Description de l'Afrique*, Penniman says,

> His method has much of the precision of Spencer's *Descriptive Sociology*, and his understanding of the position of the various customs in their several societies entitles him to rank as the first of the functional anthropologists.[11]

Harris asserts that the concept of culture without either the term or formal definition started with Locke, who argued that any innate ideas would have to be universal, and that therefore ideas that varied from place to place would have to be socially learned. This opinion was widely shared, which explains the enthusiastic insistence during this period that education (Turgot, Rousseau) rather than genetic endowment determined human development; education in this context was understood comprehensively enough to approximate the modern anthropologist's "enculturation." Harris finds the concept of culture in Turgot, Spinoza, Vico, Montesquieu, LaMettrie, d'Holbach, Condorcet, and Ferguson, and goes so far as to say that "It was not the concept of culture that was absent in 1750, but rather the moral indifference of cultural relativism."[12]

## Missions in the Eighteenth Century

The eighteenth century, especially towards its end, saw a temporary waning of Roman Catholic missionary outreach, after three centuries of sustained effort. Spain and Portugal, which had been carrying the missionary load, were in serious decline. France, which had received the baton

---

[11]T. K. Penniman, *One Hundred Years of Anthropology* (Repr. New York: William Morrow, 1974; orig. 1935) 38-39.

[12]Harris, *Rise of Anthropological Theory*, 13.

from them, sank toward the end of the eighteenth century into the vortex of the French Revolution. Nevertheless, some Catholic missionaries, for example Lafitau, continued in the early part of the eighteenth century the tradition of serious investigation of the cultures of the non-Western peoples they served.

The eighteenth century also saw the dawn of Protestant missions. Actually, John Eliot had already in the seventeenth century begun missionary outreach among the Indians of Massachussetts, and had translated the Bible into "Moheecan" (1661–1663), one of the first of a long line of missionary translations and the first book printed in North America. David Brainerd, with the strong support of Jonathan Edwards, also did missionary work among the Indians. Several German pietists worked in Greenland and India, under the sponsorship of the king of Denmark. Though none of these did much with indigenous cultures, Ziegenbalg did make an excellent translation of the New Testament into Tamil (1714). Moravians, under the sponsorship and leadership of Count von Zinzendorf, worked in a number of countries. These did not have much sophistication, and made no specific contributions to our understanding of culture, even though they lived an intentionally incarnational life, some going so far as to become slaves to minister to slaves in the Caribbean. But throughout this period very little was done that would advance our understanding of culture.

CHAPTER 3

# The Nineteenth-Century World

The nineteenth century, for our purposes, extends from 1792, date of the publication of William Carey's *Enquiry*, to 1922, date of the publication of two pioneering works of functionalism in cultural anthropology. These 130 years were marked by epochal historical events and processes, and by a constellation of ideas that both arose from and supported these events and processes. In my view, the four major processes of the century that impinge on our concerns were the industrial revolution, the movement to abolish slavery and free slaves, the colonial enterprise, and the modern missionary movement. Though some have overstated the interconnections between these, it would be naive to suppose that they simply concurred in time but were fully independent of each other. We will examine the industrial revolution, the abolitionist movement, and the colonial enterprise in the next section, and the missionary movement in the next chapter.

## Major Historical Processes

The nineteenth century was marked by an explosive multiplication of both basic discoveries and practical developments in science and technology. These, together with concomitant new economic and political structures, are usually comprehensively summarized as the industrial revolution. This process was in one sense precisely what one would have expected from the optimism and empiricism of the Enlightenment, and from the several foundational discoveries and inventions that had emerged in the eighteenth century; yet the specific consequences and institutional embodiments of these developments were not foreseen even a decade or two before they took place. In particular, even though Adam Smith in *The Wealth of Nations* (1776) vigorously advocated some of the economic and political measures which fostered the industrial revolution, it is clear that he was far from accurately envisioning the exact shape this revolution was to take. Yet within a very few decades it had utterly transformed not only the means and methods of producing goods, but also the economics, the politics, and the social structures of most Western countries; so that it was in impassioned outrage at that full-blown process and its largely unforeseen noxious effects that Marx and Engels wrote *The Communist Manifesto* seventy-two years later. Not that they were alone: 1848 was marked by revolutionary eruptions all over Europe.

A crucial component of the industrial revolution was the enormous improvement in the technologies of transportation and communication, which affected missions in many ways. In 1793, it took Carey five months to get from England to India; by 1922, the trip routinely was accomplished in no more than three weeks. If one wanted to communicate with the mission field without going there, a letter in 1793 took the same five months; in 1922, mail took a few weeks and telegrams could be there in a day or two. This altered relations between home base and mission field in a myriad subtle ways. In particular, it radically diminished the de facto autonomy of missionaries on the field vis-à-vis the home board.

The industrial revolution also led to the need for expanded reliable sources of raw materials and expanded reliable markets for the excess production of factories. This in turn fueled the colonial enterprise which, though in some parts of the world it had already begun, really took off in mid-century, a few decades after the onset of the industrial revolution.

The reason the colonial enterprise in the formal sense started so late was that the European powers that had been involved in earlier colonial expansions were all preoccupied with other matters. Spain and Portugal were exhausted, and managed to keep only bits and pieces of their former empires. Neither country ever did anything much with what it retained. France had spent itself in the convulsions of its Revolution and the Napoleonic aftermath, and was experiencing perennial political instability. It kept some of its earlier territories, took Algeria in the 1830s, and then gradually moved into West and Central Africa. Britain was facing internal social and political stresses which made it reluctant to launch further overseas projects after its loss of the Thirteen Colonies in North America. South Africa, permanently taken in 1805, was an exception. The Netherlands were content with Indonesia, which they already had from the earlier colonial era. So the task of relating the non-Western world to Europe and North America was for a time left to business companies like the British East India Company, to explorers and adventurers, and to humanitarians and missionaries.

In fact, it was often humanitarians and missionaries who spurred on reluctant governments to get involved in Africa and Asia; this was especially true of efforts to eradicate the slave trade, which had their chief point of origin in Great Britain. As we shall see in the next chapter, British Christians, both at home and on mission fields, were in the forefront of those who pressed the British government to use a naval blocade to interdict the slave trade from the west coast of Africa to the Americas. Later Livingstone plied his considerable influence to persuade the British government to intervene in east and south central Africa to eradicate the slave trade directed towards the Arab world. In India, missionaries took the lead in urging the British government to take over from the British East India Company because the latter's policies and practices were abusive and had precipitated the uprising known as the Sepoy Mutiny. The Crown accordingly took control of India in 1858. In a wider frame of reference, social conditions in the "heathen" regions, as viewed by Western eyes, were deplorable or worse, and cried out for charitable alleviation.

In the United States, the history of the abolitionist movement is too well known to require retelling; it involved a massive campaign of public propaganda, continuous efforts to influence public policy at federal and state levels, and a project launched in the 1820s to repatriate freed slaves to West Africa. For this purpose, a stretch of coastal land was appropriated which was called Liberia.

This project came to an end after a relatively few people had in fact been resettled, with little or no regard for either the rights and interests of the populations living in the area or for the fact that few if any of the former slaves came from that area or had any knowledge of how to live under spartan tropical conditions. Nevertheless, the former slaves established themselves as dominant in the country, and to this day constitute an elite which has historically been quite oppressive and corrupt. Today's internal problems in Liberia can be traced back in part to that ill-judged project. For our purposes, it is most significant that the chief reason for the launching of the project was that even abolitionists could not with equanimity envision a society in which free African-Americans would live on a truly equal footing with whites.

In any case, it is clear that the earliest efforts of Western countries to launch a new colonial era were often overtly based on humanitarian motives. Yet not long after the middle of the century the enterprises of both humanitarians and business corporations in the non-Western world were increasingly incorporated into overarching projects of national aggrandizement by conquest and exploitation. Earlier reluctance to get involved, based on humanitarian and prudential grounds, quickly eroded, and the rush to carve up the non-Western world became a race that several times led to armed confrontations and almost to war between the European powers. We shall soon see how scholars in what became the social sciences provided intellectual and ideological justifications for the enterprise.

It is commonly said that the United States did not participate in the colonial era, that it never had colonies. This is almost true, but only in a quite superficial sense. The United States did have an empire, which was colonial in all but name. Its components were of three sorts. The first component was internal: it consisted of black people who were slaves until the Civil War, and who then became "free" but continued to be exploited and discriminated against in a host of ways; of Native Americans, whose sad history is well known from such books as *Custer Died for Your Sins*;[1] and of Hispanics, as more and more areas of Mexico (Texas, California, Arizona, New Mexico) were annexed by the United States. The continuous theft of land from the Indians and from Mexico over the entire century provided the raw material for that westward expansion which is so glorified in American history books.

The second component of the American empire was Latin America, de facto dominated by the United States ever since the Monroe Doctrine of 1823, a domination which was underlined by the Mexican-American War (1845-1846) and a hundred or more smaller invasions, as well as by the power of economic hegemony.

The third component was a number of islands: Hawaii, as well as those taken from Spain in 1898, Cuba, Puerto Rico, the Philippines and a few others. The process of subjugation, especially in the Philippines, was unspeakably brutal; the true story has never been widely known in the United States, masked as it was by the myth of American benevolence, of President McKinley on his knees praying for wisdom and finding divine guidance to proceed with the conquest "for the good of the natives"; and it

---

[1] Vine Deloria, Jr., *Custer Died for Your Sins: An Indian Manifesto* (New York: Avon Books, 1971); R. Pierce Beaver, *Church, State, and the American Indians* (St. Louis: Concordia, 1966).

seems that the worst atrocities were successfully kept even from missionaries on the scene.[2]

The official policy, once conquest was complete, was that the United
States served as a trustee to bring the "natives" to the point of independence; and this in fact did happen eventually in Cuba and the Philippines,
though that is part of the story of the twentieth century. But it may be said
by way of anticipation that independence never meant that these countries
could steer a truly autonomous course contrary to the policy of the United
States in matters of international relations or economics. All of these "colonies" did in fact contribute greatly to the wealth and power of the United
States, at minimal administrative cost.

Canada participated in the imperial process at one remove, via its participation in the British Empire, as well as in its dealings with its own indigenous populations; these latter were treated much as in the United States,
which is to say very badly. Australia and New Zealand were in a similar
position, both in being part of the British Empire and also in treating badly
their native peoples, the Aborigines and Maoris respectively.

The period 1880–1920 has been aptly called the Imperialist Era, because it was then that the major Western powers entered in earnest the
competition to seize colonies and create empires. They grabbed chunks of
Asia as well as many islands; but it was in Africa that the process was most
total. Explorers had already been over the ground and roughed out a crude
map of the major features of the continent. The handful of coastal trading
posts, as well as more developed bases in South and North Africa, became
the jumping off points for expeditions of conquest and occupation which
in short order had taken over virtually the entire continent.

The Congress of Berlin (1884-1885), under the sponsorship of the
newly-united Germany and the leadership of the redoutable Chancellor Otto
von Bismarck, effectively divided the continent among the European nations. There were still occasional confrontations: between France's de
Brazza and Leopold II's Stanley over the north bank of the Congo (France
won); between Britain and France over the Sudan (Britain won); between
France and Germany over Morocco and Cameroun (France won in Morocco, Germany in Cameroun).

---

[2]Stuart Creighton Miller, *Benevolent Association* (New Haven and London: Yale University Press, 1982); Joseph Schott, *The Ordeal of Samar* (New York and Indianapolis:
Bobbs-Merrill, 1964).

In Asia, the situation was rather more diverse. The British raj was firmly in control in India, and less firmly in Burma. The French seized Indochina in the 1860s. The Netherlands controlled Indonesia. Spain held the Philippines by inertia until the United States took over in 1898. But Japan had managed by becoming a modern big power itself to escape Western control.

China, on the other hand, though never formally conquered, had been vanquished and humiliated by Britain in the Opium Wars of the 1840s and the subsequent treaties. Thenceforward, China was often at the mercy of pressures backed up by military force from the Western powers, especially the United States, Britain, and France, and the international trade portion of its economy was hostage to these powers. Resentment of this fact in part motivated the violent uprising in 1900 called the Boxer Rebellion. Thailand was not conquered, but it came into the American orbit of influence.

Thus, by 1914, much of the world was officially or unofficially in the hands of the Western powers.

Great Britain, as we have said, already controlled India, Burma, and South Africa. Now, under the energetic leadership of Cecil Rhodes, it sought and acquired an empire in Africa that would stretch from the Cape to Cairo; it also took Nigeria and the Gold Coast (now Ghana) in the west. Britain practised the policy of "indirect rule," leaving existing authorities—rajahs and paramount chiefs and so on—in place, and imposing the British will through a civil service that was British at the upper levels and local at the menial levels. On the whole, it left education and many social services to Christian missions, for which it subsidized them. In South Africa, where there had been a sizeable white minority for almost three centuries, and in the Rhodesias and Kenya, where white settlers were strongly encouraged to come, Britain ruled more overtly in the interests of these settlers at the expense of the Africans, especially in matters of land and labor policies.

France came to possess Indochina and a vast stretch of territory from Algeria in the north to the mouth of the Congo in the south and from Senegal in the west to the borders of the Sudan in the east. It divided this huge area into two regions, French West Africa (eight colonies) and French Equatorial Africa (four colonies). France was in a unique situation: although the Concordat Napoleon had signed with the Vatican remained on the books until 1905, the Third Republic (1871-1940) was notoriously anticlerical. This led to a kind of ambivalence in practical relations with missions; on the one hand, French policy tended to favor the Roman Catholic missions (which were often in any case staffed by French citizens) at the expense of Protestant missions (which were rarely French in personnel). But anti-clericalism also led to a much tighter control over education, for instance, than was the case in the colonies of the other powers. A more detailed examination of French colonial policy belongs in chapter 5. France ruled in a more direct and centralized manner than Great Britain.

Germany for its part seized three major chunks of Africa—Tanganyika, Cameroun, and Togo—a part of New Guinea, and several other islands. Though German Romanticism tended to exalt the "Volk," so that one would have expected a tendency to respect existing cultures, this respect was in practice very fragile; in the crunch, whenever there was the possibility that German policy might be thwarted, direct intervention could be rather brutal. But of course German colonial rule came to an end during World War I, after which the various former German colonies were entrusted by the League of Nations, under mandate, to Great Britain, France, and Australia.

Little needs to be said about the Portuguese colonies, since Portugal held them mainly by default and did little or nothing with them. The Netherlands, as I have said, held Indonesia, taken from Portugal in the earlier colonial era, and did not participate in the nineteenth-century race. Their colonial policy was a kind of benevolent despotism.

Belgium came into the situation late, since Stanley took over the Congo not for the Belgian nation but for King Leopold II as a private owner. But the brutality of the exploitation of people and land became so notorious that international public opinion, roused in part by missionary agitation, forced the Belgian government to take over from Leopold early in the twentieth century. Subsequent developments belong in chapter 5.

Two things need to be said by way of overall generalization about the colonial era around the turn of the century. First, the northern countries—Britain, Germany, Belgium, and the United States—were the ones in which racism in its classic forms powerfully affected policy; that is, explanations and justifications of policy readily and successfully rested on racist assumptions and attitudes. France and Portugal did not on the whole use racist rationales as such; their national arrogance rested rather on culture and language, so that Africans who managed to become culturally and linguistically French or Portuguese were fully accepted into the society of the conquerors; but in practice these were extremely few, and what education was dispensed benefited a tiny minority who became a "detribalized" elite.

The second general observation is that, whatever differences there might be between the overt political and social policies of the various colonial powers, economically they were at one: mercantilism was in the nineteenth century practised in far more virulent forms than Britain could have dreamed of imposing on its American colonies in the eighteenth century.

It may be recalled that in the Introduction I outlined the process, five centuries long, in which hitherto separate peoples and nations gradually were incorporated into the world system which exists today. The era of colonial empires (roughly 1450-1950) was an intermediate phase. In both its Iberian and its western European periods, the colonial system established relationships of dominance and subservience between each metropole and its colonies, making of them a single structure which functioned for the benefit of the metropole. In matters of land, labor, cash crops, mineral resources, and so on, everything was done to milk the colonies. But, unlike earlier Iberian colonialism, this version was far cannier: enough resources were plowed back into the colonies to make them at least minimally viable, in terms of human survival and functioning. Education of a sort, medical services of a sort, were provided. But the details will be examined in chapter 5.

These three processes, the industrial revolution, the abolitionist movement, and the colonial enterprise, with their interconnections and their multidimensional consequences, profoundly affected the fourth concurrent process, the missionary enterprise, and also the intellectual baggage which missionaries carried with them. Not least among the intellectual influences upon missionaries were ideas about the origins and nature of human beings and human institutions.

## Intellectual Currents

Just as the early nineteenth century political world in Europe, after the convulsions of the French Revolution and the Napoleonic Era, saw a strong conservative reaction, so there was a parallel intellectual reaction against the bold, visionary, and "heretical" ideas of the Enlightenment.

But mere reaction is hardly creative enough to sustain an intellectual movement, and in the second quarter of the century the conservative tide ebbed, and Enlightenment ideas once again moved center stage. Thus, the intellectual currents which dominated the nineteenth century had their roots in the Enlightenment, and they both fed on and spurred the developments that we have described in the practical world. Probably the dominant idea of the nineteenth century, the one which may fairly be called the Zeitgeist of that century, was the idea of *Evolution*—the idea, that is, that change is inevitable, necessary, and good, that it represents *Progress*. This idea was not totally new, as we have seen, since it was part and parcel of the Enlightenment. But it came to dominate the age in every area and dimension of life and thought.

Foundational to evolutionism was the concept of uniformitarianism, propounded by Charles Lyell in *The Principles of Geology* (3 volumes, 1830-1833). This was the logical elaboration and culmination of the Enlightenment idea of natural law; and in the minds of the intellectual elite of the Western world, it was the final step: the free, direct, and miraculous activity of God in the origin and history of the universe was fully replaced by immutable and absolute natural laws operating over enormous periods of time. This geological concept laid the foundation for all later developments in the other natural sciences—astronomy, physics, and biology— and even in the late-blooming social sciences, which began to appear during the last third of the century. This, in the minds of many people, not least the thinkers themselves who created these disciplines, had two profound effects with religious consequences: it seemed to make God unnecessary (Laplace had already said baldly to Napoleon, "Sire, I have no need of that [the God] hypothesis"), and it seemed to make the Bible less than credible.

It is therefore ironic that the explosion of modern Protestant missions from the West to the non-Western world had its base in a culture in which Christianity was under heavy attack and itself not infrequently felt and acted extremely defensive. With astonishing speed, concepts of geophysical evolution, cosmological evolution, sociocultural evolution, and biological evolution conquered and determined the very shape of the disciplines within which they emerged. In not a few cases the evolutionary theory and the discipline emerged simultaneously, so that there was no alternative theory in place from which a rebuttal might have been launched. Wallace and Darwin, Comte and Spencer, and others became names to conjure with.

The Darwinian theory was sparked by the suggestion of Malthus that whereas resources increased arithmetically, populations grew geometrically, so that inevitably there would be insufficient food and the weaker members of the race would starve in large numbers. This gloomy forecast was coupled by Darwin with his own observation in the Galapagos Islands, during his voyage on the *Beagle*, of the marvelous adaptation of each species to its niche in the habitat. Darwin christened the Malthusian process "the struggle for survival," and suggested that "natural selection," favoring over long periods of time those populations of organisms which were best adapted to their environment, had produced the various well-adapted species native to each place.

As an aside, one may wonder why most Christians, faced with the various types of evolutionary theories, elected to resist Darwinian biological evolution while swallowing whole the concurrent generalized concepts of sociocultural evolution. No doubt a partial explanation is that Darwin's theory most obviously seemed to challenge the truthfulness of Scripture, understood literally. It was not as easy to point out specific incompatibilities between the ideas of Comte, Gobineau, and Spencer and the surface meaning of the biblical message. These latter ideas, moreover, were quite supportive of unrestrained laissez-faire capitalism, which was widely seen as the economic system most compatible with the Bible, if not actually taught in it. They could also be construed as compatible with the prevalent optimistic post-millenial eschatology. Yet in retrospect, it is the fallout of sociocultural evolutionism that has done far more measurable damage on the human scene by justifying all kinds of exploitative relationships between persons and groups.

In the nascent sciences dealing with human phenomena, there were several subsidiary developments that fed into the overall stream of thought. First, archeological findings led to the discovery, first stated explicitly by Councillor Thomsen of Copenhagen, that human societies had moved successively through periods when they used different materials to make tools: a Stone Age, a Bronze Age, and an Iron Age. The Stone Age was later subdivided into an old (Paleolithic) period, a middle (Mesolithic) period, and a late or new (Neolithic) period. It was on this foundation of successive periods, *progressing* one after the other, that later ideas of cultural evolution were constructed.

A second notion which quickly took hold was this: that between human populations there were significant biological and psychological differences such that these populations could be ranked on an inferior-superior scale. This, the essence of racism, was first formulated in an intellectually elaborate way by a Frenchman, the Comte de Gobineau, in his *Essai sur l'inégalite des races humaines* (1853-55). It should be noted that he was the first to use the word "race" in this sense. But the fact that racism was universally accepted and taken for granted can be seen from the speed with which the term was taken up by others: as early as 1859, Darwin gave to his blockbuster the title *On the Origin of Species by Means of Natural Selection or the Preservation of the Favoured Races in the Struggle for Life.* Supported by the genetic ideas of Galton and others, and by various other intellectual and pragmatic considerations, this noxious prejudice became coin of the realm.

It was not at first clear whether the "inferior" races would or even could ever evolve to the status of the "superior" ones. In fact, this was hotly debated throughout the century and beyond. Everything depended on whether the "inferiority" of the dark "races" was genetic, in which case there was really no hope in the short run, since biological evolution at best worked very slowly; or whether it was culturo-religious, in which case a prolonged period of cultural and religious transformation might do the job. In some circles the view prevailed that it was precisely the job of Christian missions to accomplish this latter humanitarian task.

Some racists argued for monogenetic evolution, that is the single origin of all "races" of humankind; but the more extreme argued for polygenetic evolution, which is the idea that the "races" of humankind actually sprang from different pre-human species. This latter position was defended in the twentieth century by the man who may have been the last unreconstructed racist in physical anthropology, Carleton Coon of Harvard.

The great majority of scholars were racial determinists, turning their backs on the Enlightenment insight into the crucial role of enculturation in shaping human development. Racist propaganda was also used, says Harris, for purposes of social control. In order to defuse class discontent based on economic injustice, state propagandists in several European countries labored to create "the fiction of common descent [among all the citizens of each nation] enshrined in the metaphor of fatherland and motherland."[3] The idea was that if the people of, say, Germany, could be induced to think of themselves as a single people with common interests against the rest of the world, they would submerge or sublimate their internal conflicts in the

---

[3]Marvin Harris, *The Rise of Anthropological Theory* (New York: Crowell, 1968) 106.

interests of the greater unity. Thus racism was consciously used for ideological purposes to control populations by indoctrination.[4]

A third line of thought contributed to the birth of the social sciences, flowering from Enlightenment seeds: this was expressed in the ideas of Auguste Comte (1798-1857) about society, and specifically in his views about the supposed evolution of dominant modes of thought across time. Comte, a Frenchman, has the honor of having coined the term "sociology." Building on foundations laid by Saint-Simon, he wrote a number of books, among them *Cours de philosophie positive* (6 volumes, 1830-1842) and *Système de politique positive* (4 volumes, 1851-1854).

In these he posited a three-stage evolutionary ladder whose rungs were dominant styles of thought, which he said characterized human societies at successive stages of their history. First, in his scheme, was the long period of time during which humankind thought *theologically*—obviously, to Comte, a superstitious period, in which humans felt that they were under the control of divine forces which it was folly to question or resist and to which subjection was the only sane policy. This was followed by a time when humans (at least in some societies) thought *metaphysically*; that is, they began to exercise their minds in a questioning, critical manner, investigating the world and themselves. Finally, Comte assigned to himself the privilege of announcing the birth of the age of *scientific* or *positive* thinking, when both superstition and speculation were to be replaced by positive knowledge, the fruit of scientific inquiry.

Operating with a dominant image of society as an organism, Comte believed that social phenomena— what he called social statics (which would later be called functional relations) and social dynamics (that is, evolution)—were subject to discoverable laws in the same way as the phenomena of the natural world. He was a thoroughgoing historical determinist. Yet, paradoxically, he took a quite cavalier attitude towards any idea of material causation and disdained empirical evidence! It is clear that Comte is one of the founding fathers of one of the dominant religions of the nineteenth century and of the first part of the twentieth, scientism.

John Stuart Mill (1806-1873) borrowed and blended ideas from both Locke and Adam Smith in attempting to formulate a liberal (in the nineteenth-century sense) approach to what Harris calls "the evolution of pro-

---

[4]See also Philip D. Curtin, " 'Scientific' Racism and the British Theory of Empire," *Journal of the Historical Society of Nigeria* 2 (1960).

ductive systems." He has been more influential in economics and political science than in anthropology, however.

The Englishman Herbert Spencer (1820-1903) worked and wrote over a very extended period of time, in fact during the entire last half of the century. His major works include *Social Statics* (1851), *Principles of Psychology* (beginning in 1862), *Principles of Sociology* (3 volumes, 1862-1869), and a series called *Descriptive Sociology* (begun in 1873). Some of his most seminal ideas were born toward the middle of the century, while others were still emerging towards the end of the century. His basic ideas about sociocultural evolution actually antedated the work of Darwin and Wallace, so that whoever coined the phrase which has most persistently stuck to Spencer, "social Darwinism," did him a disservice. There is no doubt, however, that in his later formulations he did borrow ideas from the biological realm, notably those of natural selection and the survival of the fittest.

Spencer came to believe so religiously in the sanctity of these processes in the human and social domain that any interference to mitigate their operation was to be totally avoided and condemned. It was the *right* of superior persons and especially of superior classes and societies to dominate inferior ones, and even, if competition led to that end, to eliminate them. No sentimental considerations should be allowed to subvert this sacred process. This, needless to say, was a welcome justification for the colonial enterprise. Harris says, in his pungent style,

> The peculiar appeal of Spencerism was that it safeguarded Christian charity by combining Malthusian pessimism about the immediate present with Helvetian optimism about the distant future. Human nature was modifiable, but not immediately. Institutions were modifiable, but not immediately. Evolution must run its course.... The utility of this position for an empire or a corporation on which the sun never set needs no special emphasis.... Missionaries, merchants, industrialists, each in their own way, used the imagined biocultural specialties of the "inferior" races as the justification for inferior treatment.[5]

Another dimension of the Enlightenment debate which persisted into the nineteenth century was that between idealists (in the tradition of Kant and Hegel), who thought that the primary causation in the universe and in history was mental and ideational, and the materialists, whose champion

---

[5]Harris, *The Rise of Anthropological Theory*, 133-34.

from the 1830s on was Karl Marx (1818-1883). Beginning in his native Germany, Marx wrote a number of philosophical works which laid the foundations of his thought. But his most famous works were *The Communist Manifesto* (1848, with Engels) and *Das Kapital* (3 vols., 1867-94, completed by Engels), the latter written in London.

In his analysis of both his own era, that of the early industrial revolution, as well as of earlier historical periods, Marx borrowed from Hegel the idea that dialectic relationships constitute the dynamic of history, but built for his version a resolutely material engine: what determined the nature of any historical period or of any social system was control of the "means of production."

In an agrarian society, for example, the means of production is land, so that whoever controls the land controls society, shapes it to suit the purposes of the dominant "class," and provides an ideology to justify the dominance of that class. In Marx's view, capitalism provided just such an ideological foundation in an industrial economy for the control of society by the owners of factories and their allies in business and politics; and religion functioned as a narcotic to allay any incipient expressions of discontent by the dominated, exploited class, labor. Yet it was labor, and only labor, which in fact created the value of manufactured products. The noxious process by which labor was robbed of the value of its products and cynically persuaded that this theft was justified, Marx called "alienation."

Whatever one may think of this analysis, not to mention the accompanying militant atheism and the conclusion that only violent revolution could ultimately remedy the problem, one must credit Marx with at least two important contributions: emphasis on the importance of the real-world, material conditions under which people actually exist; and the tools for a critique of ideology, that is for questioning prevalent explanations and justifications of any given status quo by asking such questions as "Says who? Who benefits? Who is hurt?" Just as Marx's outrage at systemic injustice made him the ethical heir of the very Old and New Testament prophets whom he rejected, so his keen insight into the mechanics of social rationalization provides us today with a powerful tool for a Christian critique of things as they are. The issue will resurface later on in our criticism of functionalist concepts of culture.

This is the best place to discuss a very important dimension of the contrast between Spencer (and most of the fathers of cultural anthropology) on the one hand, and Marx on the other. Spencer, looking at the terrible struggle between classes and between societies from the vantage point of the winning side, pronounced it good: unchecked by noxious sentimentality, it was the engine of progress. Marx, looking at it from the perspective of the losers, called it outrageous, and issued an imperious summons to revolution. At just this point, in a paradoxical way, Spencer was the forerunner of the Malinowskian and Kroeberian functionalists, the scientists of the status quo. Marx, augmented by Lenin's critique of imperialism, was to influence a later school of thought in the social sciences: the cultural materialists, whom we shall meet in the twentieth century. Ironically, both Spencer and Marx argued passionately for a laissez-faire attitude towards social conflict, because they expected opposite outcomes from a totally unmitigated struggle.

As Kenneth Hamilton has pointed out,[6] immediately after Hegel various thinkers began to use images to speak of social realities; two emerged, the organic and the mechanistic. Organic images, says Hamilton, tended to be used by thinkers of the "right" and thinkers with religious commitments, because the vegetable analogy carried with it a suggestion of life and teleology. The mechanistic image was adopted by thinkers of the "left," notably Marx. It is dominant today, as in the language of "keeping pace," but it is in principle deterministic. Ironically, the most recent revival of the organic image has been captured by proponents of what Hamilton calls "rootless freedom," the flower children of the sixties; and, I might add, the New Age people today, though perhaps this should not surprise us since astrology is quite mechanistic.

## Evolutionary Theory

*Precursors.* As we saw in the previous chapter, most if not all of the intellectual components of a concept of culture were in place by the end of the eighteenth century. Fred Eggan quotes Slotkin to the effect that "all fields of anthropology were developed by the end of the 18th century. In fact their bases were established in the 16th and 17th centuries" so that what happened in the period 1860 to 1900 was merely the professionalization of anthropology.[7] There were also precursors in the period around

---

[6]Kenneth Hamilton, *To Turn from Idols* (Grand Rapids: Eerdmans, 1973) 83-88.

[7]Fred Eggan, "Ethnology and Social Anthropology," in *One Hundred Years of Anthropology*, ed. J. O. Brew (Cambridge: Harvard University Press, 1968) 121.

the mid-century, in which foundational work was being done by Germans such as G. F. Klemm and Theodor Waitz. But these were enormously erudite compendia of information about many cultures, not formulations of any true theory of culture.

So it remained necessary for someone—actually, a number of persons—to pull all the pieces together, endow them with a label, and assign to them some sort of a coherent theory. Preliminary work was done on the continent, by such scholars as Bastian and Bachofen, and in England by Henry Maine and J. F. McLennan. These raised certain questions, made certain assumptions, and in a real sense defined and established the boundaries of the field within which the issues could be discussed.

Because a number of the scholars who became concerned with the relevant questions were lawyers and political thinkers, they naturally raised questions which their professional formation and political predilections suggested to them. So it was that for better or worse, the questions that came to dominate the field dealt with matters of social structure: family, kinship, and marriage; and economic, political, legal, and governmental institutions. And because of the evolutionary Zeitgeist of their day, they became obsessed with wondering how these things had functioned in truly "primitive" times, how the earliest humans had dealt with these matters. Thus was born—Kuper would say "invented"—the concept of "primitive society."[8]

Both the earliest scholars to raise these issues and their successors in the full-blown discipline of anthropology worked within the framework of this concept, and agreed or disagreed about the questions that were raised about it. Kuper traces what he calls the "transformations" of the conceptual components and configurations centering on this notion right up to our own times. Among the questions variously answered were: whether or not "primitive society" knew marriage or went through a period of sexual promiscuity and/or group marriage; whether "primitive society" was patrilineal or matrilineal; and whether or not the kinship terminologies of "primitive society" accurately revealed the social structure.

What was never questioned, then or later, was that there was such a thing as "primitive society." The seductiveness of this notion stemmed from its inherent ambiguity (Kuper, in my opinion, does not sufficiently

---

[8]Adam Kuper, *The Invention of Primitive Society* (London and New York: Routledge, 1988).

highlight this factor). Etymologically, it referred to a real, even self-evident fact: that there *were* such things as the first humans, and that they presumably lived in groups and therefore had to develop some sort of rules of social organization. But how these earliest humans might have resembled their closest primate cousins/ancestors in these arrangements was problematical.

Even more problematical was the fact that virtually without question, it was taken for granted that contemporary societies which displayed some of the same cultural features as could be ascertained about the primal humans from archeological evidence were *also* "primitive." The very sparsity and built-in bias of archeological evidence towards durable artefacts was ignored, as scholars happily went about the business of extrapolating from ancient humans to "our primitive contemporaries" (there was actually a book by that title in the twentieth century) and back again.

It is a significant contribution of Kuper to show that how anthropologists—whether evolutionists, diffusionists, functionalists, configurationists, or neo-evolutionists— answered the questions on the "primitive" agenda depended at least as much on ideological and even personal concerns as on the evidence. Such considerations as one's political views— conservative, reformist, or revolutionary—, whom one was feuding with, which school of thought or institution was dominant, and other matters of this non-scientific sort, profoundly affected the scholarly debates of anthropologists.

*Tylor and Morgan.* But it is to Lewis Henry Morgan and Edward B. Tylor that the consensus of the discipline assigns the honor of having developed the concept and embryo theory of culture and founded cultural anthropology.

The term "culture" was used in something like a modern sense in German in the 1840s and in English in the 1860s. But Edward B. Tylor (1832-1917) in England created the first formal definition of the term culture: culture, he wrote, is "that complex whole which includes knowledge, belief, art, law, morals, custom, and any other capabilities and habits acquired by man as a member of society."[9] It will be noticed that, though Tylor granted minimal recognition to the idea of a "complex *whole*," the definition is in effect a mere list of items. Nor, as Singer has pointed out, did this "def-

[9]Edward B. Tylor, *Primitive Culture*, 2 vols. (Repr. New York: Henry Holt, 1889; orig. 1871) 1.

inition distinguish social organization and social institutions from a general concept of culture.''[10] It was only later, with the advent of functionalism, that a sense of coherence and integration among the components of culture became a part of the concept. In any case, the crucial question for evolutionism was not how things fit or worked together, but how they came into being.

Tylor, though he wrote a massive two-volume work entitled *Primitive Culture*, and dealt at length with all of the domains of culture—material, social, and ideational—is best known for his ideas regarding the evolution of religion. He argued for a surprisingly rationalistic explanation of the origin and development of this important aspect of culture: the earliest humans, he speculated, wondered what exactly it was that happened during sleep, dreams, and death. They noted that while observers could see that a sleeping person remained inert, that person could be experiencing via dreams a great many things—traveling, conversations with others including those long dead, and the like. These prehistoric persons, Tylor said, concluded that there must be inside each person, and in fact inside each animal and each other object in the universe, a kind of nonmaterial double which could exist and move outside the body, and to which Tylor assigned the label "soul." This belief in the existence of "souls" in every bit of reality Tylor called "animism," from the Latin for "soul." It was in Tylor's scheme the first stage in the evolution of religion.

In one version of the second stage, the "souls" of the dead, especially those who had been particularly significant in life, such as culture heroes, were accorded special veneration. This was the ancestor cult, which to this day prevails in many societies, both highly sophisticated (for example, China and Japan) and preliterate. In a similar manner, the "souls" of the most prominent and powerful phenomena of nature, such as heavenly bodies, mountains, major rivers, and the like, were deified. This, according to Tylor, was the origin of polytheism. Eventually, as societies advancing in other cultural spheres developed monarchy, the same institution was attributed to the sphere of the divine, and one god or goddess became the ruler of the heavenly realm. The ultimate religious evolution was the insight, achieved only once or twice in the experience of humankind, that the chief god was in fact the only God: monotheism had arrived, the cul-

---

[10]Milton Singer, "Culture: the Concept of Culture," in *International Encyclopedia of the Social Sciences*, ed. David L. Sills, vol. 3 (New York: The Macmillan Co., 1968) 527.

mination of evolution. It was left for Freud in his fanciful writings about religion to add an extra step to this process: the evolution of humankind to the point of rejecting religion as an illusion.[11]

Lewis Henry Morgan (1818-1881), a lawyer working in upstate New York, for his part developed in great detail concepts of the evolution of material culture and of social structures, especially those of kinship. Interestingly, he seems to have used the term ''culture'' little if at all. His work represents at one end extremely careful and enduringly useful descriptive efforts regarding the Iroquois, whom he knew intimately; and at the other quite extravagant speculation, when he was working selectively but uncritically with data from the writings of others.

His scheme for the evolution of material and technical culture was spelled out in three major stages: savagery, barbarism, and civilization.[12] Each in turn was subdivided into lower, middle, and upper phases. Passage from one phase to another, or from one major stage to the next, was marked decisively by the discovery or invention of one or two specific cultural features. Thus, a society passed from lower savagery to middle savagery when it discovered the use of fire and invented fishing. Both were necessary; a society that had one but not the other remained in lower savagery, no matter what else they devised. Similar all-or-nothing diagnostic traits were assigned to every particular rung of the evolutionary ladder. No deviations or exceptions were allowed; Morgan, in other words, created a most Procrustean bed!

It should be added that even though he wrote about the evolution of material culture (techniques, implements, etc.), he was *not* a cultural materialist, since he never really examined the question of historical causation, much less material causation. In fact, though the evolutionists insisted that what they were reconstructing was real history, their theoretical and ideological agendas, coupled with the paucity of empirical evidence concerning much that they argued about, led them to erect purely imaginary constructs, that is, to do pseudo-history.

It must be pointed out in all fairness that though the builders of theory did little or no fieldwork themselves, they did sponsor and direct from afar by correspondence a number of fieldworkers of various degrees of capa-

---

[11]Sigmund Freud, *Totem and Taboo,* trans. James Strachey (New York: Norton, 1952); *The Future of an Illusion*, trans. W. D. Robson-Scott (London: Hogarth Press, 1928).

[12]Lewis Henry Morgan, *Ancient Society* (New York: Henry Holt, 1877).

bility, including the missionary Fison, who provided them with a great mass of data to serve as raw material for their constructs. Most of these carried out their investigations among the Aborigines of Australia, who were widely supposed to be the most "primitive" peoples in existence. But since for the most part the data were gathered in answer to questions dictated by the theoretical concerns of the sponsors, this process was not as fruitful as it might have been.

One question about evolution which was not resolved in the nineteenth century was whether it was always automatic and propelled deterministically by immanent properties of the universe, or whether it could be materially affected or even steered by divine and/or human intentionality. Some thinkers, Karl Marx among them, can be read as saying both things, that is as contradicting themselves; they were determinists when this suited their agenda, and they exhorted their audience to get on board, to make it happen, when this suited their agenda. By the turn of the century, any element of teleology had pretty well been banished from the sciences of the natural world, which was understood to operate entirely in accordance with blind natural laws, through the interplay of randomness and determinacy. In the twentieth century, to introduce an element of purpose, goal, or intentionality into the concept of evolution (as in the mystical thought of Teilhard de Chardin) is to incur ridicule. Teleology is simply "unscientific."

It was longer before teleology was thoroughly expelled from the sciences dealing with human beings and groups, and in some quarters one is still exhorted to take charge of the evolution of social structures and systems. The controversy over determinism and free will, in other words, is still part of the agenda in the human sciences, though overt proponents of freedom are very much in the minority.

*Assumptions and Implications.* Nineteenth-century evolutionary theory made a number of basic assumptions:

1. A teleological sense of progress was very strong. Teleology was weakest in the purely secular theory, where it has now disappeared totally, rejected consciously and vehemently; and was strongest in Christian circles, which assigned to God the role of Designer.

2. There was a single ladder of progress for culture. Tylor, significantly, never used the plural "cultures"; it is as if he thought of culture as a single thing, of which each people had a greater or lesser quantity. By way of anticipation, the *Oxford English Dictionary* assigns the first use of

the singular with indefinite article (implying pluralisability) to a book entitled *The Norman Conquest,* by Freeman (1867); it finds the first use of the plural in the *Spectator* (27 June 1891) with the citation "speaking all languages, knowing all cultures, living with all races."

But the fully pluralistic and relativistic concept was the fruit of what Milton Singer has called "the Boas revolution" in the early twentieth century. In fact, though Tylor used the word "culture" in his title and in his definition, throughout the book he used "civilisation" much more frequently as a synonym. The rungs of the ladder, whether of the technological sort adduced by Morgan, or of the ideational sort adduced by Tylor, were always in the same sequence, so that one could read from the mere absence or presence of the diagnostic features what level a given people had achieved. Morgan, as was noted above, hardly used the word "culture" at all, singular or plural.

3. The reason the ladder is uniform, some of the evolutionists argued, is that human beings everywhere and at all times are mentally alike; their minds work in exactly the same way, so that given the same conditions, they will respond in the same manner; given the same problem, they will devise the same solution. This concept was labeled "the psychic unity of mankind." As a matter of fact, says Harris, "to most of the evolutionists, independent inventions were of interest, not for demonstrating evolution, but for demonstrating psychic unity."[13] This belief constitutes, no doubt, one version of the perduring notion that reason is always and everywhere the same. It will be remembered that earlier versions of the idea appeared during the Renaissance and the Enlightenment. It also constituted the seed of a reaction against racism.

4. Western civilization was self-evidently at the acme of this ladder. It had passed through all the previous stages, and had emerged as the exemplar of where all other peoples would go if they were fortunate enough. This notion was greatly exaggerated in Christian circles, where the superiority of the West was attributed to its "Christian" character, in contrast with the starkly pagan foundations of lesser societies. Is it too much to wonder whether Christian influence was in some sense supposed to have abrogated or at least mitigated the effects of original sin in Western civilization, as conversion was supposed to do for individual persons? I have not seen this suggestion overtly made, but the uncritical manner in which

---

[13]Harris, *The Rise of Anthropological Theory,* 175.

many referred to "Christian civilization" sounds as though some such assumption were being tacitly made.

5. Culture was an inventory of items relating to the various aspects of collective human life. It should be said that this was not an explicitly argued feature, but rather a feature of the theory by default. Nothing was said one way or another about how the domains and features of a culture fit together, since this was in any case not a matter of interest.

Evolutionary theory also had certain implications, which were expressed in many practical ways in dealings between Western and non-Western societies:

1. A feeling of extreme superiority was fully justified in Westerners, especially Christian ones; and ethnocentrism was a quasi-theological obligation. That missionaries were not always and exclusively cultural imperialists and iconoclasts, as Lamin Sanneh has shown they were not, is in my view little short of a miracle of grace. Those missionaries who in any sense respected indigenous cultures were surely not being true to their cultural model!

2. Conquest and colonialism were fully justified. Herbert Spencer, I have pointed out, was the most radical in drawing out all the logical reasons why this was so; his theory amounted to "might makes right" in its most naked form. It was also he who coined the phrase "survival of the fittest." Kipling gave the idea trumpeting poetic expression. In the United States, several missionary leaders were, as we shall see in chapter 4, among its vocal proponents in Christian circles.

3. Because culture was thought of as only an inventory, it was assumed to be possible to attack and eradicate isolated cultural traits such as polygyny that were deemed offensive to Christian morals, and to introduce isolated "Christian" customs and practices at will. After all, it was reasoned, these benighted people should be eternally grateful to be granted even a fragmentary participation in the superior culture of superior whites.

### Diffusionism and the Culture-Historical Theory

Early in the genesis of cultural anthropology, while the major attention, especially in the English-speaking world, was on schemes to explain the development of culture through time, other scholars, especially in Germany, were beginning to work at explaining the development of culture with reference to the distribution of traits and complexes through space. In other words, they were interested in what came to be called "cultural diffusion.'' They were especially concerned to create a theory which could lead from descriptions of the current distribution of cultural features to descriptions of the processes by which things had come to be that way.

Several of these scholars, such as Ratzel and Frobenius, traveled extensively and investigated the distributions of cultural traits in various parts of the world. But the honor of producing theories of diffusion goes to two men, Fritz Graebner and Wilhelm Schmidt.

The German Fritz Graebner (1877-1934)[14] was concerned to weigh evidence regarding whether apparently similar cultural traits had in fact been independently discovered or invented in the different places where they were found, or whether they had been discovered or invented once and then been borrowed by one culture from another. He developed four criteria designed to permit rigorous probabilistic judgments of the evidence. The "criterion of form" argued that, other things being equal, the more particularly elaborate and complex the shared form in question was, the less likely that it had been separately invented twice or more, and the more likely that it had been devised once and then borrowed.

The second criterion was the "criterion of quantity." This argued that the more numerous the inherently separate and distinct similarities of cultural forms which are found in two geographically separate places, the more likely it is that there was historical contact between those two places. The other two criteria had to do with the establishment of plausible links of travel or communication between places in which putatively similar cultural traits were found. The best-known example of an attempt to construct a convincing connection between a place of origin and a place of later distribution was the work of Thor Heyerdahl in his two expeditions with Kon-Tiki and Ra II. In the first instance, he was trying to show that features found in South America could have originated in Southeast Asia. In the other, he wanted to establish a connection between ancient Egypt and South America.

Finally, Graebner developed the concept of culture circles to represent in space the historical processes of diffusion.

Wilhelm Schmidt (1868-1954)[15] in fact transcends the limits of the nineteenth century, but his work did begin in the latter part of that century. Working chiefly in Vienna, he developed for his Roman Catholic mis-

---

[14]Fritz Graebner, *Methode der Ethnologie* (Heidelberg, Germany: C. Winter, 1911).

[15]Wilhelm Schmidt, *The Culture Historical Method of Ethnology*, trans. S. A. Seeker (New York: Fortuny, 1939).

sionary congregation, the Society of the Divine Word, what was in fact a very comprehensive missionary anthropology for that time. But he is chiefly remembered for his development of what he called the "culture-histori-cal" method. Through careful investigation of the distributions of many cultural traits, he devised the concept of culture areas. These he plotted on maps, in such a way as to trace the actual processes, and in some cases the actual chronology, of the way these traits came to be distributed as they were; he also attempted to explain why a trait had diffused in one direction but not in another.

Diffusionists made one key assumption: humankind is *not* especially inventive and ingenious, so that one cannot expect that the same condi-tions and the same problems will evoke the same responses in different times and places. Rather, people borrow readily from one another. It is easier to imitate than to create, so people do it whenever they can.

By twentieth-century standards, diffusionism can in fact hardly qualify as an *explanatory* theory at all. To describe how something works is just that, a description. To explain would require some kind of answer to the question "why." This the diffusionists never really attempted.

Tacitly, but only in a very low-key way, Graebner's criterion of quan-tity implied an incipient concept of connectedness between cultural fea-tures, since one was obliged to take into consideration whether feature A and feature B were distinct enough to count for two, or whether they were at some analytical level one by virtue of necessary association, as with a bow and arrow. But one must not infer from this incidental detail anything like the understanding generated by functionalism of a tight integration be-tween all traits and domains of a culture.

In spite of the involvement of Schmidt in the very development of dif-fusionism, this theory turned out to have relatively few significant impli-cations for missions. Though it is clear in retrospect that the missionary enterprise through the centuries constituted in itself perhaps the most ex-tensive intentional diffusional process of all time up to the twentieth cen-tury, it was little examined in that light. Perhaps this was because diffusionists focused so heavily on material culture, which could be in-vestigated not only by contemporary observation but by archeology. For both valid and dubious reasons, it may be that in the history of cultural an-thropology, diffusionism will become a mere footnote.

## Conclusions

To summarize: the Enlightenment bore fruit in the fundamental concept of evolution as progress, and—for some, at least—the concept of human autonomy and human power to change the human condition at will. This both led to and fed on extraordinary advances in science and technology, with the industrial revolution and the colonial enterprise as its most conspicuous manifestations. We have also seen that all of this produced in the West an extremely heady mood of optimism, self-confidence, and arrogance. We have seen that the combined impact of the material and economic pressures of the industrial revolution, the humanitarian impulse to eradicate slavery, and the overweening sense of Western destiny and superiority led to the colonial enterprise, in which the advanced societies of Europe took on the "White Man's Burden," the right and duty to rule the "inferior" peoples for their own good.

But it may not be inappropriate to use the tools of Karl Marx and to ask a probing question: is the convergence of developments in the "real world" and the ideas I have been describing really fortuitous? The obvious "fit" between them makes this convergence seem exceedingly suspect. Is it really credible that the people who were blithely developing these ideas and thereby placing themselves, as members of dominant societies, in a highly privileged position, were totally innocent? One need not go to the length of postulating conscious sinister conspiracy to think that there was a great deal of overt and covert self-interest in the arrogance and ethnocentrism the ideas expressed.

We have also said that it was in this atmosphere that the modern Protestant missionary movement, the third major historical process of the nineteenth century, took its most explosive development. This is the subject of the next chapter, where we will see that the missionaries were, by and large, children of their time, motivated indeed by love for Christ and love for their "unfortunate" fellow-humans, but also subject to the views and attitudes, the prejudices and blind spots of their age.

# CHAPTER 4

# Nineteenth-Century Missions

## The Historical Context

It was in the context of the world described in the previous chapter that the modern Protestant missionary movement took its rise and its extraordinary, explosive development. There were, it should be noted, precursors in the seventeenth and eighteenth centuries—German Pietists and Moravians, American Congregationalists, and British Anglicans—whose work is described in another volume of this series.

But it is more than a purely symbolic notion that assigns the real birth of the modern missionary movement to the publication in 1792 of Carey's *Enquiry*. The British Baptist churches thus had the honor of launching the movement; Carey and his colleagues Joshua Marshman and William Ward constituted the Serampore Trio, which registered great achievements from the beginning of their work in 1793 well into the 1830s. Neill gives an excellent brief description of Carey's policies and methods, lauding especially his emphasis on "a profound study of the background and thought of the non-Christian peoples."[1] It was not long before other British missionaries, sent by an increasing number of missionary societies, went to many different countries. From the United States, Adoniram and Ann Judson went to Burma in 1812. They were followed by an ever-spreading flood of others from several Protestant countries, sent by various missionary societies to many different countries, until the whole period from Carey to

---

[1]Stephen Neill, *A History of Christian Missions* (Harmondsworth, England: Penguin Books, 1964) 263-64; see also A. Christopher Smith, "The Edinburgh Connection: Between the Serampore Mission and Western Missiology," *Missiology* 18 (1990): 185-209.

the Edinburgh Missionary Conference of 1910 could appropriately be called by Latourette "the Great Century."[2]

The relationship of this movement to the colonial enterprise is, of course, a most interesting and significant one, which has been studied by many scholars.[3]

In the early part of the century, missions in many cases preceded the expansion of the colonial empires. Later, as the colonial expansion accelerated, missions arrived at the same time as, or soon after, the colonial powers. The areas which first attracted missions were the Asian countries of literate civilizations: India, China, Burma, Indonesia; the parts of Africa along the western and southern coasts which had already experienced Western influence for some time; a rapidly growing number of Pacific island societies; and the internal indigenous "colonies" of the United States and Canada. Japan was added in the 1850s. Later in the century, as the colonial enterprise burgeoned, missions continued to move onward, either just before or just on the heels of the colonizing powers. By the end of the period, and especially after the "faith" missions entered the fields, many of the interior parts of Asia and Africa were at last touched by missionary work.

It did not seem to make too much difference whether or not the missionaries were from the colonizing country. One might expect that the missionaries who were "at home" with the colonial power would be more supportive and less critical of that power than foreigners. This was indeed sometimes the case. But in the face of the massive presence of non-Western peoples and cultures, Westerners tended to stick together and to support and defend each other as Westerners. Furthermore, missionaries who were not citizens of the colonial power were acutely aware that they lived and worked in their fields by sufferance of that power, and they tended to be correspondingly circumspect. A significant exception was in the Congo, where it was missionaries, none of them Belgians, who led the hue and cry that forced Belgium to take the colony from its king because of the atroc-

---

[2]Kenneth Scott Latourette, *The Great Century,* vols. 5 and 6 of *A History of the Expansion of Christianity* (New York: Harper, 1943, 1944; repr. Grand Rapids: Eerdmans, 1970).

[3]E.g., Torbin Christensen and William R. Hutchison, eds., *Missionary Ideologies in the Imperialist Era 1880-1920* (Aarhus, Denmark: Aros, 1982); John K. Fairbank, ed., *Christianity in China* (Cambridge MA: Harvard University Press, 1974); Max Warren, *The Missionary Movement from Britain in Modern History* (London: SCM Press, 1965).

ities they witnessed. But by and large missionaries, citizens or not of the colonial power, were supportive of the colonial enterprise as such and saw it as favorable for the spread of the gospel.

Missionaries for the most part also applauded the results of the Opium War of Britain against China, which compelled China to admit opium and more missionaries. Later, they applauded when they did not actually call for intervention by Western powers to defend Western and mission interests. And by the end of the century, missions led the chorus in praise of American conquest of the erstwhile Spanish colonies.

Late in the century, Latin America was "discovered" as a Protestant mission field by North American and British agencies. In a period when the established Roman Catholic Church was still monolithically aligned with the privileged classes and where the poorest masses were only nominally Christianized, Protestants initially brought a breath of fresh air. They represented progressive, "liberal" ideas from the home of democratic values. But as time passed and notions of "manifest destiny" came to the fore, the more activist mainline Protestant missionaries became protagonists for the ideas and interests of their North American and European home countries in the name of the civilizing mandate. Meanwhile, the more conservative missionaries, rejecting the liberal theology and social gospel of their mainline opponents, saw themselves as politically uninvolved. But their attitudes, reflexes, and influence turned out in fact not to be all that different.

One can roughly divide the century into three partly overlapping phases: (1) the period of beginnings, from the time of William Carey's *Enquiry* in 1792 to the mid-century, during which only voluntary societies sponsored missions; (2) the period of consolidation, which began in mid-century and lasted beyond the Edinburgh 1910 conference, during which the voluntary societies expanded and settled in, and denominations began to establish missions; and (3) starting in the last third of the century, the rise of the "faith" missions, with their very particular ethos.

The period of beginnings lasted from 1792 until the mid-century. Voluntary ad hoc societies launched the movement when the regular church authorities declined to do so. They pioneered in many fields, evangelized, founded churches, produced and printed Bible translations, and built clinics and schools. By the middle of the century, their work was in many cases substantial, and they were dealing with second-generation Christians and the need of churches for discipline, teaching, and leadership.

This led, about the middle of the century, to a process of consolidation. In the United States especially, denominations began their own missions and joined in the enterprise. As the number of missionaries increased, as their work became more and more institutional and therefore complex and expensive, it became necessary to develop more efficient administrative structures, and it also became necessary to appeal to richer donors, most of whom were businesspeople. These dynamics, together with the needs of the more mature churches on the field, pressed missions into a mode of consolidation and maintenance. It became less and less urgent to move out to the vast areas not yet reached with the gospel.

Simultaneously with the move to social ministries, and as more and more people were sent to foreign fields and missions thus became bigger, the major boards, especially in the United States, became more and more formally structured in accordance with the patterns of business organizations. This was calculated to inspire the trust of wealthy potential donors, who would have little confidence in pious groups run by preachers. More and more board executives had business experience or talents, and ran their organizations efficiently, like a business.

Part of this approach involved a transformation of the public relations appeals; this was an important reason for the emphasis on social and civilizational activities, and in particular for the presentation of missions as good for American trade and American influence in the world. But we must not think that was all there was to it. Missions continued to exercise a spiritual ministry, continued to evangelize and plant churches. Mission executives continued to exercise a pastoral as well as an administrative role in relation to their missionaries. But some mainline missions did become big businesses and could be thought to have lost sight of the primary reason for their existence, at least from the perspective of the more conservative constituencies.

It was into this picture that the "faith missions," pioneered by James Hudson Taylor's China Inland Mission in 1865, brought a new element. In proportion as the older missions settled down and shifted their emphasis from evangelization to church maintenance and institutional work and were increasingly caught up in the civilizational and national ideologies of their homelands, the faith missions renewed the emphasis on primary evangelism, especially in the great interior regions of the continental land masses. The mystique that was developed, and that made a virtue of the rural and small-town mentality of many of their supporters, focused not merely on the interior regions but specifically on their more remote and "bush" areas. One thing needs to be added: the independent faith missions were, as we shall see before long, powerfully motivated by a premillennial eschatology which emphasized that the world must be evangelized before the imminent return of Jesus Christ (Matthew 24:14).

## Roots of the Movement

*Religious Factors.* It is fitting that we examine now the specifically religious roots of the movement, since whatever else motivated the pioneer missionaries, their most intense and most self-conscious purpose was always religious: the conversion of people to Jesus Christ, and the founding of Christian churches.

As is well known, the modern Protestant missionary movement was the spiritual fruit of German Pietism and Moravianism, and also of the Wesleyan revival, which was influenced by both. These determinative influences, superimposed on the theological ideas of the various branches of the sixteenth-century Reformation, shaped an understanding of the gospel and of evangelization that was very "spiritual," otherworldly, and individualistic, howbeit modified by the Wesleyan social conscience.

The doctrine of original sin was almost universally taken for granted. All human beings, but especially the "heathen," were depraved and lost, doomed to hell apart from the salvation made available in Jesus Christ. Persons had to receive this salvation by a conscious act of faith and repentance. The Baptist portion of the movement obviously rejected the view of the church as including those baptized in infancy; but even the Anglican and Pietistic (Lutheran) strands by and large demanded a conscious personal decision to follow Christ and a concomitant change of life, especially when they were working in "heathen" lands.

Specifically eschatological motives were also powerful in the nineteenth century. Piggin[4] has described four relevant positions which affected his sample of British missionaries to India in the first half of the century: postmillennialism moved some people to work to bring in the kingdom of God through missionary outreach; premillennialism moved other people to evangelize the world in view of the imminent return of Jesus Christ; pure dispensationalism of the Darbyite sort was, however, an in-

---

[4]Stuart Piggin, *Making Evangelical Missionaries 1789-1858* (N.p.: The Sutton Courtenay Press, 1984) 142-45.

hibiting factor for Piggin's sample in the circles which espoused it; finally, some assigned priority to evangelizing the Jews in light of Romans 1:16.

There is every reason to generalize from this sample to the movement at large, especially with regard to the two major positions. Later in the century, in North America, postmillennialism became the dominant view of the mainline churches; its optimism blended with the emerging social gospel, and with the notion of the "civilizing mission" and "manifest destiny" of the United States, to create a most heady brew. In sharp contrast, as Dana Robert has shown,[5] the faith missions were motivated by premillennial dispensationalism, which took a gloomier view of the present evil world, and whose sense of urgency eclipsed the inhibitory effects which the strictly dispensational component had had earlier in Britain.

Other religious motives listed by Piggin, which can also be widely generalized, include the hope of heavenly rewards, a sense of duty, love, pity, and the glory of God.[6]

*Humanitarian Factors.* It should surprise no one that a movement influenced by the Wesleyan revival should also have a strong humanitarian component in addition to the purely religious aspect. For most missionaries, there was a close link between Western "Christian" civilization and evangelization, which implicitly demanded that the instruments of the civilizing process—chiefly schools—should be an integral part of mission. But there were other humanitarian factors that played an important motivating role in missions.

The first and most general was that, from the point of view of Western missionaries, life in the non-Western world was obviously harsh and miserable. Disease, starvation, violence, vice, illiteracy, corrupt and repulsive customs were all rampant. Causes of these conditions, in addition to original sin, which as we have seen most took to be universal, included the "inferiority" of the people and their cultures, the darkness of "heathenism," the incidence of tribal warfare, and in many cases the ravages of the slave trade. These social ills constituted an unavoidable challenge for the spiritual children of Wesley, or for that matter for any disciples of Jesus of Nazareth.

---

[5]Dana L. Robert, " 'The Crisis of Missions': Premillennial Mission Theory and the Origins of Independent Evangelical Missions," in *Earthen Vessels: American Evangelicals and Foreign Missions, 1880-1980,* ed. Joel A. Carpenter and Wilbert R. Shenk (Grand Rapids: Eerdmans, 1990) 29-46.

[6]Piggin, *Making Evangelical Missionaries,* 124-55.

But what was the solution? A debate occupied much of the century about the nature of the link between evangelization and civilization. Early in the century, such voices as those of Henry Venn and Rufus Anderson insisted that Christianization was primary, and that civilization would be a by-product of the gospel.[7]

But they did believe in the superiority of Western civilization. Anderson, for example, assumed cultural superiority and a de facto cultural establishment of Christianity. He wrote, for instance, that New England civilization had been "conferred" by the gospel, and hence was "the highest and best, in a religious point of view, the world has yet seen."[8] Accordingly, he actively encouraged and founded humanitarian and "civilizing" missionary efforts. However, he thought of "transforming civilization" not as a task in its own right but as a by-product of evangelization.

So when they developed the concept of the indigenous church, with its three-self slogan, there was little in it of real cultural indigeneity, apart from a pragmatic recognition of the need to use vernacular languages and to appoint "native" church leaders. That the churches founded by missionaries should in all major features be identical with the churches that had sent the missionaries was axiomatic. Late in his career (1868), Venn did in a letter to missionaries of his Church Missionary Society speak in favor of "native" culture, but the call went unheeded.

The sense of the inferiority of "heathen" cultures was backed up by a strong sense of the inferiority of people with dark skins. It is notable that northern Europe and North America, the regions from which the Protestant missionaries came, were also the regions in which racism developed its most virulent forms. Motivated in part by the need to find ideological justification for the harshest, most degrading version of slavery the world has ever known, both Christians and non-Christians mustered what "proof" they could find for the notion that dark pigmentation signaled inferior intelligence, inferior morality, and inferior sensibility. Christians used pseudo-exegesis to argue that the so-called "curse of Ham" (Genesis 9:18-27) applied to the black races, supposedly descendants of Ham.

---

[7]Henry Venn, *To Apply the Gospel*, ed. Max Warren (Grand Rapids: Eerdmans, 1967); Rufus Anderson, *To Advance the Gospel*, ed. R. Pierce Beaver (Grand Rapids: Eerdmans, 1971).

[8]Anderson, *To Advance the Gospel*, 73.

I mentioned briefly in the previous chapter the works of Gobineau, Darwin, Spencer, Galton, and others which placed racism on pseudo-scientific foundations. These ideas were powerfully influential, even when they were known only at second or third hand. And, especially once the complete evolutionary scheme was in place, the arguments for racial and cultural "superiority" and "inferiority" supported each other in an unholy spiral of misunderstanding and misrepresentation. The love of Christ, which undeniably motivated the missionaries powerfully, did much to mitigate racism, but it never really eliminated it. Missionaries often protested the worst effects of racism when translated into colonial policies, but few indeed were themselves free of the taint of racist attitudes.

Venn and Anderson also took for granted the racial superiority of whites. Venn wrote of the missionary being of "another and superior race than his converts"; but he paradoxically argued from this *against* the missionary playing the role of pastor in the "native" church, lest dependency be fostered.[9] His successors, more arrogant than he, drew the opposite conclusion from their sense of superiority and hunger for power, and postponed indigeneity indefinitely.

A significant case in point is the history of the Anglican Niger Mission, an effort of Venn's Church Missionary Society, in which Samuel Ajayi Crowther, a Yoruba educated in England, had been installed as bishop. His authority was accepted in this isolated post. But when missionaries arrived, attitudes changed; then it was suddenly intolerable for white missionaries to answer to an African bishop. So a pretext was seized and he was replaced by an Englishman. Unfortunately, this was not an isolated case. Long after racism and ethnocentrism were generally recognized as wrong and ostensibly repudiated in missions, power struggles and jealousy between missions and indigenous churches and their leaders often continued to be the order of the day.

The ready use of vernacular languages, which Lamin Sanneh adduces[10] to rebut the stereotype of missionaries as cultural iconoclasts, and which as he points out was in fact interpreted by converts as validating their cultures before God, was by and large not so interpreted by the missionaries. For we must remember that these missionaries did not understand the tight nexus between language and culture as it is understood today. They seem

---

[9]Venn, *To Apply the Gospel*, 78.

[10]Lamin Sanneh, *Translating the Message* (Maryknoll NY: Orbis Books, 1989).

to have assumed without much thought that language was a mostly neutral instrument of communication which they were obliged to use, and did use gladly, in sharing the gospel with people. Though there was of course often a good bit of soul-searching about the appropriateness of using vernacular terms for God or other biblical realities, and a frequent wringing of hands about the absence in language A of a term for biblical concept X, the implications and entailments of the use of vernaculars to communicate the gospel were for the most part very poorly understood. This inability to understand the embeddedness of language in culture, ironically, was no doubt in part the fruit of the analytically disjunctive approaches to learning that were both the glory and the failure of the Enlightenment. In dividing to conquer, and thus in establishing academic disciplines with their distinct methods and their separate institutional embodiments, Western scholarship inevitably split things that belonged together.

What Sanneh's book powerfully demonstrates is that evangelism, especially cross-cultural evangelism, is by no means a simple process of communication in which one party knows the message and is active, while the other party does not know the message and is passive. In this respect, the communication model often used in missiology too easily lends itself to misunderstanding and abuse. Rather, evangelism is, as Sundermeier put it,[11] a *hermeneutic* process, in which both parties are actively interpreting the message and the situation. Under ideal conditions, the parties carry out this process in dialogue, in which case there is a good chance of creative convergence. But ideal conditions rarely prevailed in the nineteenth century: missionaries took it for granted that they knew the gospel ex officio, as it were, and that they communicated it perspicuously. Missionaries and hearers thus carried out their hermeneutic activities largely out of each other's awareness. Hence the gulf between what was intended by the missionaries and what was heard and acted upon by the hearers.

But what should catch our attention in all of this is that Bible translations and vernacular literatures were produced; and once these were available, they lived a life and exercised an impact all their own, no longer under the control of the missionaries who had produced them. This goes a long way to explain the range and depth of the impact of the gospel, far beyond what the missionaries imagined was going on.

---

[11]Theo Sundermeier, "Missiology Yesterday and Tomorrow," *Missionalia* 18/1 (April 1990): 259-69.

The high civilizations of south and East Asia posed a special problem for the ideology of Western superiority. Missionaries had to shout much louder to convince even themselves that these were clearly inferior to Western civilization; and the fact that they never convinced the Indians, the Chinese, and the Japanese is partly evidenced by the massive resistance of these peoples to the missionary message. What was from the perspective of the missionaries undeniable, however, was the demonic nature of the great religions of Asia, since these led to a host of degrading and disgusting customs and practices which provided endless fuel for the promotion of the missionary cause.

The second humanitarian factor was much more specifically focused: this was the hearty determination of Christians, especially in Great Britain, to abolish the slave trade from Africa to the New World on the one hand and to the Middle East on the other. Slavery as an institution in Britain had already been abolished; but it became a major element of the British Christian agenda to eliminate the trade itself, which perpetuated and increased slavery in other places. Thus, Christians were in the forefront of the successful effort to make interdiction an important concern of the Crown and an important activity of the British navy. British naval ships were therefore deployed along the West African coast and intercepted slaving ships with fair regularity, usually taking the slaves aboard back to the African coast. Sierra Leone was established as a haven for such freed slaves, much as Liberia had been by Americans.

But these efforts to eliminate the slave trade also comprised early on a determination to replace it with more legitimate forms of economic activity. Henry Venn pushed for the introduction of cotton cultivation in Africa, and Buxton argued for the introduction of legitimate trade.[12]

Somewhat later, and as a result of the work of David Livingstone, efforts were made to eliminate the slave trade in eastern and southeastern Africa, which sent slaves to the Arab world. Livingstone also called for the introduction of ''legitimate commerce'' to create sound economies in place of those ravaged by the slave trade. He was also, incidentally, a partisan of direct involvement by the British Crown to suppress the trade if no other means sufficed; thus he became a de facto advocate of the colonial enter-

---

[12]T. F. Buxton, *The African Slave Trade and Its Remedy* (London: Pall Mall, 1968 [1838]); Wilbert R. Shenk, *Henry Venn—Missionary Statesman* (Maryknoll NY: Orbis Books, 1983) 69-71.

prise. In his wake not a few other missionaries also became such advocates.

Thus, Buxton, Venn, and Livingstone added a third element, commerce, to the duo of Christianity and civilization as a goal for mission, because they saw a great need to substitute it for the slave trade as the basis of a viable economy; and this third component increased greatly in importance as the century wore on, especially in the eyes of wealthy supporters of missions. Venn and the others may be forgiven if they did not foresee the less desirable effects of modern commerce and a cash economy in replacement of barter and subsistence. They were sincerely trying to root out the evil they knew was evil. It is only in retrospect that we realize how profoundly disruptive was the integration of these economies into the colonial system, and then into the present global structure. Whatever the motives, this process of substitution was in itself a powerful force for cultural dissolution.

As the century moved towards its close, the two motives, the religious, conversionist one on the one hand, and the humanitarian, civilizing one on the other, increasingly merged. Though this phenomenon was widespread, it was especially true in the United States. Alfred Krass in at least two of his writings analyzes this process with great insight; he shows convincingly that what H. Richard Niebuhr and others have written about the "kingdom of God in America"[13] in nineteenth-century church thought was at least as true of the missionary movement as of the church at large.

Tracing back to Jonathan Edwards in the early eighteenth century the idea that America occupied a special place in God's plan to establish the kingdom, Krass shows how that idea came to full flower in the late nineteenth century. Millenarianism, which had hitherto been the preserve of marginal enthusiasts and sects, captured the mainline, and missionaries were stirred by the vision that extending American civilization *was* extending the kingdom of God. Krass quotes an 1870 lecture by Samuel Harris:

---

[13]Alfred C. Krass, *Five Lanterns at Sundown: Evangelism in a Chastened Mood* (Grand Rapids: Eerdmans, 1978); "Mission as Inter-Cultural Encounter—A Sociological Perspective," in *Down to Earth,* ed. Robert T. Coote and John Stott (Grand Rapids: Eerdmans, 1980) 231-56.

God has always acted by chosen peoples. To the English-speaking people more than to any other the world is now indebted for the propagation of Christian ideas and Christian civilization.[14]

In "Mission as Inter-Cultural Encounter," Krass describes in detail the methods of American Board missionaries in inland Angola from 1880 on, and finds both the Board's instructions under which they went and their approach in the field to be thoroughly in keeping with dominant American messianism and millenarianism. "In a slip of the tongue," he writes about a Board meeting in 1880, "one speaker lets the secret out: 'The gospel of Jesus Christ, let us remember, is the power of God unto civilization . . . for civilization is included under salvation.' "[15]

We will thus not be surprised when we discover the ways in which Christian mission became thoroughly intertwined with American national aggrandizement around the turn of the century.

The specifically American version of expansionism was called "manifest destiny." Concerning this idea in the context of the Spanish-American War (1898), Pierce Beaver has written:

"Manifest Destiny," a powerful sentimental factor in the expansion of the United States to its present boundaries and then in both the acquiring of overseas territories [such as Hawaii, the Philippines, Puerto Rico, Cuba, and Samoa] and the exertion of influence in international affairs, was one motive in the enormous growth of American foreign missionary endeavor during the last half of the nineteenth century. Many Protestants believed that God had raised up the new nation to play a decisive role in the winning of the world for Christ.[16]

This view entailed on the part of the missionaries a measure of wilfull blindness to and a selective interpretation of the actual process by which American hegemony was established. As we saw in the previous chapter, the worst atrocities were probably concealed by the authorities from the missionaries; but they could hardly have been totally ignorant of what was going on. It is to be feared that in the minds of some, the heinousness of the brutality involved was partly mitigated by tacitly racist considerations.

[14]Krass, *Five Lanterns*, 30.

[15]Krass, "Mission as Inter-Cultural Encounter," 240-41.

[16]R. Pierce Beaver, *Ecumenical Beginnings in Protestant World Mission* (New York: Nelson, 1962) 134.

It is true, of course, that other Western nations developed similar justifying ideologies and myths; this process seems to be inherent in the existence of modern nation states, and is particularly important for those with expansionist ambitions. But the particular mixture of national aggrandizement with Christian eschatological themes, millennial and messianic, which is displayed in "manifest destiny," seems peculiarly American.

More and more, it was taken for granted that in their civilizing efforts, missions had the right to appeal to the Western powers to enforce conditions favorable to their work and their personnel. One of the chief grounds for widespread resentment of missions in China, for instance, was the extraterritoriality which Western powers forced China to grant to missionaries and their proteges. The Boxer Rebellion of 1900 was largely motivated by the accumulation of such resentment over the decades which had intervened since the treaties of the 1840s; and few among the missions in China objected to the indemnity extorted by the Western powers from China for the damages done to missions during that uprising.

Finally, towards the end of the nineteenth century and more and more in the twentieth, one finds an aggressive and arrogant apologetic for the expansion of Western civilization through the direct exercise of the dominant power of Western nations. Already in 1860, one Presbyterian missionary had described the "agitation" that prevailed among the Chinese after the British and French attacked some Chinese forts in an attempt to extend the coolie traffic: this, he wrote, "shows the instability and excitability of the Chinese."[17]

However, it should be pointed out as a broad generalization that this kind of attitude was much more characteristic of "mainline" missions than of "faith" missions; it was usually more characteristic of mission executives and supporters at home than of missionaries on the field, though not a few missionaries enthusiastically subscribed to the idea; and it was usually more characteristic of missions from colonial and imperial powers than from countries that had no such program. With respect to the first distinction, "faith" missions generally partook of the dark view of Western culture that characterized their conservative supporters, as we have seen above. With respect to the second, it was executives of mainline boards and enthusiastic promoters of missions who were among the chief cheerleaders. Certainly, powerful lay persons in the United States—Theodore Roose-

---

[17]*The Missionary Chronicle* (1860).

velt, William Howard Taft, and Woodrow Wilson among them—explicitly saw missions as advancing United States interests and "standardizing life in foreign countries as well as in the United States by Christianity" (Wilson).[18]

There were, it must be pointed out, dissenting voices. Hutchison shows that liberalism in some of its forms wanted quite early to relinquish missionary control and questioned "the right of Western Christendom to lecture the rest of the world"; he adds in an end note that "Some of these views—for ex., those involving doubts about Western or American culture—were echoed in conservative theology; conservatives were very likely to see the home culture as morally declining or bankrupt."[19] Hutchison goes on to mention debates over this issue within liberalism and among advocates of the social gospel, with George A. Gordon a rather ambivalent advocate of American superiority and Walter Rauschenbusch an opponent. The latter strongly deplored the increasingly crass commercial rationale that was being used to promote missions among rich businessmen as exponents of Western civilization and trade. But Hutchison documents a decline of resistance to the civilizing mission as colonialism grew "or by the gradually-perceived need for modernization as an accompaniment to Christianity."[20]

## Social Origins of Missionaries

But the modern Protestant missionary movement was not only a broad, sweeping phenomenon; it also recruited and sent out particular kinds of people. Where did these missionaries come from? What kind of people were they? How were they educated? What ideas did they take for granted? In other words, what was *their* culture? One could answer these questions in very general terms by saying that they were children of their age and milieu.

Piggin in a fascinating study has analyzed the social origins of several hundred British missionaries to India in the first half of the century.[21] It is

---

[18]Jane Hunter, *The Gospel of Gentility: American Women Missionaries in Turn-of-the-Century China* (New Haven: Yale University Press, 1984) 8-9.

[19]William R. Hutchison, "Modernism in Missions: The Liberal Search for an Exportable Christianity," in *Christianity in China,* ed. John K. Fairbank (Cambridge MA: Harvard University Press, 1974) 116, 393.

[20]Christensen and Hutchinson, eds., *Missionary Ideologies,* 7.

[21]Piggin, *Making Evangelical Missionaries.*

fair to say, I think, that his sample is widely representative of the movement. He found that, in a British society with rigid hierarchical distinctions, the large majority of missionaries came from either the lower reaches of the professional classes or from traditional artisanal classes, classes which were as a whole socially ambitious and which sometimes found in the ministry or in teaching a means of upward mobility. They were generally "individuated," "non-deferential" people, with a propensity for radicalism.[22]

Many of them, including William Carey, David Livingstone, and Mary Slessor, were at least partly self-educated, though the earliest Americans, Adoniram Judson and his colleagues, were seminary graduates, and for many American missions this continued to be the prevalent pattern. On the European continent, notably in Germany, missionaries were from the beginning educated in specialized institutes, which were separate from and generally deemed to be inferior to the university faculties of theology which educated clergy for the state churches at home. This latter fact reflected what was throughout the century and beyond a standard dichotomy between "missions," which were carried out in "heathen" lands, and the rest of church work, including "evangelism," which was carried out in "Christian" lands. The distinction became very explicit later in the missiology of the German Gustav Warneck. It was based four-square on the idea that Western civilization was Christian, and hence supportive of the work of the gospel, while non-Western cultures were intrinsically "heathen," and hence inimical to the work of the gospel. As for Britain, Piggin describes the slow development of missionary training institutions and the debates between proponents of classical education and "practical" training.[23] In the early period, few missionaries were university graduates.

Andrew Walls aptly summarizes the social status of the missionary body of the early nineteenth century:

> It is now a common-place that the typical early nineteenth century missionary—visualized by David Livingstone as "a dumpy sort of man with a Bible under his arm"—was a fairly homespun character. . . . His formal education was not high, and, if an Anglican, his social and educational attainments were not such as would have brought him ordination to the home ministry. It is almost equally accepted that by the end of the nineteenth

---

[22]Ibid., 40-41.

[23]Ibid., 151-238.

century the situation had changed; not only were the numbers of missionaries immensely swollen, but the universities and the public schools could
now supply a quota.[24]

In other words, late in the century, many missionaries of the mainline missions from Great Britain came from somewhat higher social origins than
their predecessors, and often had university education. These typically
brought, along with their Christian faith and their sincere dedication, a
considerable freight of upper-class prejudices which aggravated the underlying racism and ethnocentrism of the missionary movement in general. Missionaries from the upper classes tended to lend themselves more
enthusiastically to the civilizing mission and to the agenda of empire.

As I have said, the earliest American missionaries had the same education as ministers for home churches; and social distinctions were not
nearly as rigid as in Britain or the continent. But many American missionaries were of humble origins and found in missions a means of becoming
somebody, or making an impact on the world.

The faith missions, when they started, on the whole recruited missionaries of modest social origins and mediocre education, in some cases re-
flecting the social situation of the supporting constituencies. For especially
in North America, in the absence of a religious establishment and in the
presence of a plethora of Christian bodies, denominations have tended to
comprise persons of rather homogeneous social status and thus to reflect
the social class structures of society.[25]

The majority of missionaries from all countries were of modest social
origins. They were in general deeply earnest, highly motivated, highly
disciplined persons, inured to deprivation and struggle. It is understandable that they would prize greatly those elements of "high" civilization
for which they had had to work so hard themselves. Unlike many persons
of the upper classes, they were deeply religious and strongly shaped by what
Weber later called the "Protestant ethic," as well as by the rigorous personal morality which characterized their sociocultural roots. They were very
conscious of the "pit" of lower-class culture from which some of them
had been "rescued," partly by Jesus Christ and partly by their own efforts.

---

[24]Andrew F. Walls, " 'The Best Thinking of the Best Heathen': Human Learning and
the Missionary Movement," in *Religion and Humanism*, ed. Keith Robbins (Oxford: Basil
Blackwell for the Ecclesiastical Historical Society, 1981) 341.

[25]Niebuhr, *The Social Sources of Denominationalism* (repr. Cleveland: World/Meri-
dean Boods, 1962; New York: Henry Holt, 1929).

## Missionary Understandings and Attitudes

*General Considerations.* It is completely understandable that, coming into contact with cultures which were in their eyes even worse than those of the European or American lower classes, missionaries should react negatively. And while they were not aware for the most part of the work of the intellectual pioneers we discussed in the previous chapter, the general ideas which were part of the evolutionistic Zeitgeist were absorbed with the air they breathed. The superiority of Western civilization as the culmination of human development, the attribution of that superiority to the prolonged dominance of Christianity, the duty of Christians to share civilization and the gospel with the "benighted heathen"—these were the chief intellectual currency of their lives. The image evoked by Reginald Heber's hymn, of lands "where every prospect pleases and only man is vile," moved these missionaries powerfully. Just how powerfully, history relates: the sufferings they endured, the sacrifices they made, the deaths they died in their hundreds. Would that those of us who preen ourselves on our greater understanding of culture were as dedicated and as full of the love of Christ as they.

*Concrete Examples.* But it is time to look at concrete examples. Rather than wander at random through the vast literature, I have chosen to cite a few cases from the various missionary-sending countries. I have accordingly selected as highly representative of the North American missionary experience in the nineteenth century the unusually full documentation of missions of the Presbyterian Church (USA) which is found in a sequence of mission periodicals.[26] A less intensive but representative sampling of other missionary literature justifies the affirmation that other missions displayed most of the same attitudes in the same sequence and in roughly the same time frame.

In 1833, for example, we read about the "heathen" that among them "Justice is disregarded; mercy is trampled underfoot; woman is degraded and unpitied; children are reared amidst ignorance and vice; the present is full of misery, the future of despair." Later in the same year, we find a catalog of "testimonies of different writers as to the character and moral condition of heathen and anti-Christian nations": Bedouins are "addicted

---

[26]The periodicals are *The Missionary Chronicle* (1833-1849); *The Home and Foreign Record of the Presbyterian Church* (1850-1870); *The Presbyterian Monthly Record* (1871-1886); *The Church at Home and Abroad* (1887-1898); *The Assembly Herald* (1899-1920).

to robbery''; in Tahiti one finds ''sanguinary details of barbarous wars,'' and ''drunkenness is almost universal''; the ''Buschemen'' are said to ''live by plunder and murder'' and ''their miserable condition, as it regards their domestic and social relations, is another proof of degradation.'' From a note in 1836, we learn that in Haiti ''Polygamy, concubinage, and all licentiousness, prevail.'' This violently condemnatory note never fully disappears to the end of the period of our concern; but more moderate notes gradually begin to sound and somewhat qualify it.

Coupled with antecedent theological ideas such as the doctrines of original sin and the indispensability of Jesus Christ for salvation, this attitude led to a harshly negative interpretation of the religions of non-Westerners as ''heathen,'' ''pagan,'' or ''demonic.'' This judgment was reinforced by the dominant ideas, discussed in the previous chapter, that non-Western cultures were inferior to Western civilization, were ''barbarian,'' or ''savage''; and that non-Western persons were inferior to Western persons. It was also undoubtedly reinforced by the revulsion many Western missionaries experienced as they met concrete alien cultures—a revulsion arising from culture shock, homesickness, loneliness, sickness, and frequent deprivation.

It was very apparent to these sincere people that if even persons brought up in ''Christian'' Western civilization often needed to experience a radical conversion and change of life, how much more did ''heathen savages'' need such a conversion—a conversion which, as we have seen, combined civilization and Christianity. For many, the only real question was in what order these experiences should occur: should the ''heathen'' be first civilized so that they could become real Christians, or should they be Christianized so that they could become civilized? Especially in the early part of the century, however, evangelization was a task unanimously affirmed, while civilization was more controversial. I have pointed out that both Henry Venn and Rufus Anderson strongly pressed for evangelization, and saw civilization as its by-product.

The balance shifted as the century progressed; but, as we shall see, the imposition of Western civilization was never unanimously advocated. Warneck, for instance, was strongly opposed to it for reasons which we will examine later.

By the 1840s we begin to find in the Presbyterian records a few brief descriptions of cultural traits, as for example marriage customs, and even of religious beliefs and rites, which show some degree of understanding.

This line, punctuated by the occasional snide or horrified aside, also continued and grew as time passed. By the end of the nineteenth century and the beginning of the twentieth, quite sustained and sophisticated descriptions of customs were appearing, often with a sympathetic tone; but there was never anything like a concept of culture as a whole.

The promotional and apologetic motif also persisted, as in an 1856 piece which argued that demonstrations in mission schools that Western science was true while the science in Hindu books was false would persuade and convert the youth. This, insisted the author, was better than attacking religion frontally. But frontal attacks on religion continued nevertheless. In 1864, for example, one writer affirmed forcefully that "the Devil is regularly, systematicaly, and ceremoniously worshipped by a large majority of the inhabitants of the island of Ceylon."

Beginning in the 1850s, one finds a dawning recognition that some of the problems missionaries found among the peoples they encountered were products not of indigenous culture, but of the noxious influence of Westerners. One writer in 1855 pointed out that white people corrupted American Indians in order to "obtain their assent to being defrauded." In a similar vein, by the way, the *Report of the Centenary Conference on the Protestant Missions of the World* (1888)[27] contains several sobering assessments of missionary errors. A Danish missionary discussed the "sin" being committed when polygamists were forced to repudiate their extra wives; there were scattered comments about the mistake of imposing European customs and church buildings; and Hudson Taylor expressed a remarkably flexible view of polygamy.

Yet another note was sounded with increasing insistence from the 1870s in the Presbyterian journals, once the churches were established and a second generation of Christians appeared: the need for church discipline, for vigilance on the part of missionaries, for a spelling out of what practices were permissible and what were impermissible for converts. Here the standard applied was unabashedly Western and pietistic, not to say legalistic.

It was found necessary, from about 1880, to combat what was perceived as incipient universalism and tolerance of other religions. This reflected the early dawn of the influence in the West of historical and comparative studies of religion, which gradually pushed many people, in-

---

[27]James Johnston, ed., *Report of the Centenary Conference on the Protestant Missions of the World,* 2 vols. (London: James Nesbit, 1888).

cluding church people, in the direction of religious relativism. We will examine the full flowering of this influence in other chapters.

Two dimensions of the missionaries' home culture, especially of those from the English-speaking world, greatly affected their attitudes and actions. The first was the fact that the nineteenth century was a period of intense reaction against the sexual libertinism of the eighteenth century; it was, of course, this reaction which gave its most conspicuous trait to the "Victorian Age." In many cases, as social historians have shown, the emphasis was at least as much on the appearance of propriety as on true virtue. But the general prudery of the age with regard to matters sexual goes a long way to explain the revulsion which many missionaries felt at the sight of naked people, and the near-universality with which they condemned and proscribed polygamy as well as "native" music and instruments, which were associated in the missionaries' minds with lascivious dancing. In fact, anything which could be construed as giving public visibility to any expression of human sexuality was strongly condemned by most missionaries.

The other dimension of the missionaries' culture which heavily influenced how they viewed both themselves and the peoples they served, was an unabashed nineteenth-century sexism. In North America the century saw the rise of a strong theologically inspired movement for the emancipation of women. But this affected the missionary enterprise obliquely rather than directly, even though, as Beaver has shown,[28] the missionary movement was itself an early manifestation of women's liberation. The way missionaries treated their own wives was diagnostic: wives were typically subservient, not involved in decision-making, not having their own spheres of missionary service. Single women were accepted as missionaries only reluctantly, though many in fact did extraordinary work. On the other hand, the missionaries by and large emphasized what they saw as the aspects of "native" cultures which degraded women, and trumpeted the claim that the gospel elevated women; though in not a few cases, as in Southern Ghana, the limitations placed on women by Victorian notions of a "woman's place" restricted women who before had enjoyed considerable freedom of action within their own sphere. But since this is the theme of another volume in this series, I will say no more.

---

[28]R. Pierce Beaver, *American Protestant Women in World Mission*, rev. ed. (Grand Rapids MI: Eerdmans, 1980).

Other areas in which the missionaries' nineteenth-century views of morality were imposed legalistically on "natives" included for many the use of beverage alcohol; "worldly" amusements; "sabbath" observance; and the like.

One churchman who differed sharply with the majority on a number of issues of African culture, notably polygamy, was the Anglican Bishop John William Colenso of Natal, who led his diocese during the middle of the century. But since he was highly unconventional and controversial in many other ways, to the point of being deposed and excommunicated by the Church of England, his example was not widely followed.

The situation in Great Britain followed a quite parallel path to the one outlined for the United States. The nineteenth century saw the development of some surprisingly modern-sounding views of mission. Venn and Anderson, already discussed, are of course well known. Less well know, but well worthy of consideration, is Melville Horne's *Letters on Missions* (1815), which spell out a number of insightful methodological proposals for missions.[29] Throughout the century, there were exhibited both an increasing degree of understanding of and even sympathy with indigenous cultures; and, as the colonial enterprise evolved, an increasing degree of cultural and political imperialism. The cultural imperialism came first, and was usually expressed via schools which did their best to inculcate British Christian values into Asian and African children. The outstanding proponent of this approach was Alexander Duff in India. Duff, supported by Thomas Macauley, strongly advocated the use of English in education. But Venn and others were equally firm about the priority of the vernaculars. By and large, this latter view prevailed in British colonies.

Political and economic imperialism naturally came to the fore as the British Empire expanded. As we have already seen, racism was a marked trait of both American and British missionaries throughout the century. But, as we shall see, to at least one British missionary go the honors for having produced a respectable and responsible ethnography in the nineteenth century. And it was also in Britain that there was produced in 1868 a remarkable document entitled "On Foreign Missions in Connection with Civilization and Anthropology."[30] This fifteen-page tract was read in 1868

---

[29]Melville Horne, *Letters on Missions, Addressed to the Protestant Ministers of the British Churches* (Andover: Flagg and Gould, 1815).

[30]George Harris, "On Foreign Missions in Connection with Civilization and Anthropology" (London: Bell and Daldy, 1868).

at the Manchester Anthropological Society, of which its barrister author, George Harris, was president.

In this paper, Harris forcefully argued for the mutual usefulness of missionaries and anthropologists and against what was apparently already a problem in his day, mutual rejection and recriminations between missionaries and their supporters on the one hand, and anthropologists on the other. Missionaries, wrote Harris, provided the exemplifying data for anthropologists' syntheses (we must remember that this was written *before* the publication of Tylor's *Primitive Culture*); but anthropology provided for missionaries insight into ''human nature'' and the human situation. Taking for granted, as everyone did in that century, the superiority of Western civilization, Harris argued that non-Western peoples were capable of being both Christianized and civilized. He also asserted that missionaries needed to be people of the highest capacities and attainments. It is not clear how many missionaries were aware of this discussion going on about them, or of the infant literature of anthropology.

In a very incisive paper, Andrew Walls discusses British missions during the imperial period, 1880-1920.[31] He begins by saying that ''Before 1880 one can make a much better case than after it for Seeley's belief that the British Empire was acquired in a fit of absentmindedness.'' He emphasizes that British missionaries took the Empire for granted; and that, as we have seen, in the high imperial period missionaries of a new type—public-school-and-university educated—were recruited in very large numbers. So many missionaries went out, in fact, that for that reason among others the three-self ideal was on the whole abandoned.

The extent to which British missions sometimes saw themselves as playing a major role in the advancement of ''civilization and commerce'' can be seen from an 1878 editorial in *The Christian Express*, organ of the Lovedale mission school in South Africa. The context was a discussion of government policy to expel blacks from the land and tax them in order to compel them to become a cheap labor force for white employers. The editorial says in part:

> We want to see the natives become workers. . . . And . . . we believe
> Christianity will be a chief cause of them becoming a working people. . . .

---

[31]Andrew F. Walls, ''British Missions,'' in *Missionary Ideologies in the Imperialist Era: 1880-1920,* ed. Torbin Christensen and William R. Hutchison (Aarhus, Denmark: Aros, 1982) 159-66.

Christianity creates needs. . . . If you want men to work, then, you must get them to need. . . .

Now the speediest way of creating needs among the people is to Christianise them. As they become Christianised, they will want more clothing, better houses, furniture, books, education for their children. . . . And all these things they can get only by working.

But Christianity also teaches the duty of working, and denounces idleness as a sin.[32]

The agenda of civilization and empire was not quite unanimously accepted among British missionaries. Forman points out[33] that in Papua New Guinea, the London Missionary Society, which had been present before the British rule was established, was rather ambivalent, while the high-church Anglican Mission idealized the people "as childlike, . . . as saints," but had a most naive and superficial grasp of the culture.

In Germany, the culturally decisive influence on missiology was that of romanticism, which exalted the particular and glorified the *Volk*, the "people," in the narrowly ethnic sense. It is not accidental, as we saw in chapter 3, that Germans were the first to use "culture" in something like its modern sense. In missions, this apotheosis of the particular and of peoplehood found its expression in the thought of Gustav Warneck, the premier missiologist of the latter nineteenth century.[34]

At just that period of history when German ethnicity and nationalism were being given belated expression in a single nation state (1871) and the German people were being taught to be proud and aggressive, missiology was emphasizing the distinctiveness of each people, of each culture, of each language, of each set of institutions; all of these, German theologians and missiologists were asserting, were gifts of God, to be affirmed and preserved. Thus, as the gospel moved into new areas and touched new peoples, each such group should bring with it into its new faith all of its existing cultural and social arrangements, especially kinship and marriage patterns

---

[32]Quoted in Charles Villa-Vicencio, *Trapped in Apartheid* (Maryknoll NY: Orbis Books, 1988) 44-45.

[33]Charles W. Forman, "Missions in Papua New Guinea," in *Missionary Ideologies in the Imperialist Era: 1880-1920*, ed. Torbin Christensen and William R. Hutchison (Aarhus, Denmark: Aros, 1982) 23-33.

[34]E.g., Gustav Warneck, *Outline of a History of Protestant Missions from the Reformation to the Present Times*, trans. and ed. George Robson (New York: Revell, 1901?).

and political structures, so that the new church would have, as it were, a ready-made and well-understood style of operation.

This approach was justified partly in terms of Luther's doctrine of two kingdoms; but it also rested on a novel exegesis of the phrase *panta ta ethne,* "all the nations" in the traditional English versions, in Matthew 28:19 and elsewhere. The phrase, which in the Septuagint had been used primarily to refer collectively to the Gentiles, was reinterpreted by Warneck in a distributive sense, that is, as meaning "all of the peoples, each taken as a unit." We are not far at this point from the enumeration of the "cultures of the world" soon to be implied by Malinowskian functionalism, which will be discussed in chapter 5. We will encounter in chapter 6 a recent reincarnation of the idea in McGavran's "Homogeneous Unit Principle" and in the attempt by Winter and others to enumerate the unreached peoples of the world.

On the mission field, the Warneck program was implemented by a number of missionaries, notably Bruno Guttmann among the Chagga in Tanzania[35] and Christian Keysser in Papua New Guinea.[36] What Guttmann explicitly set out to produce was a Chagga church, which is to say a church following traditional Chagga social and cultural patterns and *in which a Chagga and only a Chagga could ever feel at home.* Guttmann also passionately resisted all efforts to bring the Chagga into the orbit of modern Western civilization, since that would be to destroy the integrity of Chagga peoplehood.

Keysser, for his part, went very far in making a personal adaptation to the local culture, and even wondered what that culture might have to say to Christianity. In other words, while missionaries from the English-speaking world were for the most part energetically trying by all means to accelerate the process of Westernizing the non-Western peoples of the world, some Germans were just as strenuously trying to stop or reverse the process.

The German approach appears on the surface to be respectful of culture. But it fell by way of anticipation into some of the pitfalls of Mali-

---

[35]See Donald C. Platt, "An Ethnological Approach to Mission: Bruno Guttmann in Kilimanjaro," in *The Gospel and Frontier Peoples,* ed. R. Pierce Beaver (South Pasadena: William Carey Library, 1973) 139-53; also Ernst Jäschke, "Bruno Guttmann's Legacy," *International Bulletin of Missionary Research* 4/4 (October 1980): 165-69.

[36]Forman, "Missions in Papua New Guinea," 27; see also Christian Keysser, *A People Reborn,* trans. Alfred Allin and John Kuder (Pasadena: William Carey Library, 1980).

nowskian functionalism, to be described in chapter 5: it attempted to deal with each culture in isolation from all others, and even to prevent cultural contact as much as possible; it also tried to hold back culture change, even when it was wanted by the people. In their efforts to preserve the "pure" culture, the German missionaries were thus often paternalistic. And they failed to give due weight to the New Testament vision of a church which would incorporate people from all human groups, relativizing and transcending but not homogenizing their differences.

Not all Germans followed this line. The Allgemeine Evangelisch-Protestantische Missionsverein in Papua New Guinea explicitly intended to "propagate Christian knowledge and Christian culture."[37] This mission, says Glüer, was founded outside Pietist circles, and held a more centrist theology, à la Harnack, who affirmed that "the aim of missionary effort is . . . 'the creation of one great family of civilized nations.'" In a similar vein, the Rhenish Mission thought that Europe had "world-historical significance," that mission was a vehicle of culture, and that mission should work in alliance with the state.[38]

In the Scandinavian countries, missions did not have to cope with the issue of colonialism by their home governments, but the Lutheran ones were of course established at home. Hallencreutz[39] writes that in Sweden, missions were sent by three constituencies: (1) some rather radical free-church groups, which related rather ambivalently to the centers of culture and power at home and followed a narrowly conceived evangelistic program on the field, motivated primarily by a somewhat apocalyptic theology; and (2) state church missions and (3) free agencies of the mainline churches, both of which held to the Lutheran doctrine of the two kingdoms, emphasized indigenous structures and leadership on the field, often questioned

---

[37]Winfrid Glüer, "German Protestant Missions in China," in *Missionary Ideologies in the Imperialist Era: 1880-1920,* ed. Torbin Christensen and William R. Hutchinson (Aarhus, Denmark: Aros, 1982) 51-61.

[38]Gerhard Besier, "Mission and Colonialism in Friedrich Fabris," in *Missionary Ideologies in the Imperialist Era: 1880-1920,* ed. Torbin Christensen and William R. Hutchison (Aarhus, Denmark: Aros, 1982) 84-93.

[39]Carl F. Hallencreutz, "Church-Centered Evangelism and Modernization-Emphasis in Swedish Missions 1880-1920," in *Missionary Ideologies in the Imperialist Era: 1880-1920,* ed. Torbin Christensen and William R. Hutchison (Aarhus, Denmark: Aros, 1982) 62-74.

the abuses of colonialism, but accepted modernization and civilization as intrinsic to missions.

Nils E. Bloch-Hoell describes the ambivalence of Norwegian missionaries in South Africa in their relationships to the British government.[40] They cared for people's external welfare with great sincerity, "could appreciate good Zulu qualities," and "could be very critical of the evil elements in European civilization," but opted on the whole to get along with the powers that were in place.

One should say a word about French and Swiss Protestant missions and missionaries. Though they were, and are, few in number, they did work in a number of countries, notably in southeastern and south central Africa. By a quirk of history, French Protestant missions did not work in French colonies until after World War I; and of course Switzerland never had colonies at all. So these missionaries could and usually did adopt a stance rather detached from the policies of the British and Portuguese authorities in whose colonies they served. Some of them showed great cultural sensitivity, and one of them, as we shall see, contributed a major ethnography.

To summarize a very lengthy and complex section: First, the process of *understanding* the cultures of the peoples progressed in a more or less straight upward curve throughout the nineteenth century (1792-1922). From initial shock and horror, missionaries moved to a fairly high level of working comprehension of the customs and practices of the people and a lesser but appreciable level of ability to work within these cultural parameters.

Second, *respect* for indigenous cultures rose considerably in the English-speaking world from the initial period to the beginning of the period of high imperialism, and then declined as the juggernaut of aggressive Western civilization swept missions into its train and absorbed its enthusiasm and its energies. On the European continent, views of indigenous cultures and of the civilizing task of the West varied widely across the spectrum.

Third, it was only at the very end of the period that genuine appreciation for the *religious* traditions of non-Westerners became more than a minority parlor game in missiological circles.

[40]Nils E. Bloch-Hoell, "Norwegian Mission to South Africa 1880-1920: Colonialistic Confrontation or Apostolic Approach?" in *Missionary Ideologies in the Imperialist Era: 1880-1920,* ed. Torbin Christensen and William R. Hutchison (Aarhus, Denmark: Aros, 1982) 13-22.

Fourth, there were always, especially among the more conservative and apocalyptically motivated missions, dissenting views and practices, which promoted superficial cultural adaptation for pragmatic reasons and refrained from civilizing impulses for theological reasons.

### The Self-Evaluation of Missions.

The turn of the century saw a number of books describing in glowing terms the beneficial effects of Western missions in non-Western countries. Already in 1881 Thomas Laurie was trumpeting the contributions of missions and missionaries to geography, geology, meteorology, natural science, archeology, philology, literature, music, Bible translation, history, education, medicine, commerce, arts, and especially ethnography.[41] From 1897 to 1906, James S. Dennis published three massive volumes describing in detail the contributions of missions to the social well-being of humanity.[42] After describing in extenso "the social evils of the non-Christian world" (a picture as sordid and gloomy as anything written in 1833), Dennis sings an anthem to "the dawn of a sociological era in missions," in which civilizing barbarians was becoming the major business of missions. A few years later, in a more popular vein calculated to appeal to rich businessmen and induce them to support missions, Isaac Taylor Headland attributed all real cultural advances in recent human history to the superiority and ascendancy of the West in all areas of life: government, trade, science, "civilization," civic life, intellectual development, moral and religious education, music, and art. The reason: the West was Christian.[43]

### Missionary Life and Work

But missionary understandings and attitudes did not remain mere ideas: they necessarily translated directly into styles of life and work. It is therefore time to give this matter consideration.

---

[41]Thomas Laurie, *The Ely Volume: or, The Contribution of Our Foreign Missions to Science and Human Well-Being* (Boston: American Board of Commissioners for Foreign Missions, 1881).

[42]James S. Dennis, *Christian Missions and Social Progress,* 3 vols. (New York: Revell, 1897, 1899, 1906).

[43]Isaac Taylor Headland, *Some By-Products of Missions* (New York: Methodist Book Concern, 1912).

In the pioneering stage of missions in any field, but especially in the "primitive" areas, missionaries were quite prepared to endure hardship as a matter of course. They lived extremely frugally, using local resources, local housing, local food, and the like. But as soon as they were to some extent established, the question naturally arose as to how they should now live. What kinds of houses should they have? What kinds of food should they eat? What kinds of clothes should they wear? What kinds of recreation should they enjoy? What kinds of social relationships should they participate in?

Hypothetically, they faced the following options:

First, to live like the local people in all or some of these dimensions of life. But this in fact seems not to have been seen by most as a serious option, even for those who worked in China or India, and a fortiori for those who worked in "primitive" places. Rationales for the refusal to consider this option were several. It was argued that the physical and mental health of missionaries and their families precluded it; and it is true that the pioneering phase, when missionaries had approximated this style, was costly in lives and broken health. Furthermore, it was argued, the people themselves did not expect it and would not respect missionaries who lived just as they did. Finally, missionaries should set an example of a "better" way of life.

A second option, in countries where there was social stratification and hence a local upper class, would have been to live like these people. Some missionaries made modest motions in this direction, at least to the extent of accepting mutual social relationships and mutual invitations to social occasions. This choice could have been said, following the example of the Jesuit missionaries in seventeenth-century China and India, to accord with a top-down evangelistic strategy; which was in fact advocated by not a few Protestant missionaries of the nineteenth century.

The third option, and the one the great majority of missionaries in fact adopted, was to live as much as possible as they would have back home; with the significant proviso that for those of modest social origins, life on the mission field was much more like the life of upper classes back home than the life they had been used to: having servants, living in increasingly large and elaborate houses, and so forth.

Closely connected with style of life was the choice of social networks. When they could, missionaries tended to socialize with other missionaries, though an abundant literature suggests that missionaries often did not get along well together. But missionaries isolated from their own kind typically chose their social circles from the following groups, in descending order of priority: fellow-citizens of their homelands, Christian or not; other "Europeans," Christian or not; and finally local people. It is clear that for purposes of social intercourse, for the majority of missionaries cultural congeniality overrode considerations of Christian fellowship.

A related consideration has to do with the famous missionary compound. In most fields, as soon as it was feasible, missions obtained by purchase or grant a substantial piece of land, often isolated from local communities or enclosable by walls and gates, and built on that land all the buildings they needed: missionary housing, churches, schools, printing presses, dispensaries, and hospitals. This was justified by the missions in terms of economics, security, and efficiency in the work—which considerations may well have a certain validity. It was also justified as a place where the mission could establish a "Christian" village for their converts to separate them physically from their "heathen" neighbors and preserve them from the danger of reversion to "heathenism."

But missionary compounds immensely exacerbated the social and cultural isolation of missionaries from the people they meant to serve. As a result, missionaries and local people tended to meet only in "official" capacities, when one or the other had some practical need that would motivate crossing the gulf between them. Ordinary casual human neighborliness was made virtually impossible.

Harris Mobley has done a careful analysis of the consequences of missionary attitudes and lifestyles in Ghana.[44] He found that Ghanaians deeply deplored and resented several aspects of the missionary pattern. He uses the phrases "white man's town" to describe the isolated compound, "coast conscience" to denote attitudes which maintained social distance, and "white man's burden" to refer to vocational dominance of missionaries over Africans; and he quotes from a large number of Ghanaians from the late decades of the nineteenth century to the mid-twentieth century to demonstrate how pervasive the patterns were and how much Africans detested them.

"In 1906 Mensah Sarbah warned the missionary to beware of his identification with other Europeans, lest his image become distorted"; and Ag-

---

[44]Harris W. Mobley, "The Ghanaian's Image of the Missionary: An Analysis of the Published Critiques of Christian Missionaries by Ghanaians, 1867-1965" (Ph.D. diss., The Hartford Seminary Foundation, 1966).

grey insisted in contrast that "the Christian man who comes among us must be one of us."[45] Mobley quotes the Rev. T. B. Freeman, who in 1898 was attracted to the black American mission of Bishop Small's A.M.E. Zion Church because white missionaries "are an alien race who are *not above the colour question*."[46] And in 1930, J. W. De Graft Johnson "predicted an end to Christianity in West Africa unless 'our white friends who preach to us' reconcile their actions to their message."[47]

What about the style of missionary work? How was it pursued? Missionaries, of course, preached a great deal, evangelistically, didactically, and pastorally. But in the heritage of the Protestant Reformation, as modified by the Enlightenment, their message was often quite nakedly cognitive, appealing by logic to the intellect of their hearers; it tended to deal inadequately with the emotional, existential, esthetic, and even noumenal dimensions of religious experience.[48] By the grace of God as well as for a variety of human reasons, people did respond, sometimes in large numbers; but they often experienced a gap in their Christian lives that had to be filled somehow or other in other ways. One way was to retain contact with those elements of their traditional past which did deal with those things the missionaries failed to deal with; another was to establish their own independent churches in which they could fill the holes by means of their own devising.

In order to buttress their preaching and teaching ministries, missionaries in this period, following in the train of Eliot and Ziegenbalg, became heavily involved in Bible translation and publication, seeing it as an indispensable part of evangelization, civilization, and planting indigenous churches. Carey personally translated the Bible into Bengali and promoted and was involved in a score of versions in other Indian languages; Morrison at the peril of his life translated the Bible into Chinese; Judson produced a Burmese version; a host of others followed. Of course, once the "Bible" genie was out of the bottle, missionaries had less and less control over how it was used and what it accomplished, and the total impact of missions did indeed produce the results described by Sanneh. But this

---

[45]Ibid., 14-147.

[46]Ibid., 160.

[47]Ibid., 171.

[48]Ibid., 202-15.

enormously important component of the missionary enterprise is described in another volume in this series, so I will not pursue it further here.

As for addressing the intellectual and physical needs which loomed so conspicuously, what these missionaries in fact did—found schools, hospitals, orphanages, agricultural and artisanal programs, economic cooperatives, and the like—was exactly what one might have guessed they would do. They were, after all, children of their age as well as children of God. In their minds the link between a problem and its often technical, often expensive solution was simple and direct. They could not possibly have foreseen that these charitable and often excellent institutions would in time themselves become problematic. After all, these were the inventions of choice of a "Christian" civilization which it was their duty and privilege to share with lesser peoples.

But the cultural inadaptation of much that was done, especially in medical work, also stemmed from the cultural specialization and fragmentation which missionary doctors and nurses brought with them; their professional education, after all, was exactly like that of their non-Christian colleagues. Though they usually loved the people with a sincere Christian love, and often gave much better care than was available in secular hospitals, from the point of view of many an African or Asian they dispensed exactly the same medicine as the others, and failed to make the holistic connection between body and soul that the local people sensed was needed.

Missionary work also was dominated by a cluster of Western cultural values: strong task-and-goal orientation; efficiency and "rationality"; directness and explicitness; and the spontaneous resort to methods requiring money and technology. Andrew Walls, writing about American evangelical missions, but pointing out that the U.S. represents "the ultimate development of the West," discusses these missionaries' "frank and unembarrassed attitude to money and high technology."[49]

What these approaches did, apart from their effect on the work in the narrow sense, was widen yet further the gulf between missionaries and local people that already existed because of social distance. In many parts of the world, human relationships traditionally have high priority over any

---

[49]Andrew F. Walls, "The American Dimension in the History of the Missionary Movement," in *Earthen Vessels: American Evangelicals and Foreign Missions, 1880-1980*, ed. Joel A. Carpenter and Wilbert R. Shenk (Grand Rapids: Eerdmans, 1990) 1-25.

and all utilitarian concerns; the missionary attitude was widely seen to give pragmatic concerns priority over the human, and was correspondingly resented. And when local people tried to remonstrate by means of sensitively indirect ways of expressing their feelings, missionaries either did not notice the objections, or considered the local people to be secretive and dishonest. Mutual misunderstanding and resentment were rampant. We will discover in chapter 6 that, surprisingly, understanding of "culture" did not eliminate these problems.

### Contributions to the Understanding of "Culture"

In the nineteenth century, missionaries were the cross-cultural brokers par excellence. Whatever the image developed by missionary writing and speaking during this century, that was the image that was taken as true by the home audience; for good or bad, few if any other sources were taken to be as trustworthy as the missionaries who lived and labored for a lifetime in the remote regions of the world. In other words, long before the *National Geographic* or travelogs or television pictures, an avid readership learned what it did about the world from those who had been there.

As we saw in the previous chapter, even when anthropology began to emerge as a recognized discipline, most of its practitioners were armchair theorists, working with data provided by travelers, of whom the most notable and prolific were without doubt the missionaries. The missionaries were thus cultural brokers between their home societies and the peoples among whom they worked. In this role, there were both conscious, intentional components, things which the missionaries wanted to teach their supporters and their converts respectively about each others' cultures; and unconscious, incidental components, things which were learned even though the missionaries did not communicate them intentionally.

It is not possible to establish a firm periodization for the representation of non-Western cultures by missionaries. One can rather discern gradual processes, in which understanding seems to increase and evaluation seems to relax a little. The first bits of description were just that, bits: raw observations of cultural details, usually of the sort that shocked the missionary deeply. We have already seen that these fragments represented at once the missionary's cry of anguish in a very painful situation, the expression of the missionary's theological perspective, and the need to promote the cause of missions among churches back home.Gradually, the picture eased,

and missionaries understood culture better and described it more objectively.

The culmination of this process was the appearance, one at the end of
the nineteenth century and the other early in the twentieth, of two monumental and ground-breaking ethnographies. In 1891 there appeared *The
Melanesians,* by R. H. Codrington.[50] This monograph was based on work
in the field from 1863 to 1887. The term "culture" does not appear in either
the index or the table of contents. Codrington showed not the slightest interest in the theoretical debates between evolutionists and diffusionists that
raged in his day, and seems to have had little if any sense of the wholeness
or integration of culture. He does use the term "ethnology" in the table of
contents, and the index comprises references to agnatic descent, animism,
couvade, exogamy, levirate, polyandry, polygamy, and totems; in other
words, he had some substantial acquaintance with the terminology which
was coming into being in anthropology. There are references to Andrew
Lang and Max Müller, though oddly enough none to Edward B. Tylor, inventor of the term animism.

Codrington chronicled in great and careful detail both the similarities
in belief and custom that prevailed throughout Melanesia, as well as many
of the particularities of the various island peoples. He paid close attention
to social structure, political structure, religion, magic, life cycle rites, and
many other things. His account, notably of religion, is scrupulously and
even sympathetically objective. One thing for which he continues to be cited
in the literature is the introduction and explanation of the Melanesian term
*mana.* Altogether, an epochal contribution, especially at a time when the
official anthropologists never saw "natives."

The second ethnographic monograph produced by a missionary at the
turn of the century was *The Life of a South African Tribe,* by the Swiss
missionary Henri Junod.[51] Once again, we have a monumental and metic-
ulous account of the social and "mental" life of a people. Junod like Codrington did not use the term "culture" and was not interested in theory.
But he handled with confidence a good bit of the terminology current in
his day.

---

[50]R. H. Codrington, *The Melanesians* (Oxford: The Clarendon Press, 1891; repr. New
Haven CT: HRAF, 1957).

[51]Henri A. Junod, *The Life of a South African Tribe,* 2nd ed. rev. and enl. (London:
Macmillan, 1927).

It must not be thought that these two were alone; they are simply the monographs which deservedly made the most impact in anthropology. But there were others. C. G. Baëta cites Duff MacDonald in Malawi, "whose book *Africana*, written in the 1880s, revealed a penetrating understanding of African culture in this area."[52]

## Conclusions

How to conclude this chapter? I think no better closure could be used than a citation from the Report of Commission V, *The Preparation of Missionaries,* of the Edinburgh 1910 World Missionary Conference. We are accustomed to hear the glowing optimism and self-congratulation which are associated with that conference. But there was also a more sober note which bears quoting. The report (quoting Dudley Kidd at length) questioned Huxley's optimism regarding commerce as a "civilising force," and raised questions about other matters along the way.

> Western commerce and politics thoroughly arouse the natives, and yet have a fatal way of Europeanising the Kaffir and of destroying in him some of his original and peculiar virtues. Of the factors which help to elevate a backward race the most beneficent might be the Christian religion; it can, when suitably presented, do more to quicken, control, and purify the Kaffirs than can all the combined forces of commerce, politics, and education. *But having confessed my missionary faith, let me discriminate. Christian missionaries do not always show consummate wisdom in their methods. Christianity is under no inherent compulsion to impose any special form of civilisation on its adherents, else we should all be Judaised. It is certainly strange that we should take an Eastern religion, adapt it to Western needs, and then impose those Western adaptations on Eastern races. . . . It need cause us no surprise to note that we have more Europeanised than Christianised the Kaffirs, to their loss, and to the Church's loss.*[53]

A sobering and salutary note indeed!

-----

[52]C. G. Baëta, ed., *Christianity in Tropical Africa* (London: Oxford University Press, 1968) 15.

[53]World Missionary Conference, Report of Commission V, *The Preparation of Missionaries* (Edinburgh: Oliphant, Anderson, and Ferrier; New York: Revell, 1910); italics added by the Commission.

# CHAPTER 5

# Modern Theories of Culture

## The Historical Context

*Before World War II.* As I have already suggested, for anthropological and missiological purposes the twentieth century can usefully be said to have started in 1922. The period from 1900 to 1922 was in many ways transitional, with World War I (1914–1918) as a watershed. The world situation in 1922 was as follows.

The United States continued to control the territories taken from Spain in 1898, despite the formal recognition of independence for Cuba in 1901. During the transitional period, the United States had created Panama ad hoc out of territory taken from Colombia, and seized the Panama Canal Zone. It continued to dominate Latin America, less directly but no less surely. It was taken for granted, not only in Washington but in the country at large, with few dissenting voices, that the United States had the right as well as the might to determine on behalf of Latin Americans what kind of government they could have; and the decisions were made unabashedly on the basis of their effects on American business corporations in the area. In addition, the United States seized Hawaii.

Of course, the United States continued to have its internal colonial populations: Native Americans, African Americans, and Hispanic Americans, who in various ways all suffered for their lack of economic and political power. The prevailing ideology was the melting pot, which pressed minorities and immigrants towards cultural assimilation; but when some members of the minorities tried to take advantage of this approach, they were excluded on racial grounds. The story of reservations, the story of Jim Crow, the story of wetbacks and migrant workers, is too well known to be rehearsed here in detail, though it must be taken into consideration as a backdrop for anthropology and for mission.

A fair share of the work of American anthropologists during the entire period of the existence of anthropology was focused on the Native Americans; very little attention was paid to Hispanics or African Americans, though some linguists have studied their speech forms.

From 1922 to World War II, American policy in relation to its de facto empire changed very little. The Marines several times overthrew Latin American governments, American business interests dominated the Latin economies, and the United States kept a close rein on international relations and defense matters. The same was true in the Philippines, which was not able to take any real steps toward independence until 1933.

The period between the wars was the heyday of British, French, and Belgian colonialism. Administrative structures were elaborated, and legislation defined the relations between metropolis and colonies to the major benefit of the former and the minor benefit of the latter. Though in almost all colonies there were movements for national independence, cultural survival, and economic self-defense, these were for the most part contained, though Mahatma Gandhi did give the British raj a hard time in India. Repressive measures, as in the massacre at Amritsar in 1919, could be quite brutal.

The colonial governments did provide some social services such as education and medical care; and what they did not provide themselves they sometimes subsidized missions to do for them. It must be pointed out, however, that right up to independence and beyond, these services were almost always woefully inadequate, especially in the poorer colonies.

Policies differed on some points. The French tended to think globally and to legislate uniformly for France and its colonies in a highly centralized way. The more absurd effects of this were sometimes mitigated by creative local administration, as when my father was given oral permission to practise medicine in French Equatorial Africa despite the law restricting medical practice to French citizens. The British, on the other hand, tended to rule ad hoc in their various colonies, sometimes to the point of incoherence.

The French had a highly centralized educational system, and rigorously imposed the French language and culture in all schools, whether government- or mission-run; they had no respect for indigenous cultures and vernaculars. They strongly preferred that education be dispensed by the government, but tolerated and even subsidized mission schools, under heavy regulation. The British left much more leeway to the missions and accepted the use of vernaculars in the lower levels of education. The French actively subsidized the higher education in France of a tiny assimilated elite; the British permitted a good number of colonial people to obtain higher education, but with less active government sponsorship.

The Belgians were most paternalistic and repressive: education, mostly provided by missions, was regulated to ensure that Africans did not obtain anything other than basic skills and vocational training.

The German colonial empire was dismantled and its parts severally awarded by the League of Nations to Britain, France, and Australia under mandate. Though the mandate status did afford nominal protection for the rights of the populations involved, for most practical purposes the territories were very little different from their neighbors which were outright colonies.

The Dutch continued to rule Indonesia paternalistically. The Portuguese continued to hold their colonies and to foster the settlement of Europeans there, but did little by way of development.

All the colonial powers constructed some basic infrastructures: railroads, bridges, roads, seaports, later airports. But it is characteristic that all of these were designed exclusively for mercantile purposes, as a glance at the map shows: roads and railroads led from some inland center of population and agricultural or mineral production to the nearest seaport. Connections between colonies were neglected. As late as 1970, moving a truckload of household goods from Abidjan, Ivory Coast, to Accra, Ghana, an airline distance of 230 miles, I had to go far inland and travel over 600 miles on often abominable roads.

The rationale for colonialism continued to be basically economic, with a strong overlay of national power and glory. In many colonies the people were, by legislation, regulation, and outright coercion, forced to shift from subsistence agriculture to the monoculture of cash crops: cotton, coffee, or peanuts, for instance; or to work in mines or other European enterprises. The exploitation of native populations was often brutal. In 1928 the French novelist André Gide traveled in French Equatorial Africa, then wrote a scathing exposé which forced the government to institute some reforms.

*Since World War II.* World War II was a much more decisive turning point than World War I. Instead of strengthening colonialism, it proved to be the beginning of its end. The colonial empires collapsed over the period from 1945 to 1975, with many colonies becoming independent around 1960. In some cases—in Indonesia, Algeria, Viet Nam, and Zimbabwe, for instance—the process was violent, in others relatively peaceful. Some powers prepared purposefully for independence, others, notably Belgium, closed their eyes until the last minute and made no preparations.

The period from World War II to the present in the United States remains a part of the awareness of every American adult: the civil rights movement, the parallel movements of the other ethnic minorities, the resistance in some white quarters, the support in other white quarters, and the present situation. Cuba broke free from American dominance in 1959 only to become tributary to the Soviet Union. The Philippines increased its political independence, though not without trauma, but remained economically under American domination. Hawaii became a state in 1959, but Puerto Rico is still trying to decide whether to continue its territorial status, to work for statehood, or to work for independence.

But the same historic era that saw the disintegration of the colonial empires saw the coming into being of two new global realities: the East-West confrontation called the Cold War, and the North-South polarization embodied in the global economic system.

The East-West Cold War was founded on clashes of ideology and in the exercise of power in the world. The Western nations were self-identified with freedom, democracy, and capitalism; the eastern nations were self-identified with economic and political communism and had their own imperial ambitions. The ups and downs of this conflict during the more than four decades after World War II are well known: the nuclear standoff, the Korean War, the Vietnam War, and the cautious and precarious détente culminating in the dramatic events of 1989 and 1990 in eastern Europe.

Many of the countries of the southern hemisphere, erstwhile colonies coming to independence or small, weak states, tried desparately to steer clear of the clash of the giants and to remain unaligned; at Bandung, Indonesia, they created in 1954 a bloc which tried to define a posture unaffiliated with either the West or the East. Few were successful, mostly because the giants did not permit uninvolvement; it was required, in the 50s, 60s, 70s, and 80s that a country declare its allegiance to one or other of the major blocs.

But though the Cold War filled the headlines, a perhaps more significant development was the simultaneous emergence of a new global economic order. The old colonial empires had been, at least in intention, each a distinct, self-contained system based on asymmetrical relations between metropole and colonies. Now there emerged fully into view a global economic system, which absorbed the old separate parallel structures of bilateral dominance and dependency into a single worldwide structure. Dominance in the system lay in the North— erstwhile colonial powers, the United States, and Japan; the South—including many former colonies— found themselves still dependent.

The major actors in this system are transnational corporations, which are so huge, so dispersed, and so diversified that they escape accountability. Governments in the North are in general highly supportive of the system; in fact, it is one of their chief roles to exercise their power on behalf of the transnationals. Governments in the South are sometimes supportive, sometimes opposed. But they have little room to maneuver, and either option can lead to dire consequences. The flow of wealth from the poor South to the rich North continues unabated; and most northern governments, especially the United States, have consistently opposed the efforts periodically launched to establish a more just economic world order.

One of the chief devices used by the northern countries to mask the North-South polarization, especially the United States and Great Britain in the Reagan-Thatcher years, was to subsume it under the East-West clash. This ploy painted every effort in the South to gain a modicum of justice as being inspired and controlled by the East and its communist menace.

Finally, a parallel process has been going on for several decades in which Northern/Western cultural products—publications and media, films, consumer goods—have been aggressively exported for commercial and ideological purposes. This is often experienced in the South as a new form of cultural imperialism, more powerful and more pervasive even than that which characterized the colonial era.

Anthropology and missions were both carried out in this very complex and shifting scene, and interacted with it in a wide variety of ways. We will discuss anthropology in this chapter and missions in the next.

### Functionalism

*Precursors.* What forms of anthropology have prevailed during the twentieth century?

Evolutionism and diffusionism continued to dominate the field of anthropology as it became a recognized discipline with academic status around the turn of the century, and in fact for the first two decades of the twentieth century. But a great deal of new fieldwork was being done, the results of which called into question the confident overarching schemes devised by Morgan, Tylor, and others. Two things especially precipitated the demise of classical evolutionism: the appearance of Westermarck's *A History of Marriage*,[1] which undermined the grand evolutionistic scenarios; and Boas's criticism of evolutionism and of its misuse of the "comparative method," which had served as a tool to make all kinds of sweeping generalizations on the basis of tenuous empirical evidence. As was happening at the same time in the physical sciences, though with nothing like the same level of sophistication and of course nothing like the depth of background in time, the existing paradigms were more and more seen to be inadequate to account for the growing volume of empirical data coming from all parts of the world.

The massive work of James G. Frazer entitled *The Golden Bough*,[2] which unaccountably continues to be influential in nonprofessional circles, turned out in fact to have been the last attempt at a comprehensive analysis of a major body of data used completely uncritically and speculatively. Henceforth, theories in cultural anthropology would have to be far more accountable to data, and data would have to be gathered in the field and scrutinized with far greater rigor than ever before.

The theory which constituted for anthropology a major paradigm shift in the twentieth century was functionalism. I will place most emphasis on this theory, though not because it is the last word, far from it. What makes functionalism particularly important for our study is the fact that it dominated cultural anthropology in the English-speaking world during the second quarter of the twentieth century, which was precisely the period when missionaries and missiologists became fully aware of this discipline as one that could be useful to their endeavors; "missionary anthropology" thus became, for good or ill, an adaptation of functionalism. Moreover, functionalism poses some philosophical questions that Christians will have to look at more critically than they have done heretofore in relation to the social sciences.

---

[1] Edward Westermarck, *A History of Marriage*, 3 vols. (London: Macmillan, 1891).

[2] James G. Frazer, *The Golden Bough: A Study in Magic and Religion*, 12 vols., 3rd ed. (New York: Macmillan, 1935; orig. 1890).

Functionalists continued the major focus of the discipline on the exotic, small-scale, "primitive" societies of Africa, indigenous America, Papua New Guinea, and other remote parts of the world. Radcliffe-Brown, and especially Malinowski, whom we will discuss later, established the firm pattern of fieldwork in a remote exotic nonliterate community as an indispensable part of professional education, a sort of professional "rite of passage." Though there was never as far as I can discover a formal "comity arrangement" between anthropology and sociology assigning "primitive" societies to the former and "civilized" societies to the latter, this division of labor did in fact come to be largely taken for granted.

This became a source of great satisfaction to anthropologists, since there seemed to be an almost inexhaustible number of "tribes" in the "primitive" world: every anthropologist could have his or her own "tribe," not to be approached by anyone else. On the few occasions when someone did revisit an anthropologist's research site, this was widely regarded as trespassing, almost theft.

What this did to the normal scientific expectation that one investigator's findings ought to be rechecked by others should be evident. Restudy did in fact occur a few times; and in each case, interesting differences of interpretation turned up that resulted, at least in part, from the different predilections and theoretical orientations of the investigators. Thus, both Redfield and Lewis studied the village of Tepoztlán in Mexico,[3] and both Goodenough and Fischer studied the people of Truk, in the Pacific,[4] and came up with significantly different conclusions.

The division of labor between sociology and anthropology was greatly reinforced as functionalism came to dominate anthropology, since it became a matter of principle and a point of honor that the ethnographer should, after fieldwork, write a monograph describing a single, "whole culture." No one was foolish enough to tackle such an assignment in relation to a modern society, but at least two generations of anthropologists thought that was what they were doing in relation to "their" individual communities:

---

[3]Robert Redfield, *Tepoztlán, a Mexican Village: A Study of Folk Life* (Chicago: University of Chicago Press, 1946); Oscar Lewis, *Life in a Mexican Village: Tepoztlán Restudied* (Urbana: University of Illinois Press, 1963).

[4]Ward H. Goodenough, *Property, Kin, and Community on Truk*, 2nd ed. (Hamden CT: Archon Books, 1978); John L. Fischer, *The Eastern Carolines* (New Haven CT: HRAF, 1970).

their tribe, their village, their hunting and gathering band. It is only in retrospect that one gasps at the presumptuousness of this notion.

As it happened, an early attempt to analyze a body of data from so-called "primitive" cultures from a quite different point of view had already been done by the French sociologist Emile Durkheim (1858–1917) in 1912, toward the end of a long and distinguished career. In *The Elementary Forms of the Religious Life*,[5] Durkheim attempted to explain what social purpose religion served and how it worked to serve that purpose in a particular sociocultural context. It is important to note that Durkheim's understanding of "purpose" or "function" bore no relation to the classical theological ideas of transcendence, ultimate truth, or salvation; it concerned a determinedly this-worldly, empirically restricted focus on the needs of societies and persons. The putative truth or falsity of the claims of any religion with respect to any other world or life was of no interest at all to Durkheim, who was an agnostic.

In order to examine his subject matter in its "simplest" and in its chronologically earliest, most "primitive" form, untrammeled by the complexities of modern societies, he took as his specimen societies the Australian Aborigines. Ironically, this was itself a work of armchair analysis, based in part on a corpus of data which Durkheim had neither the means nor the experience to evaluate critically. In this sense, Durkheim's isolated venture into the subject matter of cultural anthropology has not stood up to subsequent scrutiny.

However, he had asked a quite different kind of question from those asked by either evolutionists or diffusionists: he asked what social purpose a cultural trait served and how it did so. In other words, he asked *functional* questions. He was chiefly interested in how social systems functioned, that is in how their various parts contributed to the existence and well-being of society as a working reality. In addition to his work on religion, he had previously studied in more complex societies and from the same theoretical perspective topics as diverse as suicide and the division of labor. For Durkheim, the ultimate reality was the group, the society, and scientific explanation consisted in showing how everything concurred to make the group survive and prosper.

---

[5]Emile Durkheim, *The Elementary Forms of the Religious Life*, trans. John Ward Swain (New York: Collier, 1961).

Durkheim followed Comte in seeing society as an organism, not a mere collection of persons. And just as a biological organism has ways of functioning that are not reducible to the functioning of its individual parts, let alone its cells or its constituent chemical elements, so society, said Durkheim, has its specific ways of functioning that are not reducible to the functioning of individual persons. It was Durkheim's passionate lifetime commitment to create a science of society that would be fully independent of psychology; this he felt he accomplished by assigning sui generis properties and workings to society as a whole which could not be accounted for by describing the mental functions of its members; and also by studying what he considered to be the most basic foundations of any social order: family, morality, and religion.

So it is not surprising that when cultural anthropologists started asking functional questions, they should have found in Durkheim a ready model.

*Radcliffe-Brown and Malinowski.* Two men, the Englishman A. A. Radcliffe-Brown (1881–1955) and Bronislaw Malinowski, a Pole who was naturalized British (1884–1942), were the founders of the new theory in anthropology called functionalism, to which they had come by very different intellectual routes and different field experiences. They both published seminal works in the same year, 1922: Radcliffe-Brown published *The Andaman Islanders*[6] and Malinowski, *Argonauts of the Western Pacific.*[7] Both of them, of course, wrote many other works in the course of busy careers. These two men not only were rivals for the title of founder; they also conceived of functionalism in rather different ways. For these and other reasons, there were deep personal incompatibilities and hostilities between them. They were in full agreement on one thing only: decrying the focus of the work of their predecessors on questions of historical origins and processes.

Malinowski in particular argued, first, that the question of the historical origins of cultural features was uninteresting and unimportant; and second, that for most societies there was in any case no possibility of discovering probing data to come to any conclusions one way or another, since there were no written documents. In assessing this move on Malinowski's part, we must remember that the "history" he was so vehemently and con-

---

[6]A. A. Radcliffe-Brown, *The Andaman Islanders* (Cambridge: the Cambridge University Press, 1922).

[7]Bronislaw Malinowski, *Argonauts of the Western Pacific* (London: Routledge, 1922).

temptuously rejecting was in fact the pseudo-history of the evolutionists, made up to suit the ideological and theoretical needs of nineteenth-century Western arrogance. If we deplore the fact that he threw out the baby with the bath water, we must not forget that that particular bath water was rather foul.

It is interesting to reflect that the rejection by cultural anthropology of historical considerations came at precisely the point in the history of the discipline when it wanted most desparately to be a ''science,'' for which the model was the physical sciences. Functionalism, in other words, is in this respect the social science reflex of uncritical imitation of the ahistorical natural sciences. But it is doubtful that the human scene can be accurately described, as atoms can, with little or no concern for specific historical antecedents, since the processes of history, unlike those of chemistry, result from the convergence of numerous often unique circumstances and are irreversible. Thus, in dealing with human phenomena, to forsake the historical perspective is to forsake any hope of truly *causal* explanations.

As I have indicated, functionalism was not the same thing in the minds of Radcliffe-Brown and Malinowski. The former followed Durkheim and for that matter the nineteenth-century ''primitive society'' theorists much more closely than the latter, with the result that he dealt with social-structural questions in a more systematic way than his rival. In particular, Radcliffe-Brown placed heavy emphasis on the group and its structure, whereas Malinowski made much more room for the individual. Malinowski therefore was more open than Radcliffe-Brown to psychological questions, psychological methods, and psychological answers. He readily described the human needs which culture satisfied in terms of individuals.

One outcome of this contrast was that where Radcliffe-Brown was more influential and where the relations between anthropology and sociology have been emphasized, as in Great Britain, the discipline came to be called *social* anthropology. In the United States, on the other hand, where Boas and Kroeber established anthropology, Malinowski has been more influential; it has therefore been the connections between anthropology and psychology that have been stressed, and the focus has been on culture rather than on society. As a consequence, the discipline is in the United States more commonly called *cultural* anthropology.

It is Malinowski's approach which has also been the more influential in missiology, especially in the United States. For this reason the functionalism we will describe will be essentially Malinowski's, with comments where appropriate about the differing emphases of Radcliffe-Brown. We will explore various dimensions of the contrast as we enumerate the major conceptual components of Malinowskian functionalism. I will identify six such components as crucial.

1. Not only are there many cultures, but each one is discrete, bounded, and self-contained. It is only lack of information that prevents us from giving the exact number of the cultures of the world. A corollary assumption is that what is interesting in the social sciences is what is happening *internally* within a social group or culture, not how it relates to other groups. Functionalists did study "culture contact," but only—at least initially— as an applied chore, not in order to further theory. "Culture contact" was in fact what messed up the real field of scientific study, the isolated culture.

We have seen that Tylor did not use the plural of "culture," and that in fact it was rare in the early decades of the discipline. The *Oxford English Dictionary,* as we saw in the previous chapter, assigns the first use of the plural to 1891. This novel use apparently expanded very gradually outside of anthropology, for the singular in a quasi-Tylorean sense was still being used in some missiological quarters as late as 1943.[8] But functionalism, especially in the Malinowskian mode, took this concept to its logical conclusion— or perhaps to its reductio ad absurdum. Radcliffe-Brown, on the other hand, was not nearly as doctrinaire. One can illustrate the contrast between the two approaches by comparing them in the South African situation, in which ideologues were bent, then as now, on emphasizing in a quite Malinowskian style the discreteness of the various component cultures. Radcliffe-Brown, on the other hand, insisted on regarding South Africa as a single complex system, in which the component cultures, however hostile to each other their bearers might be, impinged on each other in ways that made explanation impossible without taking this mutual impact into consideration.[9]

---

[8]Edmund Soper, *The Philosophy of the Christian World Mission* (New York: Abingdon-Cokesbury, 1943) 155.

[9]I am indebted to Robert Gordon for calling attention to Radcliffe-Brown's views in "On the Myth of the 'Savage Other,' " in *Current Anthropology* 30 (April 1989): 205, and in "Radcliffe-Brown in South Africa and the Origins of the Intellectual Critique of Apartheid" (unpublished paper).

As a matter of fact, further study has demonstrated beyond the shadow of a doubt that, from the dawn of the human adventure, cultural isolation and "purity" have been the rare exception rather than the rule, and that even in the most so-called primitive areas cultures have undergone intense and continual contact and mutual influence. How else can we explain the numerous detailed similarities between the hundreds of "cultures" of New Guinea, for instance, or between the many jungle "cultures" of Amazonia? But the dogma of cultural singularity, discreteness, and purity so totally shaped functionalist thought that the extraordinary concept of the "ethnographic present" was invented to describe a period— purely imaginary, as it turned out—before contact with outside cultures had hopelessly contaminated the culture under study. Ethnographic descriptions were supposed to portray this "real" culture, not the tangled situation the ethnographer could actually see. Thus, ironically, while pseudo-history of one kind was being expelled out the front door of anthropology, pseudo-history of another kind was sneaking in the back door.

2. Each culture is unique and sui generis, not truly comparable to any other. Malinowski quite consistently decried cross-cultural generalizations and the notion of cultural universals. The corollary of this was a full-fledged cultural relativism, which was limited in practice only by the strength of each anthropologist's stomach. Radcliffe-Brown, as we have just seen, rejected this hermetic notion of cultural isolatedness. Moreover, he not only did not reject cross-cultural generalizations and universals, he actively sought them and attempted to formulate a good number. That most of these ended up rather vacuous, as Marvin Harris has shown,[10] does not negate the considerable contrast in method between Malinowski and Radcliffe-Brown.

3. Whatever exists, exists because it "functions," that is, it "works"; and, as the saying goes, "If it ain't broke, don't fix it." In other words, functionalism is preeminently conservative; it is the social science of the status quo: whatever is, is right. In fact, given the notion of the ethnographic present, one might even call it reactionary.

4. Proper functioning in a culture means that everything is basically harmonious: there is a tight fit between the various domains: technology, economy, social structure, political structure, religion, the arts, and the

---

[10]Marvin Harris, *The Rise of Anthropological Theory* (New York: Crowell, 1968) 524-32.

worldview, so that each reinforces the others. This was, of course, an indispensable corrective to the earlier notion of culture as a mere inventory, but it exaggerated the harmony egregiously. Furthermore, within each domain the parts were thought to function properly, each in its niche, as for example in role distinctions based on age and sex. In everything, there was a beautiful complementarity leading to a high level of stability.

5. Under such edenic circumstances, change could not be anything but a pathology, usually perpetrated by outsiders like missionaries. Applied anthropology, to which Malinowski devoted much of his career, consisted in such a framework in minimizing the effects of outside influences (but since most applied anthropology was commissioned by colonial governments and the United States Bureau of Indian Affairs, the governmental type of external agency was taken for granted!).

6. The proper sources of information about a culture are its most successful and influential members, those for whom the culture works most effectively. It is highly unwise to use as informants women, children, or persons in any way marginal to the power structures of society, since they would give either an incomplete or a distorted view of the culture. Beyond this caveat, it was usually assumed without much thought that, because there was little or no division of labor or socioeconomic stratification in the small-scale, face-to-face societies anthropologists studied, all persons—read all adult males—experienced the culture in exactly the same way and were thus virtually interchangeable as informants. It was common, indeed almost the rule, that "the culture of village X," with 200 inhabitants, was adequately described on the basis of information from one or two persons. One simply worked with whoever was available and whomever one found congenial.

Students and followers of both Radcliffe-Brown and Malinowski were very numerous in Great Britain and other parts of the British Commonwealth, especially in South Africa, Australia, and New Zealand. Not all of them were orthodox disciples of either man, but on the whole they focused their fieldwork and their theorizing on "primitive society," that is, on matters of social structure, especially kinship and marriage and political systems. Some few studied religion from a more or less Durkheimian point of view. A large number of very useful monographs resulted.

*American Functionalism.* We have been discussing functionalism as though it were a purely British phenomenon. But the fact that Singer could call the development of "the pluralistic and relativistic conception of culture a product of the 'Boas revolution' '[11] should alert us to recognize that North American anthropology was not simply a tributary of Malinowskian functionalism. Franz Boas (1858–1942) firmly established the discipline in American academia around the turn of the century, and his direct and indirect influence created a rather distinctive sort of functionalism and gave a number of characteristic foci to anthropology in America. Boas himself wrote voluminously[12] and taught a large number of major figures in the field in his department at Columbia University.

Boasian anthropology was determinedly focused on the gathering of huge amounts of data through fieldwork, and he personally set a prodigious example in this regard. It has been alleged that Boas was hostile to theory, but this is a misrepresentation. He was indeed hostile to vast speculative schemes invented in the armchair. But both explicitly and implicitly his data gathering was always controlled by some theory-based question. In fact, it has been plausibly argued that sometimes for Boas and his students theory controlled what they saw and recorded as ostensibly "raw" data. This is the gist of Derek Freeman's criticism of Margaret Mead's findings from Samoa.[13]

Mead had gone to Samoa with the assignment from Boas to discover whether the tension over sex and sexuality experienced by American teenagers was universal or whether it was a product of peculiarly American values and mores. The presumption was strongly in favor of the latter view, and that is what Mead in fact reported after interviewing a number of teenage Samoan girls. According to Mead, in an atmosphere of total sexual permissiveness there was no tension over sex among adolescents. Freeman's criticism is that Mead allowed herself to be gulled by her own starting hypothesis and by taking at face value as confirmation the imaginative yarn spinning of her young informants. Furthermore, he says, she failed to discover available counterevidence of an unimpeachably empirical sort. The debate continues as to whether Mead or Freeman was right, aggra-

---

[11]Milton Singer, "Culture: the Concept of Culture," in *International Encyclopedia of the Social Sciences,* ed. David L. Dill, vol. 3 (New York: The Macmillan Co., 1968) 527.

[12]E.g., Franz Boas, *Contribution to the Ethnography of the Kwakiutl* (New York: Columbia University Press, 1923); *General Anthropology* (Boston: Heath, 1935); *Race, Language and Culture* (New York: Macmillan, 1940).

[13]Derek Freeman, *Margaret Mead and Samoa: The Making and Unmaking of an Anthropological Myth* (Cambridge MA: Harvard University Press, 1983); Margaret Mead, *Coming of Age in Samoa* (New York: William Morrow, 1928).

vated by the charge of some Mead champions that Freeman was unfair in waiting until after Mead's death to publish his critique. Whatever the merits of the case, it should serve as a cautionary tale regarding the danger of assuming one's hypothesis to be true and discovering only supporting data.

Boasian anthropology was also passionately opposed to racism, and it was a major item on his agenda to show that human potential was determined by culture, not genetics. Closely connected with this was a firm insistence on cultural relativity, as a means of undercutting ethnocentric and racist cross-cultural generalizations.

As I said at the beginning of the chapter, Boas condemned doctrinaire evolutionism and the uncritical use of what had been called "the comparative method," which in its earliest incarnation had involved taking isolated cultural features which seemed in some sense to be comparable from a number of cultures and basing on these comparisons sweeping generalizations. He did not reject what he considered to be carefully circumscribed, functionally founded comparisons between meaningful cultural units of two or more cultures.

Boas, like Malinowski, saw a close connection between culture and the psychology of the individual. Accordingly, a number of his students, beginning with Mead, explored the uses of psychology and psychological theories in anthropology.

One of the manifestations of this openness in American anthropology to psychological and individual factors in relation to culture is that a great many studies have focused on the relations of the individual to the group. Such studies have included a major emphasis on the role of culture in shaping personality, both individual and "national," often from a quite deterministic point of view.

Child-rearing practices of many cultures have been intensely and extensively compared, and their different results in terms of personality have been analyzed, sometimes on the basis of explicitly Freudian presuppositions, and sometimes also with the use of projective instruments such as Rohrschach inkblot tests or thematic apperception tests. Anthropologists have sometimes called in psychologists and psychiatrists as collaborators.

In other instances, anthropologists have attempted to identify a dominant or favored personality type for a whole society. This approach was especially prevalent during World War II, when anthropologists were called in to help the United States government try to understand what made the Japanese, for instance, act the way they did. This approach had been pioneered by Ruth Benedict's 1934 *Patterns of Culture*, but her *The Chrysanthemum and the Sword* was specifically a wartime effort.[14]

Marvin Harris emphasizes the important—and, from his point of view, noxious—influence of a particular type of philosophy on the social sciences: idealism. Kant and Hegel in their quite different ways affirmed the important causal role in human history of ideas, as distinct from the material conditions of existence. Harris traces a very complex chain of connections from certain Enlightenment and post-Enlightenment philosophers to some contemporary schools of thought in the social sciences.[15] I have neither the time nor the competence to trace the whole line as Harris has done, but will sketch a very rapid and no doubt simplistic picture of the basic assumption and the implications of this kind of thinking.

There is really only one relevant fundamental assumption in idealism: it is that the driving power in culture is ideas in people's heads. Culture, as we have seen, does consist preeminently in collectively held ideas— knowledge, beliefs, attitudes, values, rules—which shape people's behavior in relation to the physical world and to each other. But the crucial question is, where do these ideas come from? How do they originate? What *causes* them? Many anthropologists vehemently deny any significant causal role for the bare material conditions of existence; these, it is maintained, merely provide the base line and the raw materials for the endless diversity of cultural solutions which are created by the collective ingenuity of human groups. As a matter of fact, we have already seen that the rejection of history was also a rejection of questions of origin and causation, so that functionalist-idealists barely noticed that they were begging important questions.

Another major figure in American anthropology, Alfred L. Kroeber (1876–1960),[16] was Boas's first Ph.D. student, and then developed his own ideas and his own academic empire at the University of California at Berkeley. Kroeber's central idea during the first part of his career was a kind of formidable reification, almost a personification, of culture; his way

---

[14]Ruth Benedict, *Patterns of Culture* (Boston: Houghton Mifflin, 1934); *The Chrysanthemum and the Sword: Patterns of Japanese Culture* (Boston: Houghton Mifflin, 1946).

[15]Harris, *The Rise of Anthropological Theory*, 267-73, 319-26.

[16]See Alfred L. Kroeber, *Anthropology* (New York: Harcourt, Brace, 1923); *Configurations of Culture Growth* (Berkeley: University of California Press, 1944); *The Nature of Culture* (Chicago: University of Chicago Press, 1952).

of saying this was to call culture "the superorganic." Culture, according to Kroeber, was really out there, it really shaped and even determined people's personalities, people's opinions and feelings, people's worldviews, people's actions. This scheme was extremely deterministic. Kroeber later had second thoughts and somewhat moderated his position, but he still represents the extreme exponent of idealism in American anthropology. Kroeber, like Boas, taught and otherwise influenced a large number of younger anthropologists.

A lasting contribution of Kroeber and his disciples was the decades-long project, based in his department, to do "salvage" ethnography and linguistics, that is to study a large number of the cultures and languages of California Indian peoples before the last survivors died out.

*Problems of Functionalism.* It should be evident that Malinowskian, Boasian, and Kroeberian functionalism, heavily colored by idealism, carried a good bit of acknowledged and unacknowledged ideological freight. I want to identify five problems in particular.

1. The overemphasis on functionality and relativism leads to a dulling of ethical sensitivity; almost anything can be excused because "it works." I am forcibly reminded of the muckraking American journalist who visited the Soviet Union in the 1920s and reported: "I have seen the future, and it works"; and of people who praised Hitler and Mussolini because they restored pride and efficiency to their countries. But to praise what "works" without asking what the "working" produces—suffering, for example, or tyranny—is to be amoral. This pragmatic glorification of working institutions also leads some Christians to assign all the evil in the world to the sins of individuals, and to underestimate drastically the amount of evil that is deeply entrenched in systems and structures. For historical theological reasons, this effect has been strongest among Lutherans, Calvinists, and the heirs of Pietism; but even Anabaptists have not been entirely consistent in their critique of worldly institutions, especially in the economic domain.

2. Ignoring minority and dissenting voices exaggerates the harmony and consensus of a culture, and overlooks the extent to which it may be *dys*functional for at least some of its members. To accept unquestioningly the version of a culture purveyed by those who are in charge and who benefit from the status quo is to be easily duped by prevalent ideologies; numerous American missionaries have fallen for such lines in places like South Africa, South Korea, Taiwan, the Philippines, Chile, and elsewhere. For ob-

vious reasons, they have usually been less easily duped by left-wing ideologies. It was also discovered, once women began to do fieldwork, that a woman working with women in an alien culture could draw a quite different picture of that culture from the one drawn by male investigators working with male informants.

3. Exaggerating the stability and harmony of a culture also leads us to underestimate both the need for and the possibility of change through the impact of the gospel. A relativistic paralysis about the need of *all* cultures to submit to the judgment of God and to be transformed in appropriate ways is not the most appropriate reaction against the errors of the past.

4. Assigning sole causative power to ideas and denying or ignoring the impact on culture of the material conditions of existence has much the same effect as the old-fashioned physician's approach to psychosomatic illness: "It's all in your head." In other words, it makes it easy for us, if we are so inclined, to assign the blame for any cultural or social problems to the heads of the "problem" people rather than to the circumstances in which they live. A particularly blatant example, especially since it was the work of a basically very decent and compassionate man, was Oscar Lewis' concept of the "culture of poverty." He described various aspects of the mentality of poor people in various societies: they were improvident, they failed to plan for the future or to save when they did have money, and they did not look for jobs or hold them when they got them.[17] It's a familiar litany.

But given the idealist basis of his work and its functionalist insistence on the supposed self-contained nature of culture, he simply found no way *not* to lay full responsibility for the characteristics of this culture on the poor themselves: they are poor because they create and partake in the culture of poverty. But the very fact that he found the same culture of poverty in different societal matrices but with similar material conditions should have suggested *some* connection between that culture and the common objective conditions of life. The fact that in all instances, these people are embedded in dominant cultures for which they are ill prepared, in which they have consistently failed to gain ground, and in which they are continually the butt of society's contempt must surely be at least a contributing cause to their plight. Might it not be the case, in other words, that they have fallen into the culture of poverty as a desparate means, admittedly

---

[17]Oscar Lewis, "The Culture of Poverty," *Scientific American* 215 (1966): 19-25.

counterproductive, to cope with what could realistically be seen as inescapable poverty?

At a higher level of structural reality, a functionalist view of cultural discreteness lends itself to denying the existence of the world system, in which there is a center (rich, powerful, dominant nations) and a periphery (poor, powerless, dominated nations). The fact that an idea essentially similar to this was proposed by Lenin as a corrective to Marx no doubt makes it even harder for North American Christians to swallow. At the Willowbank Consultation on Gospel and Culture held in Bermuda (1978), some of the Western participants strenuously resisted discussing concrete power relations between have and have-not countries and their concrete effects, on the grounds that "That's not culture!"

A related point: Nicholas Wolterstorff has shown how a focus on bounded social units—in his example, nation states—actually fosters conflict between those units. This was notably the case with nineteenth-century German Romanticism, which aspired to establish a nation self-determined, organically constituted, diverse from other nations, and *fortified by struggle with other nations*.[18] Immanuel Wallerstein has devoted his career and a couple of books[19] to making the case for the existence of the global system I described above, and to explaining its origins, its workings, and its consequences. The punch line is that no human group is truly exempt from some degree of participation in that system, with incalculable effects on its culture.

5. In Christian circles, anthropological idealism reinforces our centuries-long tendency to be dualists, to emphasize the spiritual, the heavenly, and the eternal to the neglect of the material, the earthly, and the temporal, in ways that are quite congenial to gnosticism but quite alien to the Bible itself. Both Old Testament and New Testament underline the divine concern for all aspects of the human predicament and divine intervention to redeem all of human existence, bodies and all. Can you visualize Jesus ignoring a hungry child or a sick old woman just because it was time to preach? He himself gave the decisive rebuttal to this kind of thinking in

[18]Nicholas Wolterstorff, *Until Justice and Peace Embrace* (Grand Rapids: Eerdmans, 1983) 110-11.

[19]Immanuel Wallerstein, *The Modern World-System: Capitalist Agriculture and the Origin of the European World-Economy in the Sixteenth Century* (New York: Academic Press, 1974); *The Capitalist World-Economy* (Cambridge: Cambridge University Press, 1979).

the story of the Good Samaritan. But our missiology is replete with this sort of unbiblical spiritualizing, probably in part because we are members of the small privileged minority of humanity, and we find it easy and comfortable to accept uncritically the ideological justification of that privilege vis-à-vis the multitude of the world's poor.

*Other American Emphases.* On the whole, American functionalism was less narrowly focused on the "primitive society" agenda than British functionalism, so that it pursued a number of other lines of investigation and developed a variety of subsidiary concepts.

One was the development by Robert Redfield and others of an embryo typology of societies and cultures.[20] Both in his fieldwork and in his theorizing, Redfield distinguished between urban societies and their cultures, and peasant or folk societies and their cultures. He described in a more or less evolutionary way how early urban civilizations emerged from a peasant base, how and why urban culture came to differ from peasant culture, and how the two kinds of cultures related in a symbiotic but asymmetrical system.

Two American anthropologists in particular investigated cultural change quite thoroughly, along different but complementary lines. Homer G. Barnett[21] studied the processes of innovation internal to a culture. He argued that fundamentally, innovation is the same phenomenon, whether it is accidental (a slip of the tongue, for instance), or ad hoc (using a rock as a hammer), or purposeful: old elements are suddenly seen in a new combination or a new context, and take on a new meaning. Barnett described the characteristics of successful innovators, and also of successful advocates of innovation (seldom the same people). Finally, he described the processes by which an innovation is adopted into a culture and thus becomes a change in that culture.

Melville J. Herskovits, on the other hand,[22] recognized the importance of contact between persons of different cultures. He argued that in addition

---

[20]Robert Redfield, *The Folk Culture of Yucatan* (Chicago: University of Chicago Press, 1941); *The Little Community and Peasant Society* (Chicago: University of Chicago Press, 1960); and esp. *The Primitive World and Its Transformations* (Ithaca NY: Cornell University Press, 1953).

[21]Homer G. Barnett, *Innovation. The Basis of Cultural Change* (New York: McGraw-Hill, 1953).

[22]Melville J. Herskovits, *Acculturation: The Study of Culture Contact* (Gloucester MA: P. Smith, 1958).

to studying "pure" cultures, anthropologists should look carefully at what happened when people of two cultures enter into extended contact. For this situation, he used the term acculturation, to distinguish it from diffusion, which can result from even ephemeral contact. He emphasized that in acculturative situations, the influence and the change occur on both sides, not only on the side of the less powerful or prestigious culture.

Yet another style of investigation developed in interaction between anthropology and linguistics (many scholars were educated in both disciplines as a matter of course). This was the approach called the "componential analysis of meaning"; it was created by such scholars as Floyd Lounsbury, Ward Goodenough, Eugene Nida, and others.[23] This method was generally applied to a bounded set of terms relating to a definable cultural domain: kinship terms, color terms, terms for local fauna, terms for sickness and health, and so on. The idea was (a) to discover the entire set of relevant terms, (b) to discover how they related to one another structurally in a taxonomy, and (c) to break down their meanings into components in such a way that a specific configuration of components defined each term uniquely and specified its exact contrasts with every other related term. This was deemed to be an important way to open a path into the worldview of a culture. It was, in the best instances, correlated with other lines of evidence, such as concrete human behavior, in order to understand the working of each cultural domain. Elaborations and extensions of this approach have more recently been called ethnoscience, cognitive anthropology, and the new anthropology. These in some ways led to the still more recent work of Geertz and others, to be described in a later section; but, as we shall see, they differed from it in crucial ways.

For the most part, introductory textbooks in anthropology during this century have tended to be mildly functionalistic in orientation, with eclectic additions to cover topics not handled well by functionalism. Ethnographic works in North America have also had a generally functionalist flavor, but only a minority were designed, like Mead's Samoa work, to make a theoretically polemical point. In Britain, however, a certain num-

---

[23]E.g., Harold Conklin, "Hanunoó Color Categories," *Southwestern Journal of Anthropology* 11 (1955): 339-44; Floyd G. Lounsbury, "A Semantic Analysis of the Pawnee Kinship Usage," *Language* 32 (1956): 158-94; Ward H. Goodenough, "Componential Analysis and the Study of Meaning," *Language* 32 (1956): 195-216; Eugene A. Nida, *Componential Analysis of Meaning* (The Hague: Mouton, 1975).

ber of monographs by leading figures did constitute the weapons of theoretical combat.

## Neo-Evolutionism and Historical Materialism

A theory, or rather a cluster of theories, which goes in a totally different direction is neo-evolutionism, though the single label covers several disparate and incompatible models.[24] But the name does suggest what they all have in common: a renewed emphasis on the importance of origins and process for understanding cultural reality. Julian Steward's approach is known as multilinear evolution; in it Steward and his disciples attempt to avoid the Procrustean nature of the evolutionism of Morgan and Tylor in favor of a more nuanced model which allows for a diversity of sequences, depending on the geographical and other physical factors of the environment. While this model gains plausibility by sticking much closer to verifiable data, it loses generality and therefore explanatory power, at least in terms of a physical-science model of "science."

Leslie White tried to get around this by postulating a model based on a highly complex and abstract analysis of each culture's total per capita use of energy, understood in the most inclusive way possible. Thus, the most primitive cultures used little energy beyond human muscle power, augmented by a few simple tools. The control of fire, the use of domestic pack animals, the improvement of tools, the use of wind and water power, the use of fossil fuels, the invention of ever-more-complex machines—all added over time to the effective control of energy by humans and thus constituted cultural evolution. More recently, scholars have used ideas from both Steward and White in a more eclectic manner to describe how cultures change—evolve—over time.

A related school of thought has adopted the label "historical materialism." This is best exemplified by Marvin Harris, who along with Ross and others of his followers[25] has done much to insist on—and to demonstrate in often quite convincing ways by means of rigorous empirically based studies—the powerful role physical and material conditions play in the or-

---

[24]Julian H. Steward, *Theory of Culture Change* (Urbana: University of Illinois Press, 1955); Leslie A. White, *The Evolution of Culture* (New York: McGraw-Hill, 1959); also V. Gordon Childe, *What Happened in History?* (New York: Pelican Books, 1946).

[25]Harris, *The Rise of Anthropological Theory*; Edwin B. Ross, ed., *Beyond the Myths of Culture: Essays in Cultural Materialism* (New York: Academic Press, 1980).

igin and functioning of any culture. They have shown that under similar material conditions, people often come up with very similar cultural responses to the problems and opportunities offered them by those conditions. Though the advocates of this school have been influenced by Karl Marx, they differ in the degree of rigor and in the specific emphases with which they follow him. Their critique of idealism and of the forms of functionalism shaped by idealism is not easily refuted, especially at those points where I have identified problems from a Christian perspective.

### European Theories

Meanwhile, anthropology on the European continent was moving in a number of directions. One took the form of elaborations on diffusionism. Another was shaped by the heavy influence in some quarters of Karl Marx. Yet another was the work, mainly in the 1920s, of the French philosopher Lévy-Bruhl.[26] He is best known for the proposal, which later he had the integrity to repudiate, that there was a profound difference in kind between the "civilized" mind and the "primitive" mind. Whereas the former could reason abstractedly, make generalizations, and distinguish clearly between subject and object, the latter could not. In fact, said Lévy-Bruhl, primitives thought much like the children of civilized societies: animistically, mystically, intuitively, assigning life and purpose to inanimate things, participating in the things around them rather than differentiating self from their surroundings. Various persons with ideological agendas happily adopted the ideas of Lévy-Bruhl, which of course lent themselves all too readily to racist applications.

A quite distinctive French variant of the emphasis in anthropology on underlying, mentally based meanings in culture, often combined with the "primitive society" agenda, is structuralism, the creation of Lévi-Strauss.[27] This theory, which was later applied by others to a host of subject matters, including literary criticism, was by its founder applied most especially to

---

[26]Lucien Lévy-Bruhl, *How Natives Think*, trans. Lilian A. Clare (New York: Washington Square Press, 1966; orig. 1910); *Primitive Mentality*, trans. Lilian A. Clare (New York: Macmillan, 1923).

[27]See, e.g., Claude Lévi-Strauss, *Structural Anthropology*, trans. Claire Jacobson and Brooke Grundfest Schoepf (New York: Basic Books, 1963); *The Elementary Structures of Kinship*, trans. James Harle Bell and Richard von Sturmer, ed. Rodney Needham (Boston: Beacon Books, 1969); *The Raw and the Cooked*, trans. John and Doreen Weightman (New York: Harper, 1969).

two cultural areas: the analysis of myth, and the analysis of kinship systems.

Structuralism is basically an attempt, not unlike a more formalized componential analysis, to get beneath the surface phenomena of culture to putative universal underlying structures of human thought, which are supposed to have certain highly abstract properties, such as being binary and contrastive. Lévi-Strauss, in other words, explicitly and forcefully rejected Lévy-Bruhl's notion of different kinds of thinking among human beings of different cultures. On the contrary, he insisted, once one gets beneath the surface diversities of cultural content, one discovers that all human beings think in exactly the same way. A number of criticisms can be addressed to structuralism: it has proved inordinately difficult to operationalize it in such a way that two scholars come up with the same results when they analyze the same body of data; it is so powerful that it obliterates the data; and, even in the hands of its inventor, it turns out to be two quite different things when it is applied to such different themes as myth and kinship.

### Contemporary Debates

A number of debates have occupied American anthropology in recent decades. We shall discuss those which are of most interest to our missiological concerns. It will be noted that these topics flow into each other and affect each other in varied and complex ways; and it will also be noted that they are all profoundly philosophical.

*Objective, "Applied," or "Action"?* One important discussion took place between those anthropologists who in the name of "objective science" adopted a determinedly detached view of the human scene they were studying, and those who argued on various grounds that the anthropologist could or even should be humanly involved in his field of study. (Some, on epistemological grounds, argued that the anthropologist could not avoid being involved in and affecting the field of study; but that will be discussed later.) The former insisted that human societies and cultures must be studied with no personal involvement or evaluative judgment, for anything of that sort necessarily contaminated the field and clouded the investigator's judgment with his or her personal hopes, fears, and anxieties.

The first break with this adamant objectivism was made by a number of anthropologists, in Britain, the European continent, and the United States. These accepted employment, usually with colonial or quasi-colonial governmental agencies, for example the U. S. Bureau of Indian Affairs, with the intent to help the agency "understand" its subject populations, and to help the subject populations "understand" and submit to the agency's policies with as little trauma as possible. The label for this activity was "applied anthropology." Many applied anthropologists sincererly believed that in using their knowledge and skills in this way they were acting in the best interests of the "natives," since implementation of the policies in question was inevitable and (usually) "good for the natives, if they only understood it."

But an anthropologist at the University of Chicago named Sol Tax became convinced that this was in fact unjust and unethical, since it added the anthropologist's power (knowledge) to the already overwhelming and oppressive power of colonial governments. He reasoned that the people he studied were helping him by sharing their knowledge of themselves and their culture with him. It was therefore not fair to use the power conferred by that knowledge against the people by lending it to the oppressive outsiders. Rather, the anthropologist had the duty to place his knowledge of both the dominant culture and the dominated culture at the disposal of the victims, by helping them understand and respond more freely and effectively, in ways that furthered their interests as *they* understood them. Tax coined for this approach, which he himself implemented in field situations, the term "action anthropology."[28]

*Freedom or Determinism?* The predominant position in anthropology has been quite deterministic; as racial or genetic determinism has been discarded, sociocultural determinism has replaced it. The major difference is that culture (social environment) is more amenable to alteration and amelioration by human action than are genes and chromosomes. This has made cultural determinism more appealing than genetic determinism to the liberal mind, with its frequent reformist impulses, and to the radical mind, with its revolutionary aspirations.

Almost alone among anthropologists, David Bidney discussed the question of freedom and determinism at length. In a book which was an extended polemic against the determinism of Leslie White, he concluded that human beings are partially determined, but that they enjoy an irred-

---

[28]Sol Tax, "Action Anthropology," *Current Anthropology* 16/4 (December 1975): 514-17; Sam Stanley, "The Panajachel Symposium," *Current Anthropology* 16/4 (December 1975): 518-24; James O. Buswell III, "From 'Anthropology in Action' to 'Action Anthropology,' " *Practical Anthropology* 8 (1961): 111-24.

ucible measure of freedom.[29] The debate was sharpened by the fact that White was a materialist, Bidney an idealist. Embedding the discussion in a comprehensive theoretical matrix, Bidney argued that human beings have both a determinate psychobiological aspect and an indeterminate "historically acquired cultural personality." It is the latter which affords us freedom, because we are not only products of culture but creators of culture. The indeterminacy of linguistic symbolism also allows for a range of freedom. In short, though human beings are not absolutely free, neither are they totally determined in the sense suggested by B. F. Skinner.

*Cultural Relativism.* The relativism debate does indeed continue within anthropology. Herskovits had given the classical expression to the concept,[30] but it was most succinctly summarized by Bidney.[31] He distinguished between four forms of cultural relativity. As a method in anthropology, it permits one to work with "scientific detachment, or, ideally, from the perspective of participants . . . of a given culture." As a "theory of cultural determinism and a philosophy of cultural reality" (Herskovits's emphasis), it insists that we live in a world of our own imagining which determines our perceptions and conceptions. As "a guide to the evaluation of value systems," it does not lead to "moral skepticism and nihilism" since "morality is a cultural universal and is essential to the corporate existence of any society." It also serves as the ground for a particular attitude toward practical problems of reform and change. We might include them all under two headings: evaluative or ethical relativism; and epistemological relativism.

More recently, Elvin Hatch has written an important book under the title *Culture and Morality: The Relativity of Values in Anthropology.*[32] He traces the history of relativism in the thought of Boas and others as an explicit rejection of the racism and cultural arrogance of the past. He distinguishes, as did Bidney, between types of relativism; his terms are "ethical

---

[29]David Bidney, *Theoretical Anthropology* (New York: Columbia University Press, 1953).

[30]Melville J. Herskovits, *Cultural Relativism,* ed. Frances Herskovits (New York: Vintage Books, 1973).

[31]David Bidney, "Cultural Relativism," in *International Encyclopedia of the Social Sciences* 3:543-47.

[32]Elvin Hatch, *Culture and Morality: The Relativity of Values in Anthropology* (New York: Columbia University Press, 1983).

relativism,'' the ''relativism of knowledge,'' ''historical relativism,'' and ''methodological relativism.'' But he also acknowledges the limits inherent in a concept of relativism and tolerance of what exists.

Possible limits to cultural relativism of the ethical type have in fact been discussed ever since it was discovered that unlimited relativism left one no base from which to condemn even the grossest abuses. Alison Dundes Renteln[33] has attempted to define a basis for universally valid value judgments on the basis of cultural universals. Herskovits had long ago warned against the fragility of trying to build an *ought* on the basis of an *is*, however universal its occurrence. But this ploy is perennially attractive to those who find it necessary to make judgments but allow for no Absolute above all cultures as a ground for those judgments.

Ethical relativism arrived early in the scene. It took longer, as we shall see immediately, for the implications of epistemological relativism to sink in.

*Epistemology: How Do Anthropologists ''Know''?* Epistemological relativism is all very well for other people's cultures. Until quite recently, it was simply assumed without argument that the anthropologist's perspective, as distinct from almost all others, was valid per se; it was somehow exempt from relativism (for many people, simply by virtue of being ''scientific''). But what if the anthropologist's own perspective is relative to something else rather than absolutely and universally true? How can one do valid science if one cannot achieve ''true knowledge''?

A very preliminary approach to some of the problems posed by this difficult question was offered by Kenneth Pike.[34] On the basis of the well-known linguistic terms ''phonetic'' and phonemic,'' he created the apocopated words ''etic'' and ''emic.'' In linguistics, phonetics is the science which describes and represents symbolically all possible human speech sounds; it thus provides a universal inventory of sounds and symbols for sounds, with which the field linguist can represent in fine detail all the variations of informants' speech. Phonemics, on the other hand, is the science which describes exactly and only the speech sounds and contrasts which function in a specific language. Extending this distinction to culture

---

[33]Alison Dundes Renteln, ''Relativism and the Search for Human Rights,'' *American Anthropologist* 90/1 (March 1988): 56-72.

[34]Kenneth L. Pike, *Language in Relation to a Unified Theory of the Structure of Human Behavior*, vol. 1 (Glendale CA: Summer Institute of Linguistics, 1954) 8-10.

at large, Pike proposed that "etic" description was description in a more or less universal set of categories brought by the investigator to the field, categories such as "marriage" or "government."

The "etic" perspective, then, was the sophisticated outsider's perspective. The "emic" perspective, on the other hand, was the insider's perspective, which gave an account of a culture in its own terms and categories. Pike also believed firmly that the emic perspective was real, and that it was discoverable by a careful outsider. Pike himself argued pragmatically that both perspectives were valid for different purposes. But others, wanting to be ideologically purer, took what they saw as principled stands for ethnography *only* from an emic point of view, or *only* from an etic point of view.

It should be clear that the emic perspective was most congenial to people influenced by Malinowski, while the etic perspective was favored either by functionalists who wanted to make cross-cultural generalizations or by scholars such as Harris who held to other theoretical positions and who wanted to make generalizations for other purposes.

Not long after Pike's proposal, there arose in the field of anthropological linguistics a related question: what was the status of the results of componential analyses of semantic domains such as kinship or color terms? Did the results of the anthropologist's efforts constitute a "real" representation of the workings of native minds? Or were they a purely synthetic creation of the anthropologist which, in the best of cases, would duplicate the real-life results but not necessarily the mental workings of native minds? Scholars who affirmed the former position were called advocates of "God's truth," while their opponents believed in "hocus pocus." These jocular labels were coined by Harold Conklin.

Today, the debate continues on even more difficult and precarious ground. There is, most fundamentally, a lack of consensus about the nature and status of "culture" itself. Is it purely ideational, or is it in some sense empirically available? Is it subjective, or is it objective? Does "a culture" have enduring specifiable reality, or is it merely a shorthand method of talking about a shifting and leaky set of phenomena? Does it correspond to something which is really "out there" for its bearers, or is it merely a conceptual invention and tool of the anthropologist?

More specifically, is an ethnographic description of "a culture" a truly scientific, verifiable account of something which really exists, or is it an intuitive invention of the writer, perhaps even a work of fiction? When an

ethnographer purports to describe what goes on in the minds of the people
under scrutiny, does the description correspond to what is there, or is the
ethnographer merely projecting his or her own subjectivity? Are cross-cultural generalizations possible and valid, or not? All of these questions are
at heart reflexes of the basic question of the status of cultural anthropology:
is it a "science" dealing with reality, or is it a branch of history, or even
of fiction, dealing with more or less subjective interpretations?

One thing which evolutionists, diffusionists, functionalists, structur-
alists, idealists, and materialists all had in common was the sense that what
they were describing was really there, that it had objective reality and existence outside their heads and could be accounted for by objective and
publicly available methods. This view has been described by some who
question it radically as the last hurrah of the arrogant optimism of the Enlightenment epistemology, an optimism which in the sciences was aggravated by nineteenth and twentieth-century positivism. It is, however,
passionately defended by many others.

But the questions come from several different directions and for several reasons. Criticism has come from philosophers, who raise profound
doubts about the epistemological soundness of the cartesian and positivistic distinction between subject (knower) and object (known). It has also
come from a number of younger anthropologists who have discovered in
their fieldwork that the models and methods they learned in school leave
them with a curiously unsatisfying sense of artificiality, of superficiality,
of excessive distance from the humanity of the people they studied. Criticism has come from ethicists, who protest that detached objectivity about
the human scene is an inexcusable abdication from the duty to judge and
be involved, that it is a tacit tolerance of intolerable reality. It has come
from sociologists of knowledge, who argue that it is impossible to view the
human scene without injecting into it our ideologically loaded personal
concerns. Most significantly for our purposes, criticism has come from
some senior anthropologists of impressive credentials and experience such
as Clifford Geertz, Victor Turner, Mary Douglas, and Eric Wolf.[35]

All of these voices have been calling for a different approach to the study
of human reality, one aiming less at "knowledge" in the positivistic sense
and more at "understanding." The goal is an interpretive or "hermeneu-

---

[35]See, e.g., Jonathan Freedman, "An Interview with Eric Wolf," *Current Anthropology* 28/1 (February 1987): 107-18.

tic'' social science. Human reality, it is argued, is inescapably subject to interpreted understanding, not objective understanding. There are multiple points of view, sometimes apparently or really contradictory, none automatically privileged, each yielding its modicum of understanding. For this reason, Geertz calls for "thick," that is, multilayered, description, and gives extended examples from his own fieldwork.[36]

Geertz makes no bones about his idealistic, semiotic view of culture:

> The concept of culture which I espouse . . . is essentially a semiotic one. Believing, with Max Weber, that man is an animal suspended in webs of significance he himself has spun, I take culture to be those webs, and the analysis of it to be, therefore, not an experimental science in search of law but an interpretive one in search of meaning.[37]

One of his classic specimens of "thick" descriptions deals with a funeral in a Javanese village.[38] The description, extending for about twenty pages, deals with the idealized form of the ritual; with the disquieting impact on the ritual of certain historic trends in Indonesia; with the specific circumstances and personalities concerned; with a narrative of what took place, including a number of idiosyncratic actions by certain participants; and with the meanings the whole thing had for various involved parties. It is a dramatic and insightful exercise.

Victor Turner in a number of writings discusses the intimate connection between social structures and social processes on the one hand, and socially generated conventional meanings on the other. In *The Ritual Process,* for instance, he deals with questions of ritual classification in terms of community and liminality—the state of being neither fully inside nor fully outside.[39] In *The Forest of Symbols*[40] he gives an extended exemplification of his model in describing the ritual life of an African society.

Finally, Mary Douglas has maintained a career-long focus on the connections between symbols and other social phenomena. In *Natural Sym-*

---

[36]Clifford Geertz, *The Interpretation of Cultures* (New York: Basic Books, 1973); *Local Knowledge* (New York: Basic Books, 1983).

[37]Geertz, *The Interpretation of Cultures,* 5.

[38]Ibid., 146-66.

[39]Victor W. Turner, *The Ritual Process* (Chicago: Aldine Publishing, 1969).

[40]Victor W. Turner, *The Forest of Symbols: Aspects of Ndembu Ritual* (Ithaca NY and London: Cornell University Press, 1967).

*bols*,[41] she explores with great sensitivity the loss of appreciation of and participation in ritual in modern societies, and concludes that the reason is that modern societies are too "open" in the sense of being heterogeneous; for, she says, "The most important determinant of ritualism is the experience of closed social groups" which thereby share the same belief and value systems.[42] Douglas goes on to develop a sophisticated model involving the dynamic interactions of "group"—the social entity—and "grid"—the foundations of cultural understandings and attitudes. She has also edited a book[43] of essays by philosophers, sociologists, anthropologists, psychologists, and others, bringing to bear their various perspectives on the question of the cultural relativity of knowledge.

The fruitfulness of Douglas's model for biblical hermeneutics has been demonstrated by Bruce Malina in a book[44] applying it to the interpretation of cultural phenomena mentioned or alluded to in the New Testament.

The upshot of all these efforts is to demonstrate how dependent on social and cultural experience is all human knowledge and belief. Epistemological relativity can no longer be denied in the name of any philosophical, theological, or methodological positivism. Moreover, this relativity does not operate only at the boundaries between discrete "cultures": it also works within cultures, to the extent that people occupy different positions in society and therefore experience and interpret reality differently.

Ironically, this process of questioning earlier certainties and one-dimensional answers is in some respects not unlike what has taken place in the very paradigm of a "hard" science: physics. Bohr's complementarity, Heisenberg's uncertainty principle reflect the impossibility of achieving a stable, comprehensive understanding of atomic and subatomic particles from a single point of view.

---

[41]Mary Douglas, *Natural Symbols: Explorations in Cosmology* (New York: Vintage Books, 1973).

[42]Ibid., 33.

[43]Mary Douglas, ed., *Rules and Meanings: The Anthropology of Everyday Knowledge* (Harmondsworth, England: Penguin Books, 1973).

[44]Bruce J. Malina, *The New Testament World: Insights from Cultural Anthropology* (Atlanta: John Knox, 1981).

## Conclusions

What can we say by way of concluding this long and involved story? Is anthropology falling apart? Are its methods, its concepts, its findings to be discarded? Should we look for surer tools for missiology?

It seems to me rather—and I will raise these questions again in chapter 7—that anthropology is slowly, painfully, through much trauma, coming of age. It is moving out of its childish exuberance and overconfidence into a more mature, cautious, modest understanding of itself and of its field of study. It is finally, one hopes, abandoning the grandiose scenarios of the past and going about the painstaking job of achieving insight, of overcoming misunderstanding. Anthropology is indeed a discipline which, though vigorous in its scholarly efforts, is in considerable disarray about its philosophical foundations. It is recognizing that it cannot by and in itself move the earth. In this chastened mood, I think it can be of even greater value to missiology than in the past, since it may lead even us missiologists to a greater modesty about how much we know.

# CHAPTER 6

# Anthropology and Missions

## The Historical Context

*Before World War II.* The twentieth century after 1922 saw a number of major changes in Protestant missions. The period of transition from the nineteenth to the twentieth century had included both the acme of missionary optimism in the Edinburgh Missionary Conference of 1910 and the trauma of World War I. This was especially devastating to German missions, though they recovered surprisingly quickly. In the United States, the Roaring Twenties brought the increased polarization of the old modernist-fundamentalist controversy, which moved from its relatively civil, scholarly period (roughly 1900–1910) to a brutal nastiness after World War I; this was in turn mitigated by the rise of the Evangelical movement in the 1940s. The Great Depression of the thirties hit most Protestant missions hard, though few abandoned their fields. The convulsions of the Sino-Japanese War and of the budding Kuomintang-Communist civil war in China were especially traumatic for missions in that country.

The Protestant missionary movement in the United States and Canada increasingly diverged into two strands, the mainline missions and the conservative missions. The mainline denominations, influenced by the convergence of liberal theology and the social gospel, continued and expanded their involvement in social and institutional ministries, but for the most part without the American nationalism. The rationale for a conscious and intentional move from evangelism to social services was most radically expressed in the Report of the Laymen's Enquiry entitled *Re-Thinking Missions*,[1] whose chief author was William Hocking. This report in es-

---

[1] Laymen's Foreign Mission Inquiry, Commission of Appraisal, William Hocking, chair. *Re-Thinking Missions* (New York: Harper, 1932).

sence adopted a quite relativistic stance with regard to the other religions, dismissing as arrogant the earlier assumption that conversion to Christ was necessary for salvation.

These missions continued to consolidate their work in their historic fields, which included mostly the coastal areas of the great continental masses as well as a few interior areas. Statistically, they more or less stabilized in numbers of personnel, and then began a gradual decline. Their concerns were expressed organizationally by the International Missionary Council, which had come out of the Edinburgh conference and which ultimately (1961) merged into the World Council of Churches. Over the decades, this Council sponsored a number of major ecumenical missions conferences: in Jerusalem (1928), Tambaram (1938), Whitby (1947), Willingen (1952), and Accra (1958).

Meanwhile, the interdenominational "faith" missions, which, as we saw in chapter 4, began in the 1860s, grew to a mighty flood in the twentieth century. Their self-understanding involved three major elements: they intentionally recruited personnel and raised funds among those churches and persons in the mainline denominations who were unhappy with developments in their denominations, as well as among conservative denominations and independent congregations; as their names showed, they intentionally and aggressively went to the "inland," "interior," "heart" regions of the great continental land masses, which were not being fully reached by the mainline missions; and they insisted on the primordial, and often exclusive, importance of evangelism as against social ministries.

This last emphasis was, of course, a repudiation of the earlier sense of social responsibility which had characterized all Protestant bodies through much of the nineteenth century; but it was explicitly motivated by a reaction against the alliance between liberal theology and the social gospel that characterized the mainline bodies. Most of these missions were theologically characterized, as in the past, by premillenial dispensationalism, which radically questioned the value of anything done to improve the present world or to alleviate present sufferings. In 1917, these missions founded a cooperative body, the Interdenominational Foreign Mission Association (IFMA).

Rather later, with small beginnings around the turn of the century and gathering momentum after World War I, a number of conservative denominations began to establish their own missions and to send their own missionaries to the field. They resembled the faith missions in their orientation to the "interior" and "bush" areas as well as in their conservative insistence on the primacy or exclusiveness of evangelism. But, of course, they added their denominational distinctives to their message. The conservative denominations in 1943 established the National Association of Evangelicals (NEA) and in 1945 its missionary branch, the Evangelical Foreign Missions Association (EFMA).

Very early after the founding of the EFMA, it and the IFMA began a close cooperation which has continued through the years. They have jointly sponsored several conferences and publications setting forth the conservative position on numerous missiological issues.

In the field, both types of conservative missions leapfrogged over the mainline missions and evangelized interior areas. This resulted in an interesting situation, which is especially conspicuous on the map of West Africa: in all the countries along the southern coast of the "hump," mainline churches dominate along the coast, and conservative ones are to the north of them. Moreover, the dividing line between them happens to coincide quite closely with a significant linguistic and cultural boundary.

Missions in Britain and the European continent were not as polarized as American missions, at least in organizational terms. There were indeed a few "faith" missions founded in Europe, notably C. T. Studd's Worldwide Evangelization Crusade, and also particular conservative groups which persisted in the traditional approach within already established missions; but these were on the whole numerically and institutionally weak. There were also more liberal constituencies which pressed for a reinterpretation of missions along the lines of *Re-Thinking Missions*. But on the whole, especially under the influence of Karl Barth and Hendrik Kraemer, as well as a number of academic and field missiologists from Germany, the Netherlands, and Scandinavia, a rather more conservative position dominated mainline missions and missiology. Incidentally, a number of the North American "faith" missions recruited with varying degrees of vigor and success in Europe. The situation in the outposts of the Empire in Australia and New Zealand reflected influences from both Great Britain and North America, and so was mixed.

Needless to say, missions worked in and around the colonial situation. Their stance towards the colonial powers and their policies varied somewhat, but it is fair to say that very few questioned the colonial system as such. For instance, when Buell in 1928 published his massive *The Native*

*Problem in Africa*,[2] few if any missionaries protested the grotesque incongruity of the title. Whatever problems existed in Africa were due to the "natives," not to the colonial powers or the colonial system.

One might suppose that it would make a difference whether or not the missionaries were working in a colony of their own homeland; but in fact the difference, if it existed, was surprisingly slight. After all, foreigners could and did feel it necessary to walk circumspectly vis-à-vis the authorities, since they worked by the tolerance of these authorities. I can still remember to my shame that in correspondence with the French authorities to which my American mission applied for permission to open schools, we wrote of our entire cooperation with "the civilizing mission of France." This may stand for a less-than-admirable norm.

World War II was in some areas a kind of holding operation for missions, in that new missionaries could not get to the fields and older missionaries could not come home on furlough. In the Far East, many missionaries were captured by the Japanese and held in concentration camps, and the churches they had served were left on their own. There were other countries from which missionaries were expelled or had their movements and activities curtailed. As a result, many churches tasted de facto independence and found it good.

*Since World War II.* After World War II, the independence of many erstwhile colonies, as well as the experience by the churches of freedom from tutelage during the war, powerfully affected missions in many countries. There were also determined efforts to reach many areas not previously touched by missions.

Because many American servicemen had served in Europe during the war, North American conservative missions discovered Europe as a mission field, and a considerable number of missionaries went there. Most of these avoided contact with established Protestant churches, considering them too liberal. But many of these missionaries were not adequately prepared to cope with the level of education and sophistication of the Europeans; many did not learn the languages well enough, and few bothered to find out about the histories, literatures, or philosophies of the continent. As a result, they were often rebuffed by the Europeans, and their work was less fruitful than they had hoped. A certain number shifted focus and ended

---

[2]Raymond Leslie Buell, *The Native Problem in Africa*, 2 vols. (New York: Macmillan, 1928).

up ministering to American military personnel and their families rather than to Europeans. An excellent study of the situation in France has been written by Allen Koop.[3]

For similar reasons, and encouraged by a pressing invitation from General MacArthur, conservative missions rushed into Japan in large numbers in the postwar period. They experienced similar discouragements of widespread rejection and meager results, partly for similar reasons. But the economic resurgence of Japan from the mid-fifties also contributed to the closing of the short-lived window of opportunity.

A notable feature of postwar American missions is that the mainline missions have experienced a decline in personnel ever since World War II, while the conservative missions have burgeoned. In 1965, for example, the Southern Baptists, the Presbyterians, and the United Methodists each had about 1500 missionaries; in 1990, the Southern Baptists were approaching 4000, while the Methodists had 500 and the Presbyterians 250. Two reasons can be given to explain these statistics: first, the mainline missions tended to be much older and to work in much more mature fields, in which churches were more than ready for independence; the conservative missions, much younger, were often still in the pioneering phase. But there was also a considerable loss of missionary zeal and missionary nerve in mainline circles, while the conservatives by and large maintained the vision. So if my description of the missionary use of anthropology in the second half of the century begins to look more and more provincially conservative, and more and more North American, it is because the field has largely been abandoned to the conservatives and the Americans, and they have seized it.

One more notable trait of conservative American missions in the past couple of decades needs emphasis. Their supporting churches had had conservative reflexes in politics and economics from early in the century, but without either much power or much know-how. But in the fifties, the mainline churches against which the conservatives define themselves moved sharply to the left politically, as in the civil rights movement, and the conservative churches reacted strongly; in the seventies the conserva-

---

[3]Allen V. Koop, *American Evangelical Missionaries in France 1945–1975* (Lanham MD: University Press of America, 1986); for a summary see "American Evangelical Missionaries in France 1945–1975," in *Earthen Vessels: American Evangelicals and Foreign Missions, 1880–1980,* ed. Joel A. Carpenter and Wilbert R. Shenk (Grand Rapids: Eerdmans, 1990) 180-202.

tive churches began to occupy a more privileged and powerful position in American society, and to become more vocal on behalf of conservative causes. American politicians successfully convinced these conservatives that the American Way of Life and the American nation represented the best hope for God's cause against the godless Evil Empire to the east. The resulting close ideological and pragmatic alliance between American nationalism, capitalism, and conservative missions is carefully documented and analyzed by Richard Pierard.[4]

British and continental missions were in many ways much more like the American mainline than like the American evangelicals. Accordingly, their participation in missions through sending missionaries has declined dramatically since World War II, though churches in some countries, notably Germany, have been most generous with funds for church projects in the non-Western world. Quite a few volunteers from Europe, Britain, and the outposts of the British Commonwealth serve under independent faith missions. As a result of all these shifts, the complexion of cross-cultural missions around the world has become overwhelmingly North American in the past few decades.

One final note before we move on to the specific topic of our concern. Though anthropology came to be appreciated and used by all kinds of Protestant missions, it was less central and exclusive in influence among mainline missions than among conservative ones. The mainline missions, often structurally complex and often concentrated in urban, relatively modernized areas, also found sociology very helpful, and used it along with anthropology. This was especially the case when they began to listen to the intellectual leaders of the national churches. Conservative missions, on the other hand, which were heavily concentrated in remote rural, "primitive," "bush" situations, tended to rely more exclusively on anthropology and to neglect sociology. This distinction can be seen conspicuously in the composition of faculties and in curricula across the spectrum of missionary-training institutions.

### The Discovery of Anthropology by Missions

We have already seen that long before the nineteenth century, but especially during that century, missionaries were among those who best knew

---

[4]Richard V. Pierard, "*Pax Americana* and the Evangelical Missionary," in *Earthen Vessels: American Evangelicals and Foreign Missions, 1880–1980*, 155-79.

what there was to be known about non-Western cultures, simply by virtue of prolonged residence among and interaction with people of every kind of society, and also by virtue of taking the trouble to learn the language and something of the customs of people. Missionaries were also, of all Westerners, the ones most overtly and sincerely sympathetic and caring in relation to people, even if these attitudes were vitiated by condescension. Codrington and Junod, as has been shown, had written excellent descriptions of cultures, and had contributed key terms to the discussion, such as Codrington's introduction of *mana*.[5]

But we must conclude, if silence is any argument, that few missionaries until this century knew much of the new discipline of anthropology; nor did the great majority have any acquaintance with the term ''culture'' or efforts to define it. I have discovered not a single reference in nineteenth-century missionary writings to a work of anthropology, not even to Tylor, though Codrington and Junod did use a wealth of anthropological terminology, which argues a good knowledge of the field. But they were exceptional.

Early in the twentieth century, however, missiologists began to tap the new discipline, and eventually to use ''culture'' and even ''cultures'' with some facility and understanding. Chief among the pioneers was Edwin W. Smith, whose anthropologically informed articles were published in the *International Review of Missions* from 1912 onwards.[6] For the next few decades he made a valuable contribution by bringing basic concepts to the attention of missiologists and missionaries, and leading them to make use of these concepts to improve their work. Smith's influence was felt most directly in Great Britain and the European continent, and among Christian bodies involved in the ecumenical movement; it was less felt in North America or among very conservative missions, which were already by this time leading their separate existence. In the *International Review of Missions*, a paper by Martin Schlunk represents a less open and perceptive stance than Smith's.[7]

---

[5]R. H. Codrington, *The Melanesians* (Repr. New Haven CT: HRAF, 1957; orig. Oxford: Clarendon Press, 1891); Henri Junod, *The Life of a South African Tribe*, 2nd ed. (London: Macmillan, 1927).

[6]See, e.g., Edwin W. Smith, ''Social Anthropology and Mission Work,'' *International Review of Missions* 13 (1924): 518-31.

[7]Martin Schlunk, ''Missions and Culture,'' *International Review of Missions* 13 (1924): 532-44.

In any case, relatively few at first took the trouble to grasp and apply these novel ideas. *Saints and Savages,* a book about mission among Brazilian Indians published around 1924 by Alexander Rattray Hay,[8] shows no appreciation for Indian cultures, quite the contrary. Nor does the 1947 book *The Soul of West Africa,*[9] by the missionary leader R. S. Roseberry, though Roseberry does show high admiration for African persons, once converted from "heathenism." A rapid survey of the magazine *Congo Mission News* from 1920 to 1932 reveals that it was toward the end of that period that the fundamental concept of culture itself began to be taken seriously by the missionary editors and authors whose work is represented by that periodical.

In ecumenical circles, J. H. Oldham in *Christianity and the Race Problem* (1924) did not display much understanding of the concept of culture, though he sharply distinguished "civilization" or "social heritage" from race, assigning the observable differences between peoples to the former rather than the latter. He wrote, for instance, that

> difficulties may arise from differences in civilization. Civilization is something quite distinct from race, but since the two often coincide, they are apt to be confused. . . . The periods of greatest progress have followed on the contact of two different civilizations and their mutually stimulating effect.[10]

The Jerusalem conference of the International Missionary Council (1928) made passing allusion to culture and cultural phenomena in at least three of the report volumes.[11] Oddly enough, the official documents from the 1938 Conference of the International Missionary Council at Tambaram evidence virtually no recognition of culture.

In spite of this inexplicable oversight, knowledge of culture and anthropology was well accepted in ecumenical circles by the mid-forties. In a comprehensive 1947 volume entitled *Christian World Mission,* for ex-

---

[8]Alexander Rattray Hay, *Saints and Savages: Brazil's Indian Problem* (London: Hodder and Stoughton, 1924?).

[9]R. S. Roseberry, *The Soul of West Africa* (Harrisburg PA: Christian Publications, 1947).

[10]J. H. Oldham, *Christianity and the Race Problem* (London: SCM Press, 1924).

[11]International Missionary Council, Report of the Jerusalem Conference, vol. 4, *The Christian Mission in the Light of Race Conflict*; vol. 5, *The Christian Mission in Relation to Industrial Problems*; vol. 6, *The Christian Mission in Relation to Rural Problems* (New York and London: International Missionary Council, 1928).

ample, the American anthropologist Ina Corinne Brown contributed a paper with the title "The Anthropological Approach," in which she carefully contrasted the respective roles of missionary and anthropologist but underlined their usefulness to each other.[12] In Bengt Sundkler's 1965 *The World of Mission*,[13] there are chapters on "Mission and Culture" and "The Church and Tribal Culture" which display a reasonably sound grasp of "culture."

A second major step towards bringing anthropology to bear on missions, this one affecting primarily North American conservative missions, was taken in the mid-thirties in the context of the then new and coterminous organizations known as the Summer Institute of Linguistics and Wycliffe Bible Translators. It was through the influence of Kenneth Pike and Eugene Nida, though their central focus was on linguistics, that awareness of culture and its crucial relevance to mission came to the attention of this mission. After Nida left the Summer Institute of Linguistics and joined the staff of the American Bible Society, he continued much more systematically than Pike to emphasize the importance of cultural understanding and sensitivity in missions. His book *Customs and Cultures*[14] became must reading for a new generation of missionary candidates. This book describes culture anecdotally and popularly, in strictly functionalist terms, and provides vivid illustrations to reinforce his key points. True to its theoretical orientation, the major weakness of the book is that it lacks any sense of possible *dys*function or of evil in culture. The picture is so sunny that one might be tempted to wonder why missions should be necessary.

Increasingly, scholars involved in the preparation of missionaries began to think anthropology an important if not essential component of that preparation. This was true even in very conservative circles: the widely used textbook *Missionary Principles and Practice*, by Harold Lindsell (1955), asserted "somewhat dogmatically that the best missionaries have been good anthropologists."[15] Lindsell exemplified in that book the impact of func-

---

[12]Ina Corinne Brown, "The Anthropological Approach," in *Christian World Mission*, ed. William K. Anderson (Nashville: Commission on Ministerial Training, The Methodist Church, 1946).

[13]Bengt Sundkler, *The World of Mission* (Grand Rapids: Eerdmans, 1965).

[14]Eugene A. Nida, *Customs and Cultures* (Repr. Pasadena CA: William Carey Library, 1975; orig. New York: Harper, 1954).

[15]Harold Lindsell, *Missionary Principles and Practice* (Old Tappan NJ: Revell, 1955).

tionalism when he insisted on "pattern and symmetry" and wrote of "an integrated and systematic whole." But it must be added that in the process of conducting polemics with various others, especially Kraft, Lindsell has retreated from these insights. Other missionary textbooks have also displayed a growing awareness of and sophistication about culture.

The Hartford Seminary Foundation's Kennedy School of Missions had already initiated such studies at the level of the M.A. and Ph.D. This institution, founded in 1918, deliberately made the choice not to grant advanced degrees in missions or missiology (the latter term was not really in use back then anyway), but in several already recognized academic disciplines which were directly contributory to missions: linguistics, anthropology, and area studies (African studies, Islamic studies, South Asian studies, and Latin American studies). This decision was made precisely because these disciplines had recognized methods and bodies of theory, whereas missions constituted not an academic discipline but a task, to the doing of which various disciplines could contribute. A whole generation or more of missionaries and missiologists did their advanced studies at the Kennedy School of Missions, until the self-destruction of that institution in 1969.

Among more conservative American schools, Wheaton College had the honor of being first to offer anthropology with a view to application in missions. This occurred in the 1940s, under the leadership of Alexander Grigolia and Gordon H. Smith. Smith was explicitly interested in applying cultural anthropology to missions, howbeit in a quite antiquated and eccentric manner. His writings reflect perspectives and attitudes already decades out of date.[16] Nevertheless, not a few students were exposed to the discipline, including Billy Graham. Many of these found their way to mission fields and applied their anthropological knowledge with varying degrees of success.

In the meantime, a number of Christians interested in missions had been studying anthropology in secular colleges and universities and were examining how that discipline related to their faith. William A. Smalley and Marie Fetzer, for example, contributed an excellent article entitled "A Christian View of Anthropology" to the 1950 collection *Modern Science*

---

[16]Gordon H. Smith, *The Missionary and Anthropology* (Chicago: Moody Press, 1945).

*and Christian Faith.*[17]A notable feature of this paper for that date was the discussion not only of the pragmatic potential of the discipline for missions, but of some philosophical issues raised by the discipline for Christians.

Sparked by Eugene Nida, several of the early nucleus of linguist-anthropologists whom he was gathering around him in the American Bible Society—William L. Wonderly, William A. Smalley, William D. Reyburn, and Jacob A. Loewen—together with others, founded a little journal, *Practical Anthropology,* in 1952. For nineteen years under the successive editorships of Robert Taylor, William A. Smalley, and Charles R. Taber, this journal served to educate missionaries and missiologists all around the world—chiefly, of course, English-speaking ones—with regard to culture, cultural sensitivity, and respect for culture. Even now decades later, I am still surprised from time to time when people on meeting me tell me how helpful that journal was to them.

By the time *Practical Anthropology* found it necessary in 1972 to close down, and was providentially taken over by the new journal *Missiology,* organ of the new American Society of Missiology, the usefulness of anthropology to missions was no longer controversial. The first editor of *Missiology,* who set a pattern that has in part been followed by his successors, was the anthropologist Alan R. Tippett. In fact, a growing number of missiologists took their major advanced degrees no longer in history or theology as in the past, but in anthropology. Every institution making any serious claims to be a missionary-educating school found it mandatory to offer courses in cultural anthropology.

By all odds the most significant of these was the School of World Mission of Fuller Theological Seminary, started in 1961 by Donald McGavran as the Institute of Church Growth at Northwest Christian College in Eugene, Oregon, and moved to Pasadena in 1965. The first colleague McGavran called, the Australian Methodist Alan R. Tippett, was a veteran missionary and an anthropologist of breadth and sophistication. In time, Charles H. Kraft was added, with his emphasis on communication and related topics; and after Tippett's retirement, Paul G. Hiebert took up the baton, though in 1990 Hiebert moved to another missionary training in-

---

[17]William A. Smalley and Marie Fetzer, "A Christian View of Anthropology," in *Modern Science and Christian Faith,* ed. F. Alton Everest (Wheaton IL: Van Kampen Press, for the American Scientific Affiliation, 1950) 98-195.

stitution, Trinity Evangelical Divinity School. Each of these scholars has been prolific in print, and a number of their works will be mentioned in one connection or another in this study. Others in the School of World Mission also have anthropological understanding to a high degree. Other important schools of missiology also stress cultural anthropology, including the E. Stanley Jones School of World Mission and Evangelism at Asbury Theological Seminary and the Alliance School of Theology and Missions.

All of this is not to say that anthropology was accepted with open arms in all Christian circles. Suspicions centered on two main issues: the less sophisticated worried that anthropology was the discipline that embodied unrepentant biological Darwinism, the idea that "men descended from apes." The better informed sometimes expressed concern that the use of a secular social science would tend to depreciate the sovereign work of the Holy Spirit in missions.

### Missionary Life and Work

In chapter 4, we found that the views and attitudes of the missionaries in the nineteenth century translated into a certain style of life and work on the field. They tended, we saw, to live much as they would have back home, eating Western food, wearing Western clothes, living in substantial houses clustered on mission stations or compounds. They were thus separated from local people by a gulf of spatial and cultural distance.[18] Their work, we saw, was dominated by a very Western style: it was oriented to tasks, programs, and goals rather than to persons, and those tasks and programs involved large amounts of money and technological and institutional sophistication.

In the twentieth century, as we have just seen, many missionaries discovered anthropology. How much difference did that make? The answer is, disappointingly little. Some missionaries working in remote "bush" areas did, when they were in those areas, begin to live more appropriately simple life styles: housing of local materials, local foods, and so on. Pioneering in this approach was the Summer Institute of Linguistics; other missions, often those influenced by that giant agency, followed its ex-

---

[18]Harris W. Mobley, *The Ghanaian's Image of the Missionary: An Analysis of the Published Critiques of Christian Missionaries by Ghanaians, 1867–1965* (Hartford: Hartford Seminary Foundation, 1966).

ample. Many of these missionaries also established commendably close human relationships with persons in their communities; in fact the term "bonding" was adopted from psychological jargon to describe the particularly close relationships intentionally established with a certain family early in the missionary's residence in a community.

This level of adaptation, however, was and remains the exception worldwide. In many missions and in many places, missionaries continued to live in large houses in compounds, continued to import huge amounts of Western supplies and amenities, and continued to maintain the social gulf between themselves and the local people. In some cases, local people were welcome in the compound as clients or patients, when they had specific needs, but not as mere neighbors. Even the missionaries of the Summer Institute of Linguistics, when they went to their technical centers, moved into a Western coccoon.

But the factor which worked most strongly against the beneficial effect of anthropology was the captivity of missions to high technology. If the level of technology and institutional elaboration achieved in the nineteenth century created a problem for missions, the escalation of these dimensions has had an immeasurable effect on missions. Missionaries moved from bicycles to motorcycles to cars to airplanes; from occasional postal service to two-way radio; from breezes and kerosene to air conditioning and electric lights; from outhouse to indoor plumbing; from typewriter and mimeograph to computer and desktop publishing. Each of these steps could be, and was, justified quite satisfactorily—given the underlying presumption that efficiency defined in very Western terms was the supreme desideratum.

And that was the real problem: technology, as Jacques Ellul has pointed out, even if with considerable hyperbole,[19] creates and imposes a ruthless logic of its own, a type of mentality which finds it increasingly harder to grasp any other point of view. Looking exclusively at tasks and programs and goals, missions too often lost sight of the human dimension; which is sadly ironic, since surely from the perspective of Christ the human dimension is the purpose of the effort. They thus partially lost the ability to make use of the cultural sensitivity they had learned from anthropology. Worse, anthropology itself became for some yet another means of moving and

---

[19]Jacques Ellul, *The Technological Society*, trans. John Wilkinson (New York: Knopf, 1970).

changing others rather than the missionary. Andrew Walls has well described the unabashed fascination of Americans with money and technology, and the influence this has had in missions.[20]

It turns out that knowledge of anthropology, like any other kind of knowledge, tends to puff up rather than to edify. One of the most arrogant and overbearing missionaries I ever knew had an M.A. in anthropology. What makes the difference, it seems to me, is what it is that we expect anthropology to do. The pragmatic mindset too easily sees in it a power tool to move and change others, to bring about specific desired results. A different mindset might see in it a precision instrument designed to change the attitudes and behavior of the missionary. The former is like the applied anthropology we discussed in chapter 5, the latter like the action anthropology which focuses on the interests of the other.

The technological, rationalistic mentality continued to see the gospel in terms of a cognitive set of propositions to be "communicated" and believed. It continued to maintain that to get things done you had to be direct and blunt, not indirect and sensitive to "face." And, most clearly, programs involving mission funding and high technology required mission control for "accountability" and "efficiency."[21]

There appeared over the years a series of articles by various people, notably William Reyburn and Jacob Loewen, about the problems and possibilities of "identification" with local people, of "reciprocity" as a pattern for human relationships.[22] But in retrospect, it must be said that these had too little impact on too few missionaries.

A major symptom of the malaise created by the accumulation of grievances of national Christians about all of these problems was the cry in the 1970s for "moratorium": the removal of missionary persons and machin-

---

[20]Andrew F. Walls, "The American Dimension in the History of the Missionary Movement," in *Earthen Vessels: American Evangelicals and Foreign Missions, 1880–1980,* 1-25.

[21]Charles R. Taber, "Structures and Strategies for Interdependence in World Mission," in *Mission Focus: Current Issues,* ed. Wilbert R. Shenk (Scottdale PA: Herald Press, 1980) 453-78.

[22]William D. Reyburn, "Identification in the Missionary Task" and "Identification—Symptom or Sublimation?" in *Readings in Missionary Anthropology II,* ed. William A. Smalley (South Pasadena: William Carey Library, 1978) 746-67; Jacob A. Loewen and Anne Loewen, "The 'Missionary' Role," in *Culture and Human Values,* ed. William A. Smalley (Pasadena: William Carey Library, 1975) 428-43.

ery to allow the local church breathing room, to allow the local church to assume its full prerogatives and responsibilities. This cry came almost simultaneously from several people, most eloquently from Emerito Nacpil in the Philippines.[23] Though he made it quite clear that he and the others were *not* repudiating mission, missionary circles in the West took offense and imputed all kinds of unworthy motives to them. The outcome after two decades has been some improvement, but not nearly enough.

In the final analysis, the question is, granted the enormous utility of high technology (this book would not have been written without a computer), is it really possible to use it without falling captive to the mentality it engenders? The jury is still out, I think.

## The Impact of Functionalism

It was not just "anthropology" that had an impact on Protestant missiology from the 1920s on; it was a specific form of anthropology, namely functionalism. Thus, it was this version of the discipline that came to *be* anthropology in the context of the missionary enterprise. This fact had some truly excellent consequences, as well as some about which I think it necessary to raise questions. It is my purpose in this section to examine these consequences, both in general and with special reference to six areas of missiological concern: understanding and respecting cultures; communication and translation; the indigenous church; the homogeneous unit principle; functional (formerly dynamic) equivalence; and "redemptive analogies."

*Understanding and Respect.* The first important role of anthropology in missions was to help those involved to achieve a simple, basic understanding of the cultures of the peoples with whom they worked. As we saw in chapter 4, this understanding did not come quickly or easily; obstacles presented themselves, especially obstacles stemming from the profound differences between the missionary's home culture, which was by definition taken for granted and unproblematical, and the cultures in which the missionary served. Compounding the difficulties of understanding were the very strong emotional components of everyone's attachment to his or her own culture: how could an alien culture be legitimate if it was not only so hard to figure out, but also hurt so badly?

---

[23]Emerito P. Nacpil, "Mission But Not Missionaries," *International Review of Mission* 60 (July 1971): 356-62.

Cultural anthropology proved a very helpful tool to overcome this initial resistance. It did this by helping the missionary to come to terms with culture shock, by showing that however painful it was, it was transient and one moved through predictable stages.[24] Then it offered a way of making sense of otherwise bizarre and incomprehensible customs. This was a chief function in mission circles of the works of Nida and others in the first five decades of the century.

Functionalism also helped missionaries and missiologists to respect and appreciate the cultures they dealt with. The classic arrogant ethnocentrism which characterized the nineteenth century gradually gave way to an increasing sense of the genuine value and ingenuity of each human community's way of life. It became evident to a growing number of persons involved in mission that to be different from Western civilization was by no means to be stupid or inferior or wicked, but just different. It was realized that each culture had developed according to its own environment and its own history and provided its members with a pattern for living that was effective and satisfying, that each culture offered answers to life's questions and problems that generally worked and met the requirements of human well-being.

Closely connected with this new emphasis on respect and appreciation was another helpful influence of functionalism: a sense of cultural relativity. Not that most missionaries were ever tempted to total relativism! But they did begin to understand that standards and criteria for evaluating any culture are internal to that culture, and that it is much harder than they had supposed to discover any standards that are not intrinsic to a particular culture. Certainly, Western civilization could not possibly offer a universally applicable scale of values by which to measure other cultures, since all of its value criteria were designed to measure the success or failure of Western civilization.

It thus became necessary to ask what each culture counted as important, what each was trying to achieve, and then to inquire how successful it was in achieving its own internally assigned goals. Thus, if one discovered that a given culture placed a high premium on the peace and harmony of the community, but a very low value on technical elaboration, one did

---

[24]Kalervo Oberg, "Cultural Shock: Adjustment to New Cultural Environments," *Practical Anthropology* 7/4 (July-August 1960): 177-82; William A. Smalley, "Culture Shock, Language Shock, and the Shock of Self-Discovery," *Practical Anthropology* 10/1 (January-February 1963): 49-56.

not depreciate it for not having invented computers or airplanes; one rather complimented it, if appropriate, on arriving at the high level of peace and harmony it was striving for.

Finally, functionalism convinced missionaries and missiologists—at least those who listened—that a culture displayed some degree of integration among its many component parts, that it was not a mere inventory of customs and traits. This countered the older practice of evaluating and approving or condemning individual traits on an isolated basis, as had been done for instance in the case of polygyny. It was increasingly realized that if one meddled in a culture at one point, one could well launch a chain reaction, an avalanche even, of successive changes in areas that one had not known were involved. A case study was widely circulated describing how the introduction of steel axes to replace stone ones among the Yir Yoront in Australia had eventually led to the collapse of the social structure of that small Aboriginal people.[25]

This line of thinking gave rise to the concept of functional substitutes, which I will discuss in a later section.

*Communication and Translation.* Beyond coping with culture shock and achieving a basic understanding of cultures, anthropology was soon put to work to facilitate communication in general and translation, especially Bible translation, in particular. Here again, Nida was the chief pioneer. His scholarly but practical *Message and Mission*[26] combined insights from linguistics, anthropology, and communication theory in a very creative manner, specifically designed to cope with the problems of cross-cultural communication. The book established a benchmark against which all later work had to be measured.

But Nida also contributed a number of seminal concepts to the theory of translation; in fact, it could be said that from 1945 to 1975, Nida *was* Mr. Translation Theory. Certainly, he did more than anyone else to incorporate explicitly the implications of culture and cultural differences into the theory of translation. His major books in the field include *Bible Translation, God's Word in Man's Language, Towards a Science of Translat-*

---

[25]J. Lauriston Sharp, "Steel Axes for Stone-Age Australians," *Practical Anthropology* 7/2 (March-April 1960): 62-73.

[26]Eugene A. Nida, *Message and Mission* (New York: Harper, 1960).

*ing*, and *Theory and Practice of Translation*,[27] as well as several works in semantic theory. He founded the journal *The Bible Translator* and wrote literally hundreds of papers at every level of sophistication for every conceivable concerned audience.

Nida's contributions included both a comprehensive, formal, theoretically grounded model of translation, and a powerful and convincing explanation of the way language and culture work together in the communication process, both within a culture and between cultures. This insight, as applied to translation, can be summarized under the term "functional equivalence," formerly "dynamic equivalence."

The key principle in this concept is that a translation should be so done as to create in the minds of its latter-day readers and hearers the same impact as the original text did on the first readers and hearers. In other words, it should convey to them the "same" information and should move them to the "same" feelings and practical responses as occurred in the primary communicative event.

The reason for this emphasis was the observation that most translators, bemused by details of the form of the original text, failed to ask the crucial question, "What will *my* audience understand through this text? What will *they* feel and do as a result?" Differences in cultural and situational context created inevitable misunderstandings and confusions, as contemporary audiences missed implicit cues that would have been crystal clear to the original audience, or made erroneous analogies and applications on the basis of misleading resemblances. Since differences in linguistic structure and stylistic features between the two languages were not noticed, versions were made which rendered easy passages difficult and natural passages very unnatural and peculiar. This concept, though it has been attacked on a number of grounds, several of them not trivial, has proved immensely helpful to translators in the practical task of producing in one language and cultural context a faithful and readable translation of texts originally written in a different language and cultural context.

More recently, a number of other missiological anthropologists, notably Charles H. Kraft of the School of World Mission at Fuller Theological Seminary, have built on Nida's foundation and have contributed further

---

[27]Eugene A. Nida, *Bible Translating* (New York: American Bible Society, 1947); *God's Word in Man's Language* (New York: Harper, 1952); *Toward a Science of Translating* (Leiden: Brill, 1964); Eugene A. Nida and Charles R. Taber, *Theory and Practice of Translation* (Leiden: Brill, 1969).

refinements in the understanding of cross-cultural communication. Because his most creative and controversial contribution to missiological anthropology wants to extend the concept of functional equivalence to other areas than language, I will reserve discussion of Kraft's contribution for a later section. Various scholars of the Summer Institute of Linguistics, especially John Beekman and John Callow, have added valuable elements to the theory of translation.[28]

*Functionalism and Indigeneity.* Anthropology in the functionalist mode had a mixed impact, both good and bad, on the concepts of indigeneity, indigenization, and the indigenous church. This complex of concepts was, as we have seen, invented in the nineteenth century by Henry Venn and Rufus Anderson and elaborated through the first part of the twentieth century. As devised by these missiologists, the concept insisted on three central powers and responsibilities of the "indigenous" church, the famous "three-selfs": self-support, self-government, self-propagation. The only necessity for the realization of indigenous churches was to find local *persons* who could handle those three things. The *shape* of the church—its theology, its polity, its discipline, its style of leadership, its liturgy and music, its architecture—could be taken for granted, since it would be a reproduction of the model of the sending church in some Western country. Missionaries would have established these things on a firm foundation, and in good time a corps of prepared—that is, indoctrinated—local persons could take the baton from the missionaries and run the operation with no substantive changes.

As we know in retrospect, it proved to be far more difficult to get to this point than had been anticipated, and that fact along with others led to an indefinite postponement of implementation. It seemed as if we were *never* going to get Africans or Asians to do it *right*! So we had the bizarre spectacle of third-generation missionaries working in the same fields as their grandparents, and of nationals with advanced Western degrees still not "ready" for indigeneity. Even Roland Allen in his writings, which were in fact influential mostly long after his death, did not fully transcend this perspective.[29]

---

[28]John Beekman and John Callow, *Translating the Word of God* (Grand Rapids: Zondervan, 1974).

[29]Roland Allen, *Missionary Methods: St Paul's or Ours?* (Repr. Grand Rapids: Eerdmans, 1962; orig. 1912); *The Spontaneous Expansion of the Church and the Causes Which Hinder It* (Repr. Grand Rapids: Eerdmans, 1962; orig. 1927).

This situation was both clarified and complicated by the growing impact of cultural anthropology on missiology, starting in a small way in the 1920s and becoming a strong force in the 50s and 60s. It was in this period, as we have seen, that anthropologists began to teach in missionary training programs, and the journal *Practical Anthropology* gave expression to the increasing sensitivity to cultural realities which was appearing in missionary circles. It began to be apparent to more and more missionaries that there was a gross lack of cultural fit between the forms of church life in the missionaries' home bases and the forms that would be appropriate in truly *indigenous* churches. So increasingly it was insisted that churches should be not only self-supporting, self-governing, and self-propagating, but in a real sense culturally self-designed. There began to be a great emphasis on culturally appropriate forms of music (ethnomusicology), liturgy, architecture, organization, leadership, and the like.

But it seems to me that with all the good that this emphasis brought to missions, missions fell into a simplistic trap: they imagined the whole world on the model of isolated ''tribal'' societies, and assumed all too easily that they could use functionalist definitions of culture as the ground for defining the *what* of indigeneity.

As a result, when these new policies were applied on virgin territory and in ''primal'' societies—as in the more remote parts of Africa, South America, and Oceania, where there were not already existing churches—they often yielded quite happy results. When they were applied to more culturally complex situations, or in places where churches founded under other principles already existed, results were more mixed. As a friend of mine in Ghana once said, ''I feel no need to return to traditional Fanti music; I like *Hymns Ancient and Modern.* I'm not ready to 'return' to the music of my ancestors that I don't know.'' In other words, the chronological problem we will examine later began to surface: it proved simply impractical and counterproductive to pretend that history could be ignored and undone and that one could start over from scratch. People were no longer full participants in the ''traditional'' culture. Functionalism, however, encouraged a too rigid and limiting view of culture which contributed to the missiological error I am identifying here.

In other words, the impact of functionalism on missions was not an unmixed blessing. At several points if was deficient and misleading; at other points it encouraged tendencies already present in missionary thinking that might usefully have been challenged. Five specific weaknesses of functionalism were especially problematic. Let it be said at the outset that I will resort to a measure of hyperbole to emphasize my point: few if any missionaries followed the miscues of extreme functionalism to their reductio ad absurdum.

1. It was assumed, as we have seen, that each culture is a discrete, bounded, self-contained unit. If one only knew enough, one could draw on a map the boundaries of each culture just as one draws the boundaries of a nation state. The implication drawn from this view was that one studied what happened *inside* those limits, and ignored as much as possible what happened across them through the contacts and relations of the people of the target culture with other peoples. The most conspicuous missiological application of this view, which I will discuss in a later section, is the concept of the homogeneous unit principle.

2. The ideal culture was a "pure" culture, one untouched by alien contaminating influences. Since already in the 1920s such cultures were virtually nonexistent, anthropologists, as we have seen, invented the concept of the "ethnographic present," which in some cases was a century or more in the past. This was supposed to be the time before all of the nasty external influences began to be felt, when the *real* culture was still in unsullied existence.

The result was that despite the artificial present tense, the orientation of functionalism in any situation of culture contact and "contamination" was determinedly toward the past. As a result, indigeneity in this framework was a process of going back in time to the traditional culture. Unfortunately, as the example of my Ghanaian friend shows, people don't live in the past, they live *now,* and many of them are looking more and more to a hoped-for future. There has to be something wrong with a missiological model that faces resolutely backward while everyone else is facing forward.

3. Closely related to this point and aggravating the problem is the functionalist emphasis that the ideal culture is stable and harmonious, and therefore in principle unchanging. In such a model, as we have seen, change is a pathology, usually brought about by outside contamination or interference. This perception is one of a number of factors that account for the frequent bitter hostility of anthropologists toward missionaries, who are often caricatured as the meddlers and cultural destroyers par excellence. This will be the theme of a later section.

4. The influence of philosophical idealism on functionalist anthropology, especially in the United States, has also reinforced a strong tendency in some Christian circles toward dualism. The fact that culture is chiefly in people's heads has led to the erroneous conclusion that what goes on in people's heads is independent of what goes on objectively and materially in the world around them, and that one can therefore safely ignore the material conditions of existence in doing mission and missiology. The reason I bring this up again here is that it is an aspect of conventional indigenization that has been sharply called into question in the recent emphasis on contextualization.

5. Finally, functionalism was strongly biased in favor of what is, because "it works." This led in missions to an overreaction against the older ethnocentric judgmentalism and to an excessive readiness to approve almost anything and everything. It also led missionaries as it did anthropologists to be gullible in taking at face value the explanations and interpretations of those persons in each society who were privileged and to discount the perspectives of those persons who were not favored or rewarded by the culture, persons who might even be grievously oppressed. This is a strange position for people who intend to be followers of Jesus of Nazareth! Of course, the "top-down" missionary strategy was not invented by functionalists, it had a very ancient history; the Jesuits of the seventeeth century in particular adopted this approach. This method was also congenial to Christians who were socially ambitious at home, and who revered successful people excessively, which has been a widespread aberration in our period. But functionalism gave this questionable approach renewed impetus.

*The Homogeneous Unit Principle.* The homogeneous unit principle is a specific concept devised by Donald McGavran as a central component of his church growth theory.[30] The McGavran theory of church growth and its subsidiary concept of homogeneous units are enormously important for our purposes for two reasons: first, because they have been widely influential in missionary circles; second, because they are one of the few thoroughgoing attempts to base a missiological theory on the social sciences, and thus constitute a test case as to whether such an effort is feasible or legitimate.

---

[30]Donald A. McGavran, *Understanding Church Growth,* rev. ed. (Grand Rapids: Eerdmans, 1980); C. Peter Wagner, *Our Kind of People* (Atlanta: John Knox Press, 1979).

Over the decades, the homogeneous unit principle has had several in-carnations and been called by several names.[31] But in its essential prop-erties it has remained and remains fairly constant. This is not the place to mount a full-scale biblical and theological critique of the concept, which has in any case been done very well elsewhere.[32] The only thing that needs to be done here is to point out that (a) the principle insists that people live in bounded groups (tribes, castes, ethnic groups, racial groups, social classes); (b) that their ways of life (that is, their cultures), their attitudes, and their preferences, are also bounded; (c) that therefore one should evan-gelize them by addressing each such group in isolation from all other groups and foster the growth of a separate church within each such group, rather than try to incorporate persons from several groups into one mixed church. McGavran attempts to defend the principle on both sociocultural and bib-lical grounds, going so far as to interpret the Epistle of James as legiti-mating discrimination between rich and poor.[33] Kraft tries to establish a distinction between "cultural and linguistic criteria," which are "basic to homogeneity," and on the other hand

> geographical criteria, associational criteria, social class criteria, sexual criteria, temporal criteria, age criteria, health criteria, and religious or world view criteria, which are not legitimate bases for homogeneity.[34]

He insists that Christianity, far from conflicting with existing grounds for homogeneity and creating an alternative basis for a new homogeneity, can be added to a culture without destroying it. The homogeneous unit principle is, in his view, *the* antidote to the melting pot and ethnocentrism.

Two comments are in order. First, the reliance of the concept on Mal-inowskian functionalism should be self-evident. Second, on purely socio-cultural grounds this is a simplistic and inaccurate conceptual tool to

---

[31]McGavran, *Understanding Church Growth.*

[32]See esp. four papers in *Exploring Church Growth*, ed. Wilbert R. Shenk (Grand Rap-ids: Eerdmans, 1983): John S. Pobee, "The People of God and the Peoples," 181-90; Da-vid J. Bosch, "The Structure of Mission: An Exposition of Matthew 28:16-20," 218-48; Frederick W. Norris, "Strategy for Mission in the New Testament," 260-76; C. René Pad-illa, "The Unity of the Church and the Homogeneous Unit Principle," 285-303.

[33]Donald A. McGavran, "The Priority of Ethnicity," *Evangelical Missions Quarterly* 19 (1983): 14-23.

[34]Charles H. Kraft, "An Anthropological Apologetic for the Homogeneous Unit Prin-ciple in Missiology," *Occasional Bulletin of Missionary Research* 2 (1978): 120-26.

describe modern societies, or for that matter societies of any degree of inner complexity; we saw in chapter 5 that Radcliffe-Brown insisted on dealing with the complexity in South Africa. In many complex societies, the relations *between* bounded groups are often *the* agenda of the society's politics if nothing else, and they must be taken into consideration in describing any one component of the mixture. In the previous chapter I illustrated this fact by reference to Oscar Lewis's "culture of poverty."

It is also the case that in complex societies, people belong to many groups which do not coincide in membership; each group serves some particular purpose for the individual member: work, religion, play, and the like. And people relate to a large number of other people, but with many of them the relationship is slight and one-dimensional. This creates a fluidity and an individualism which are not well understood using the homogeneous unit principle.

Incidentally, this same perspective has led Church Growth theorists, as we have just seen, to misread seriously the New Testament evidence regarding the social composition of the first-century churches.

In contrast, Corwin argues that even apart from biblical considerations, "human personality resists enclosure" and benefits from the stimulation of cultural diversity.[35] One can quibble with this; individuals in any culture differ, some welcoming diversity, others resisting it. On balance, there is no doubt that people in general gravitate toward their "own kind." The question is whether a descriptive observation of what is the case in the world ought to be made a normative principle for the church's practice.

Meanwhile, as we saw in the previous chapter, anthropology has moved beyond bare functionalism to rediscover the facts of diffusion and acculturation, the permeability and instability of cultural boundaries, the fact of culture change, the importance of the material conditions of existence, the fact of migration, the fact of modernization, the fact of urbanization, and a host of other phenomena of the contemporary world. Any missiological model resting too heavily on functionalism now seems extremely dated and naive, even for relatively isolated areas such as Amazonia and the Highlands of Papua New Guinea.

One conceptual offshoot of the homogeneous unit principle is the attempt by Ralph Winter and David Barrett to count the number of "people

---

[35]Charles Corwin, "Cultural Diversity as a Dynamic for Growth," *Evangelical Missions Quarterly* 17 (1981): 15-22.

groups'' which have been evangelized and those which have not been, in order to get a quantitative perspective on the job accomplished and the job yet to be accomplished.[36] In some circles this idea has been enthusiastically adopted. Perhaps one can in fact divide the world into regions and populations that have or have not been evangelized, though there are subtle factors that this model does not adequately handle. And it is true, as we saw in an earlier chapter, that human social groups, as distinct from cultures, can be bounded. But the figures used by Winter and Barrett suggest an altogether spurious sense of precision.

*Functional Equivalents.* The understanding of the integration of culture fostered by functionalism led to a sense that it was unwise and unchristian simply to condemn local customs, which were now seen to have meaning and purpose. Simply rejecting them without replacing them had many bad effects, especially when the rejection was enforced by missionary fiat.

This valid insight led to a quest for what came to be called ''functional substitutes'' for customs and cultural traits which missionaries still felt constrained to condemn. Alan Tippett was an early advocate of this approach. Where, for instance, missionaries found initiatory rites offensive, they proposed a Christian replacement to serve the same function for their new converts. For some years, the pages of *Practical Anthropology,* to cite only one example, regularly contained articles along these lines. Precedent was found in the history of missions at least as far back as the instructions of Pope Gregory the Great to the party of Augustine of Canterbury as it began to evangelize Britain.

A new phase in the discussion of this topic began with the introduction in the theory of translation of the concept of functional equivalence, which was discussed above.[37]

The concept, as I said before, has been attacked from a variety of perspectives. But I want to deal with the extension of this concept beyond translation proper. Specifically, I want to examine the extension of its application from language, for which it was designed in Nida's model of

---

[36]Ralph D. Winter, ''The Scope of the WCE,'' *Missiology* 12/1 (January 1984): 41-48; David B. Barrett, *World Christian Encyclopedia* (Nairobi and New York: Oxford University Press, 1982).

[37]Nida and Taber, *Theory and Practice,* 14, 22-28, 129; Jan de Waard and Eugene A. Nida, *From One Language to Another* (Nashville: Nelson, 1986) 36-42, 182-88.

translation, to other dimensions of culture, where its applicability can be more problematic. The best-known and most prolific writer in this vein is Charles H. Kraft.[38] On many points I find no fault with Kraft's approach. His model of cross-cultural communication is sophisticated, insightful, and usually practical. But I think he has gone too far in extending functional equivalence to cultural realities beyond language.

For there are two crucial differences between language, where the translational principle of functional equivalence was designed to operate, and culture at large, differences that call into question a too ready extension of the principle from language to culture. My critique overlaps with a similar one by Harris of what he calls the "linguistic analogy," but is not identical with it.[39] Harris was aiming at certain anthropologists, notably Margaret Mead, who made what Harris considered illegitimate analogies between language and the rest of culture, specifically considering all of culture to be a "communicative system."

A fundamental property of language *as language* which has been recognized at least since the early days of modern linguistics and which underlies the validity of functional equivalence in translation is that the connection between form and meaning is *arbitrary*; that is, apart from exceptional and marginal cases, there is no intrinsic and necessary connection between the noises one makes with one's mouth and the meanings one is trying to communicate through those noises. There is absolutely no resemblance between the animal "horse" and the various noises which conventionally point to that animal in different languages: /hors/, /ševal/, /pfert/, or /hippos/. These connections are made in each distinct language purely by social convention. It may be the case that, as one rises in the hierarchy of form from the phoneme to the structure of the entire text, arbitrariness does not equally characterize all levels; there may be—I think there is— something about the form *story*, for example, that makes it especially suitable to communicate some kinds of truths. But for linguistic form and structure as a whole, arbitrariness is a basic property underlying the extraordinary flexibility of language.

The same thing simply cannot be said about many other aspects of culture. Take the form *baptism by immersion in water*; if a symbolic meaning of "washing away sin" is a part of that ritual, it is hard to see how any

---

[38]Charles H. Kraft, *Christianity in Culture* (Maryknoll NY: Orbis Books, 1979).

[39]Harris, *The Rise of Anthropological Theory* (New York: Crowell, 1968) 420-21.

other form could convey that meaning as well. I do not want to belabor the point, but invite the reader to reflect on a variety of cultural forms, religious and nonreligious, and see whether they are merely arbitrary representations of their meaning, use, and function, or whether there is not often a clear intrinsic connection in many of them. But if this is the case, it becomes difficult to apply systematically to cultural features a principle designed for use with language and founded on the fact of arbitrariness.

A second property of language that is basic and necessary to the application of functional equivalence is that it is, as such, ethically neutral. Now it is true that, in reaction against an earlier excessive negativism in missions with respect to indigenous cultures, modern missionary anthropology has emphasized the positive and insisted on respect for and acceptance of as much of a culture as is at all possible. This is in principle very good: it replaces our spontaneous inclination to ethnocentrism with a limited cultural relativity.

But it is important to realize that it is a *limited* relativity; not anything goes, since in all cultures there are expressions not only of our God-given creativity but also of our rebellion against God. The impact of functionalism on missiology has somewhat blurred this fact, because functionalism has a built-in bias in favor of *what is*, and is hostile to cultural change. This gives missiological anthropology an excessive tendency to accept any and all features of indigenous culture as legitimate, or at least as virtually ineradicable.

But mere reflection should suffice to debunk this naive optimism about cultures. It has now been accepted by almost everyone that Western culture has profound flaws; are non-Western cultures necessarily any better? I am not suggesting that we should now return to the heavy-handed negativism of the past; but we should not be too ready to see in any and all cultural forms appropriate functional equivalents for biblical ones. In other words, we should be cautious about applying to other cultural domains a principle designed to work with ethically neutral linguistic forms.

The technical term for what happens when one combines an inappropriate cultural form with a gospel meaning is *syncretism*. We have long practised such syncretisms in Western church life, as in the typical American reduction of the church to the cultural model of the voluntary society; and it is high time to assess the damage these syncretisms have done and to change them where possible. It is *not* time to foster on mission fields with one hand what we try very hard with the other to prevent.

Kraft attempts to counter this argument by saying that what he proposes is in many cases a temporary measure, to last just long enough to get the young church properly started without imposing on it an excessive load of instant change. Existing leadership patterns, for instance, are often less than ideal—authoritarian, elitist, sexist, ageist, arbitrary, and so on. Kraft acknowledges that from the point of view of the New Testament ideal (Mark 10:42-45), these cultural patterns are often quite bad; but they are what people know and understand, and in order for the church to get under way on its own as soon as possible, one may admit leaders and leadership patterns that are less than ideal. Fair enough; but then the question must be faced: at what point and by what process will more Christ-like patterns be introduced?

3. My third point is this: it is not nearly as easy as one might think to find truly functional equivalents across cultures. In this the functionalists were quite correct: the nexus between form, meaning, use, and function is an area of enormous diversity, complexity, and potential traps for the unwary as one moves from one culture to another.

In support of this point, I cite only two quick examples. I am told that a translator in an Eskimo language in Labrador, obviously not finding a word for *lamb,* chose to substitute "baby seal." But the only thing these two creatures have in common, besides their mammalian nature, is juvenile cuteness—a poor ground for the huge freight of biblical meaning carried by the term *lamb* and its attendant cultural complex! The other example comes from Ivory Coast, in West Africa. A translator, knowing that grapevines were absent, decided to translate the Greek term in John 15 with "coffee tree," a prevalent commercial crop in the country. But not only did this substitution fail to cover the necessary biblical meanings; it backfired when a local person read the French Bible, found the grapevine, and accused the translator of falsifying the Bible.

The gist of the argument is this: most cultural traits are embedded in cultural complexes and institutions; a trait that might at first glance look "equivalent" to a biblical one will almost invariably turn out *not* to cover all the biblical ground, but rather to introduce unwanted alien features instead.

In short, functional equivalence is a potentially valid and useful missiological device; but it is also one full of dangers that one needs to be aware of.

*"Redemptive Analogies."* As a kind of extension of the concept of functional equivalence, Don Richardson has proposed the concept of "redemptive analogies."[40] Richardson was a very conservative missionary among the Sawi people of Irian Jaya, the western end of the island of New Guinea which belongs to Indonesia. As he tells the story in *Peace Child*, the Sawi were among the most "primitive" people in the world. Richardson set out to learn their language and culture in order to evangelize them. But they were, in Richardson's view, very poor subjects for evangelization: when he told them the Passion story, for instance, they decided that Judas was the hero, a kind of "super-Sawi," because he had successfully deceived Jesus into trusting him before finally triumphantly betraying him. For, said Richardson, the Sawi idealized treachery, especially after a prolonged period of cultivation of the future victim had lulled all his suspicions.

This mentality had created such a climate of anger, fear, and suspicion among the diverse Sawi communities that when they came together, attracted by the Richardson family, they ended up fighting and killing each other. Despite his theology, Richardson seriously considered leaving, and in fact told the people he was leaving. This sobering threat induced them to bring out their most formidable cultural device for establishing a truce that could not be broken: the "peace child." In this rarely invoked and very drastic rite, infants from the two warring factions were exchanged, each being entrusted by its own father to his archenemy on the other side. Once that was done, it would be unthinkable, "un-Sawi," to resume treachery. In a flash of insight, Richardson told the people, "God has given us a peace child—his own Son." Now Judas was no longer the hero, but an unspeakable villain. And the Sawi were open to the gospel.

On the basis of this experience and subsequent researches, Richardson in *Eternity in Their Hearts* argues that similar "redemptive analogies" are extremely widespread around the world, perhaps even universal. These, he says, are authentic examples of pre-Christian, prebiblical understandings planted by God to prepare people for the gospel.

*Eternity in Their Hearts* takes the form of an extended reflection, studded with parallel examples from around the world, on Paul's encounter with the Athenian intellectuals in Acts 17. In that particular instance, Richard-

---

[40]Don Richardson, *Peace Child* (Glendale CA: Regal Books, G/L Publications, 1974); *Eternity in Their Hearts* (Ventura CA: Regal Books, 1984).

son bases Paul's approach—"the 'unknown god' of your shrine is the one I'm talking about"—on an old account by Epimenedes, whom Paul in fact quoted; according to Epimenedes, at a critical time in the history of Athens, a revelation had come from "god," and this "god" let it be known that there would be a further revelation at a later time. So Paul connected his message to this expectation.

There is, I think, some validity in Richardson's argument. Surely it is clear that God has been active in self-revelation, so that there is no place or people where God is a total stranger. And surely, as a consequence, some knowledge of God and even nostalgia for God's presence can be found around the world. But it is, I think, rather much to demand that this self-disclosure always take a dramatic ritual or other demonstrative form. Richardson is in many cases overinterpreting his evidence; and in many cases the evidence is sufficiently vague not to be documented at all. A much more reliable guide in this area, because much more careful and sober, is Vincent Donovan's *Christianity Rediscovered: An Epistle from the Masai.*[41] I know of no comparable document from Protestant sources.

### Missionary Contributions to Anthropology

What have missionaries and missiologists contributed to anthropology and to our understanding of culture? I will mention briefly several contributions.

Several outstanding missionary ethnographers in our century have followed the earlier example of Codrington and Junod. Most of the earlier ones were European or British. Charles Fox published in 1924 *The Threshold of the Pacific,*[42] an ethnography inspired by diffusionism which was much admired by the anthropologist Rivers. In 1927, Edwin W. Smith published a carefully researched study of *The Golden Stool* of the Ashanti of Ghana.[43] A couple of decades later came the culminating work of the outstanding French missionary anthropologist Maurice Leenhardt, *Do*

---

[41]Vincent J. Donovan, *Christianity Rediscovered: An Epistle from the Masai* (Maryknoll NY: Orbis Books, 1982).

[42]Charles R. Fox, *The Threshold of the Pacific: An Account of the Social Organization Magic and Religion of the People of San Cristoval in the Solomon Islands* (London: Kegan Paul, 1924).

[43]Edwin W. Smith, *The Golden Stool: Some Aspects of the Conflict of Cultures in Africa* (London: Holborn, 1927).

*Kamo: Person and Myth in Melanesia.*[44] On the Roman Catholic side a host of ethnographic monographs written by missionaries appeared in these decades, exemplified by the classic *La philosophie bantoue,* by Placide Tempels.[45]

Later decades were to see a growing corpus of ethnographic and semi-ethnographic writings by missionaries and missiologists. Though a few books were written,[46] the bulk of this literature appeared in periodicals such as *Practical Anthropology* and *Missiology,* as well as other missionary journals and magazines and secular scholarly journals.

Only one missiologist to my knowledge has written a general textbook in cultural anthropology which is used in secular universities, Paul G. Hiebert.[47] This is a lucid, responsible text, covering the field adequately, dealing fairly at the introductory level with theoretical issues, and full of vivid illustrative anecdotes and citations. All the other anthropology texts written by missiologists which are known to me make the missionary orientation and application explicit and central, thus restricting the range of their possible usefulness.

A number have written books in the tradition of Nida's *Customs and Cultures,* explicitly applying anthropology to missions in various ways. These include Filbeck, Grunlan, Hiebert, Jacobs, Lingenfelter, and Mayers.[48] Miriam Adeney has written a most helpful book on missionary in-

---

[44]Maurice Leenhardt, *Do Kamo: Person and Myth in Melanesia,* trans. Basia Miller Gulati (Repr. Chicago: University of Chicago Press, 1979; orig. 1947).

[45]Placide Tempels, *La philosophie bantoue,* 3rd ed. (Paris: Présence Africaine, 1949).

[46]Two examples are Alan R. Tippett, *Solomon Islands Christianity* (London: Lutterworth Press, 1967) and Darrell L. Whiteman, *An Introduction to Melanesian Cultures* (Goroka, Papua New Guinea: Melanesian Institute, 1984); two collections of *Practical Anthropology* papers are William A. Smalley, ed., *Readings in Missionary Anthropology II* (South Pasadena: William Carey Library, 1978); and Jacob A. Loewen, *Culture and Human Values,* ed. William A. Smalley (Pasadena: William Carey Library, 1975).

[47]Paul G. Hiebert, *Cultural Anthropology* (Phildelphia: Lippincott, 1976).

[48]Stephen A. Grunlan and Marvin K. Mayers, *Cultural Anthropology: A Christian Perspective* (Grand Rapids: Zondervan, 1978); Paul G. Hiebert, *Anthropological Insights for Missionaries* (Grand Rapids: Baker, 1985); Donald R. Jacobs, *Pilgrimage in Mission* (Scottdale PA: Herald Press, 1983); David Filbeck, *Social Context and Proclamation* (Pasadena: William Carey Library, 1985); Sherwood G. Lingenfelter and Marvin K. Mayers, *Ministering Cross-Culturally* (Grand Rapids: Baker, 1986).

volvement in economic and social development and social services that is profoundly shaped by her anthropological education.[49]

As might be suspected, the cultural area that was most intensely covered by missionaries was language and its ramifications. Literally hundreds of linguists, many of them affiliated with the Summer Institute of Linguistics or the United Bible Societies, wrote hundreds of books and thousands of articles describing languages or features of languages, and the connections of language with a variety of social and cultural traits of the peoples they were concerned with. In addition to the names mentioned in previous sections, a random list might include Robert Longacre, Ila Fleming, John and David Bendor-Samuel, Katherine Barnwell, and Evelyn Pike. Since these and the specifically translational contributions are covered in another volume in this series, I will not deal with them further here.

It should be pointed out here that by and large, though functionalism strongly influenced missionary anthropology in the ways I described above, most missionary use of anthropology was not doctrinaire. It tended in fact to be eclectic, partly no doubt because the missionaries had practical aims in mind, and also partly because they were much more familiar with the real situation on the ground than were anthropologists. After all, they lived in the field, they did not only do brief fieldwork, and were thus aware of the messiness of the real world, which a too-neat theory could not account for.

We have already discussed at some length the specific contributions of Eugene Nida to the fields of communication and translation. Nida's model of translation itself, as well as the accompanying semantic theory and analytical method, are recognized as highly original and creative. Others, especially Nida's colleagues in the American Bible Society and the United Bible Societies, have made a variety of more detailed contributions.

I have also described Charles Kraft's extension of the concept of functional equivalence to culture in general in a rather negative manner. But the overall model of cross-cultural communication he developed in *Christianity in Culture*[50] and in other writings is in fact a sophisticated and useful one. Kraft deals with skill and insight with the clash of worldviews, the pitfalls of cross-cultural communication, and also the tensions between cultural relativity, both ethical and epistemological, and the urge of many

---

[49]Miriam Adeney, *God's Foreign Policy* (Grand Rapids: Eerdmans, 1984).

[50]Kraft, *Christianity in Culture*.

Christians to find an absolute expression of their faith. His style blends in a stimulating way lucidity, humor, and provocativeness, well seasoned with anecdotes and illustrations, and based on a complex theoretical model. Altogether, though not without flaws, the book will be useful for years to come.

The only other Protestant work which to my knowledge explores the interface of theology with anthropology—he throws in missiology as well— is Harvie Conn's *Eternal Word and Changing Worlds*.[51] Conn handles the interaction with skill and sophistication, but the issues involved are complex and it is sometimes hard to follow the argument. His starting epistemological and theological assumptions are quite conservative, which hinders him at a number of points from going as far as the evidence might lead.

Both Kraft and Conn in different degrees partly transcend a dilemma characteristic of American conservative Protestant missiology, but their success is only partial. In less skilfull hands, the problem is that missiology seems to move along two distinct and not really compatible tracks. On the one hand, it affirms its traditional heritage: the truth and truthfulness, in an absolute sense, and therefore the universal applicability, of Christianity and its verbal expressions, vis-à-vis the other religions. On the other hand, under the influence of functionalism, it has accepted too uncritically the relativism of contemporary anthropology with respect to cultural forms. The pragmatic escape mechanism that has made this contradiction seemingly tenable is a tacit acceptance of the modern world's relegation of God to the religion "box" and its assertion of the autonomy of all the other "boxes." Thus, one can be as dogmatic as one likes in the religion box, but relative about all the others. It would be hard to find a procedure more congenial to all those powers in the modern world that do not want to be called to account before God.

Liberal missiology, on the other hand, has in its extreme form simply completed the process by relinquishing even the religion box to relativism. But then it becomes difficult if not impossible to make anything at all answerable to God.

---

[51]Harvie M. Conn, *Eternal Word and Changing Worlds* (Grand Rapids: Zondervan Academie Books, 1984).

Linwood Barney[52] offers at least the tantalizing beginning of a solution to the dilemma. He posits that only God is truly "supracultural" and therefore absolute. Everything human—language, culture, even theology—is relative. But God communicates with us through "constants," which are neither absolute nor relative to particular cultures. These, like the incarnation, bridge the gap. The idea is more fully developed in a later article.[53]

Julius Lipner was probably moving in the same direction when he asserted the relativity of theology and gospel formulations but insisted that Jesus as the incarnate Word is not relative. He wrote,

> No doubt the Bible and Jesus himself are not the products of a cultural vacuum. But I submit that as Christians we must equally affirm . . . that they are neither permanently the function of culture and social development. Pace Kant, we must recognize God's noumenal initiative into our situation as phenomenal. . . . By "noumenal" I mean coming purely from the divine initiative. . . . The divine initiative is pure grace. . . . But to be effective it must be phenomenalized— expressed in the *plurality* of the human situation [italics added].[54]

A constant preoccupation in missiology is the fear of syncretism, the blending of cultural and religious elements that are not truly compatible or that are quite incompatible, with resulting distortion of one or both elements. The fear has been through the centuries a great obstacle to indigenization: missionaries feared that if they allowed the use of native forms of expression, especially in theologizing, the gospel would be perverted and compromised.

This fear in missions went hand in hand with a blindness to the fact that in the West, syncretism had been a way of life for centuries. Consciously or unconsciously, Western Christianity has absorbed customs, ideas, and styles of thinking that are dramatically at odds with those found in the Bible. One thinks, at the superficial level, of the absorption of many pre-Christian customs into Christian celebrations of Christmas or Easter. At a more

---

[52]G. Linwood Barney, "The Supracultural and the Cultural: Implications for Frontier Missions," in *The Gospel and Frontier Peoples*, R. Pierce Beaver, ed. (South Pasadena: William Carey Library, 1973) 48-57.

[53]G. Linwood Barney, "The Challenge of Anthropology to Current Missiology," *International Bulletin of Missionary Research* 5 (October 1981): 172-77.

[54]Julius Lipner, " 'Being One, Let Me Be Many': Facets of the Relationship Between the Gospel and Culture," *International Review of Mission* 74 (April 1985): 165.

profound level, one thinks of the reduction of American ecclesiology to the voluntary society model, or the common explaining away of the hard sayings in the Bible about wealth.

Anthropology has permitted, even encouraged, both a healthy self-criticism by Western Christians[55] and a considerable openness to finding forms which are both compatible with the gospel and culturally authentic and compelling. In one way or another, all of the Protestant missiological anthropologists I have mentioned are part of the effort to find these appropriate forms.

But most of efforts I have described have ultimately been clearly within theology, and have used anthropology tangentially without really contributing to it as such. I know of no Protestant work that approximates either the breadth or the profundity of three recent Roman Catholic works, by Schreiter, Luzbetak, and Shorter respectively.[56]

I conclude this section with a brief observation: that while missionaries have been in the forefront of those who mediated knowledge of non-Western cultures in the West, they have made only very modest contributions to the theory of culture itself, apart from its component of language and communication.

## Missionaries and Anthropologists

We have already seen in several previous chapters that missionaries were present all over the world long before there were any anthropologists; that some of those missionaries wrote insightful, sympathetic descriptions of the cultures they encountered long before the word culture had been applied to them; that when anthropologists first began to spin theories, their best corpora of data were the writings of missionaries; that anthropologists used missionaries as fieldworkers whom they directed by correspondence; that anthropologists have often used missionaries to gain access to the peoples they wanted to study, and enjoyed missionary hospitality.

---

[55]Michael Drahan, "Christianity, Culture and the Meaning of Mission," *International Review of Mission* 75 (July 1986): 285-303.

[56]Robert J. Schreiter, C.PP.S., *Constructing Local Theologies* (Maryknoll: Orbis Books, 1984); Louis J. Luzbetak, S.V.D., *The Church and Cultures* (Maryknoll NY: Orbis Books, 1988); Aylward Shorter, W.F., *Toward a Theology of Inculturation* (Maryknoll NY: Orbis Books, 1988).

Yet it is a commonplace that, as Luzbetak says,[57] anthropologists are quite generally hostile to missionaries. Why should this be so? Why should it have been the fears rather than the hopes George Harris expressed in 1868[58] that were realized?

Luzbetak, in the article mentioned above, suggests that there are negative reductionistic stereotypes at work, and also that there are profound worldview barriers, especially excessive relativism, between anthropologists and missionaries. Stipe also confirms the role of conflicting presuppositions in this hostility.[59]

In the Whiteman book, Sutlive[60] points out that anthropologists and missionaries are both often marginal in their home cultures, but in quite different ways; this leads to defensiveness and suspiciousness. Anthropologists, he says, accuse missionaries of arrogant self-confidence, of violating the rights of peoples, of subverting local institutions, and of several other crimes. The background of the hostility, says Sutlive, lies in contrasting philosophical and existential backgrounds.

Frank Salamone[61] reports on a survey which confirms the views of Luzbetak and Sutlive and adds a few additional points. Anthropologists, he found, resent the fact that missionaries often control access to people and data. Significantly, the more anthropologists were obliged to use missionary sources, the more they resented the fact. Almost half of those who used missionary sources failed to give them credit. Finally, says, Salamone, hostility to religion as such affects the attitudes of many anthropologists toward missionaries.

---

[57]Louis J. Luzbetak, "Prospects for Better Understanding and Closer Cooperation Between Anthropologists and Missionaries," in *Missionaries, Anthropologists, and Culture Change, vol. 1* ed. Darrell L. Whiteman (Williamsburg VA: Department of Anthropology, College of William and Mary, 1985) 2.

[58]George Harris, "On Foreign Missions in Connection with Civilization and Anthropology" (London: Bell and Daldy, 1868).

[59]Claude E. Stipe, "Anthropologists versus Missionaries: The Influence of Presuppositions," *Current Anthropology* 21 (April 1980): 165-79.

[60]Vinson H. Sutlive, Jr., "The Anthropologist and the Missionary: Irreconcilable Enemies or Colleagues in Disguise?" in *Missionaries, Anthropologists, and Culture Change*, 1:55-87.

[61]Frank A. Salamone, "Missionaries and Anthropologists: An Inquiry into the Ambivalent Relationship," *Missiology* 14/1 (January 1986): 55-70.

An interesting case is that of the "Barbados Declaration,"[62] a document resulting from a meeting of anthropologists to affirm Indian rights in the Americas. The Declaration in effect blames virtually all of the ills suffered by Indians on missionaries.

It seems to me, then, that the most important factors in the hostility of anthropologists toward missionaries are as follows: (a) many anthropologists are personally hostile to religion, sometimes because they have rejected the religion in which they were reared, usually Christianity or Judaism, and this existential rejection gives the hostility more animus than it would otherwise have; (b) the relativism and determinism of anthropology clash with the overt or covert appeal of missions to the freedom of people to choose to change; (c) missionaries "mess up" the field of study; (d) missionaries often control access to people and data. But I take comfort from the report of Salamone that the longer anthropologists stayed in the field, the less they hated missionaries. And it is the case that some missiological anthropologists, from Tippett to Nida to Hiebert to Whiteman, have been widely accepted in the discipline.

## Conclusions

There have been in this century extensive and very fruitful interactions between missiology and cultural anthropology. Anthropological concepts and methods have greatly helped missionaries, though not as much as might have been the case if a historical accident had not restricted the anthropological perspective available to functionalism. Missionaries and missiologists have, much more than in the nineteenth century, brought to the attention of the Western world, and to anthropology, knowledge about the non-Western cultures of the world; and their accounts have been formulated with much greater insight and sophistication. But missionaries and missiologists have tended to use anthropology pragmatically, as a kit of tools for doing their job, without being sufficiently wary of the philosophical and ideological foundations of the discipline. They have, on the whole, not kept up with more recent developments within anthropology which might help them deal more effectively with the cultural realities they face. And as regards the concept of culture and theories to account for it, missionaries have been consumers rather than producers.

---

[62]"For the Liberation of the Indians (Barbados Declaration)," *International Review of Mission* 60 (1971): 277-84.

# CHAPTER 7

# The Issues Explored

We have now sketched a rapid history of the interaction between the concepts of culture developed in the discipline of anthropology and the modern Protestant missionary movement during the past two hundred years. What can we conclude from our study?

First, that missionaries and missiologists are always influenced in varying degrees by both their theological traditions and the spirit of their age. We saw this, for instance, in the strongly negative judgments of "heathen" religions which missionaries based on theological presuppositions; and also in the ease with which American missionaries at various periods have been caught up in the national ideologies of their time.

Second, that the views and attitudes they hold with respect to culture and cultural phenomena profoundly affect the way they live their lives and the way they conceive of and undertake their work. The best examples here, I think, are the impact of romantic particularism on German mission theory and practice; and the influence of Malinowskian functionalism in church growth theory.

Third, that this effect has its outcome in the results achieved for good or bad in missions.

Theological influences are of course very powerful. Especially significant are beliefs regarding human nature, personhood, and community; beliefs about the effects of the fall and the locus of sin and evil; and beliefs about knowledge and communication. Missionaries who hold to certain doctrines with respect to the fall, original sin, and total depravity will tend to see evil centered in fallen individual human beings and to see sociocultural systems and institutions as God-given means of restraining the sinfulness of persons; this is one way of reading the Calvinist heritage.

Those who take a less gloomy view of the effects of the fall—Arminians or neo-Pelagians—will be less severe in their judgments of individuals. Those in the Pietist heritage will tend to emphasize individual salvation, ethics, and religious practice, and simply ignore systemic and structural realities. Those, on the other hand, who explicitly see evil as entrenched in what the New Testament calls "the world" (*kosmos*) or "this age" (*aion*) will tend to be much more negative about most or all socio-cultural realities. This can lead, as we have seen in recent years, to an emphasis on transformation, even revolution, as in liberation theology; or it can lead, as in premillenial dispensationalism, to a sense of futility and an abandonment of efforts to ameliorate the world.

In another direction, views of inspiration which assign inerrancy to the scriptures are doctrinal in nature; but they have arisen in response to particular philosophical and therefore cultural debates in the areas of epistemology and communication. Specifically, the contemporary form of the doctrine of inerrancy is an attempt to rebut certain philosophical developments in the West during the nineteenth and twentieth centuries and would not really have been possible in earlier ages or in many other cultural contexts.

All of which is to suggest that one must by no means underestimate the degree to which Christians in general and missionaries in particular are people of their age and culture, even with respect to their theology. The missionary movement has surely not been determined by the world in which missionaries grew up, but it has been definitely influenced; missionaries have to an astonishing degree followed the twists and turns of prevalent social attitudes and values, no less really because their conformity was so largely unwitting. When the missionaries' home society was outgoing and internationalist in spirit, so were many missionaries; when the home country was isolationist, so were many missionaries; when the missionaries' society was racist, so were many missionaries; when it was aggressive, so were many missionaries; when it was pragmatic, so were many missionaries; and when it was strongly committed to laissez-faire capitalism, so were many missionaries.

There were obviously wide differences between individual missionaries, differences between groups of missionaries, and differences between missions. But by and large missionaries were shaped as much by their own cultures as by their official theological rationales.

This became perhaps more rather than less true when missionaries "discovered" anthropology as a useful discipline and adopted it as a tool without sufficiently examining its philosophical and ideological underpinnings. In Malinowskian functionalism, many missionaries found a congenial confirmation for some of their other theologically and culturally shaped views and attitudes. Individualism, pragmatism, relativism—all have been more powerful in their thinking than they have realized. In other words, to a certain extent they allowed themselves to become captive to that very specific product of Western culture, cultural anthropology. Thus, anthropology has become yet another means by which Western missionaries have ironically been agents of secularization in non-Western cultures.[1]

But it is time to examine successively some of the issues that have been raised in our investigation.

## Culture: Its Nature and Limits

Given that culture consists of ideas in people's heads, how do these ideas relate to the objective, material conditions of existence? I think Harris and his colleagues make a powerful case for the strong influence of material conditions on cultural ideas. Habitat, resources, climate, terrain, population size and density, amount and distribution of movable and immovable wealth, power relations between persons and groups— these provide the concrete framework within which people develop their descriptions and explanations of the natural and social worlds.

Thus, for example, it is much more honest and realistic to account for the common features of the ''culture of poverty'' in different social contexts by looking to the experience of poor people living in a matrix of wealth and power in which they are embedded and kept powerless, than to blame them for it. Similarly, the sunny view of laissez-faire capitalism that prevails in middle-class America stems clearly from the experience of middle-class people—until quite recently, at any rate—that this system works very well because it benefits them so generously. It would have been superhuman—or perhaps merely Christian—to ask what capitalism did to people other than ourselves, what it did to people who did not succeed according to its rules.

On the other hand, as I will point out in a bit, it is overstating the case to posit deterministic relations in the strong sense between the material conditions of existence and the rest of culture, since in very similar con-

---

[1]Elmer Miller, "The Christian Missionary: Agent of Secularization," *Missiology* 1/1 (January 1973): 99-107.

ditions people sometimes do come up with surprisingly variable cultural responses.

Is each culture a discrete, bounded, sui-generis phenomenon, coexisting but not essentially interacting with its neighbors? To raise the question in the late twentieth century is virtually to answer it. Each culture, it is becoming increasingly evident, is part of a dynamic nexus of interaction with others, both creatively and destructively. Cultural boundaries have always been relatively open, though never as much as today, and cultural traits have from the dawn of human experience been borrowed, altered, reinterpreted, embedded in new matrices, and otherwise transformed in passing from one culture to another.

We borrow techniques and religious ideas; we borrow from our friends and from our enemies; we borrow from peoples we admire and from peoples we despise. On this empirical point the diffusionists were right; what they lacked was a solid theory to account for the fact. It is no more feasible to draw a sharp boundary around "a culture" than around a definite area of the ocean. Social groups are usually bounded by definition, and a social group can lay claim to a particular configuration of ideas and practices at any given moment in its history; this configuration, the "culture" or "subculture" of the group, is relatively stable for the duration of a synchronic snapshot.

A significant bit of evidence in support of this view of the indeterminacy and impermanence of cultural boundaries comes from the recent history of anthropological method itself. A number of years ago, several anthropologists—George Peter Murdock, John Whiting, and others—tried, in the interests of a variety of research projects, to revive the comparative method that Boas had more or less placed in limbo, and to make cross-cultural statistical generalizations by comparing a large number of cultures with respect to a variety of traits. But the more they examined the question, the more difficult it seemed to isolate discrete cultural units which could be presumed to be independent of one other and therefore susceptible of providing valid comparisons. For after all, one can validly compare things only if they are indubitably separate and distinct; and cultures, it turned out, are often not that.

It is also clear that the term "culture" is applicable in a kind of concentric way to a number of levels of social reality: one can speak of Western culture, of North American culture, of southern culture, of the culture of south Alabama poor whites, in each case the smaller reality being a particular variant of the larger one. This is exactly the same pattern that exists in the relations of languages and their variants, the dialects.

One can describe both the general properties shared by all versions of a culture, and the peculiarities of each of its subcultures. And one had better recognize the mutually influential structural relationships between the subcultures of an area, as, for example, the dynamic relationship between the culture of affluence and the culture of poverty in an American city. We saw in chapter 5 that Radcliffe-Brown properly insisted on describing all of South Africa as a single system rather than describing each component separately in Malinowskian fashion, as the South African authorities wanted him to.

Both of these insights, the one concerning the nondiscreteness of cultures and the one concerning the multilevel nature of culture, will be of great interest when we look at Stackhouse's discussion of "context" in a later section.

Is culture in fact fully integrated and coherent, as Malinowskian functionalism asserted as a matter of dogma? The empirical evidence has led to a virtual consensus among anthropologists today that the degree of coherence and "fit" between parts of a culture is a subject of specific empirical inquiry, and turns out in fact to be highly variable. Some cultures at moments in their history display a relatively high degree of integration, others are more incoherent, and some few, in the words of the Nigerian novelist Chinua Achebe, are "falling apart."

One direction that ought to be pursued more than it has been is that suggested by the work of Redfield, discussed briefly in chapter 5. Redfield, it will be remembered, differentiated in useful ways between peasant or folk societies and urban societies. Elizabeth Nottingham, in a book on the sociology of religion,[2] offers a tripartite typology of societies, which I will summarize and develop here to indicate where I think we ought to go. I hinted at this typology in the opening pages of chapter 2, and will make further use of it in discussing later the relations of religion to culture. As with any typology, this is a useful oversimplification.

Type one societies are the small-scale, often isolated, nonliterate societies with simple technology and undifferentiated social, economic, and political systems, those formerly called "primitive" and typically studied

---

[2]Elizabeth K. Nottingham, *Religion: A Sociological View* (New York: Random House, 1971).

by anthropologists. In such societies, there are a few, all-purpose institutions, notably kinship and marriage, and there is little or no social stratification or division of labor, except those based on sex and age. Religion permeates all of life, but has no separate institutional embodiment. This is why some persons visiting such societies have reported that "these people don't have a religion," because they didn't find a separate institutional identity for it; and others report that "religion pervades everything"—which is often closer to the truth.

Type two societies are urban, literate societies, such as those that emerged in various parts of the world in the fourth to the second millenium B.C. and that persisted in the West until the Enlightenment and the Industrial Revolution, and in parts of Asia for longer. Here, there is a strong division of labor, social stratification, and specialization of institutions. Religion is thus a distinct institution, which often tries to dominate the others by means of its monopoly on access to the Ultimate. Such societies often exist with a tension between institutions, especially the religious and the political.

Type three societies came to birth in the West through the Enlightenment and the Industrial Revolution. The division of labor and the specialization of institutions are extremely developed, with religion only one among the others and no longer dominant; this last fact constitutes secularization.

David Filbeck devotes three rich chapters of his book *Social Context and Proclamation*[3] to a similar typology. His terms are "tribal society," "peasant society," and "modern society." One could quibble with the labels; but a more serious weakness is that Filbeck does not do justice in his "peasant" chapter to the complexities of urban society, especially its multilayered stratification. He especially neglects the powerful classes in either city or countryside. In dealing with New Testament evidence, he dwells on the Gospels and Jesus, and ignores Acts and Paul. This is puzzling, since New Testament Christianity was preeminently an urban movement in the Roman Empire.

Is there such a thing as a "deep level" of cultural reality underlying the surface phenomena of cultures, a level in which the surface diversities are brought closer together in the form of true cultural universals? The idea

---

[3]David Filbeck, *Social Context and Proclamation* (Pasadena: William Carey Library, 1985) 107-30.

comes from linguistics, where several current theories of language posit a "deep structure" accessible from the "surface structure" only by means of rigorous analytical method. The linguistic theories also posit that when discovered, this deep structure is much more alike across languages than the surface structures of the separate languages; one theory, transformational-generative grammar, argues that underlying the very diverse surface structures of all languages is a single universal deep structure. Noam Chomsky, chief architect of this theory, explicitly connects his theory to the ideas of "universal grammar" of the Port Royal scholars in seventeenth-century France.[4]

Lévi-Strauss's structuralism, discussed in chapter 5, is one non-Chomskian form which the idea of deep structure has taken in anthropology. But as we saw, this model is so powerful that it obliterates the empirical data to which it is applied; and it is often subjective in its actual application.

So what are we to make of the proposal that there are cultural "deep structures"? Are there such things? And if so, what are they like?

Obviously, all the members of such a biologically homogeneous species as Homo sapiens require the same essentials for survival and well-being: all require water and nutrition of certain definable chemical properties; all, being vulnerable to a host of natural and human perils, require protection from those perils; all require a sense of belonging and acceptance and of shared meanings; all require guidelines for the expression of sexuality; all require means of exercising their physical bodies in useful ways; all require means of putting their minds to work to understand their world; all have esthetic impulses; and all require some means of reaching out and relating to Ultimate Reality.

Each culture correspondingly provides a wealth of particular means for meeting these requirements; but underlying the particulars there seem to be universal and fundamental rationales which are rooted in the reality of humanness; years ago the anthropologist Goldschmidt observed that human beings are more alike than cultures.[5]

To take a specific cultural domain as an example, that of morality and ethics, it is possible to make a plausible case that underlying the extreme

---

[4]E.g., Noam Chomsky, *Language and Mind* (New York: Harcourt, Brace, and World, 1968).

[5]Walter Goldschmidt, *Comparative Functionalism: An Essay in Anthropological Theory* (Berkeley and Los Angeles: University of California Press, 1966) 134.

diversity of ethical systems discoverable in the field, there are certain constants or universals which sound amazingly like the clauses of the second tablet of the Decalogue: show respect for age and status, don't commit murder, don't steal, don't commit adultery, don't perjure yourself, don't be consumed by envy for your neighbor's belongings.

From a purely naturalistic perspective, a little reflection leads to the conclusion that such rules *must* be universal because no society could long survive without them. Of course, enormous differences appear as soon as we begin to define what behaviors are included in each of the proscribed categories, and to whom they apply, and when exceptions can be made. Even as violent and treacherous a society as the Sawi—accepting Richardson's description at face value for the sake of argument[6]—could not survive if there were not some group, however small, within which one could relax and trust others without being set up for murder. It turns out, as I have said in my classes, that a chief difference between the Sawi and modern Americans is that we experience relative trust within a much larger group; on the other hand, when we as a society do kill, we kill wholesale rather than retail. So who are the "savages"?

Theologically, I am prepared to attribute the ethical "deep structure" described above to the design of God, who created us in the divine image and likeness, and who made us in such a way that, even after the fall, we would not commit species suicide by totally disregarding the laws God had given us for the successful carrying out of the human experiment. God's laws are implanted in each of us (Romans 2); and where their internalization is not strong enough to restrain our worst impulses, culture provides guidelines and society provides sanctions to keep us in line. Goldschmidt, no Christian, gives an excellent empirically based discussion of these mechanisms of social control.[7]

To conclude: "culture" is a useful concept, a shorthand way of referring to something worthy of study; but only provided we do not become dupes of our own terminology and reify it.

## Cultural Change

Is culture essentially static, so that change is a pathology; or is it inherently dynamic, so that change is normal and natural? Obviously, some

---

[6]Don Richardson, *Peace Child* (Glendale CA: Regal Books, G/L Publications, 1974).

[7]Goldschmidt, *Comparative Functionalism*.

change is destructive; but it seems to be the consensus, based on a growing body of empirical evidence, that cultures have always changed under the impact of a plethora of forces, and that moments of relative immobility are from the perspective of history just that, moments. Obviously, change sometimes moves fast and at other times slowly; but change is the normal way for cultures over time.

The factors that make for change are both internal and external. Internal forces include all forms of disequilibrium or dysfunction intrinsic to the culture; a culture may become increasingly lopsided, it may be experienced as unfair by some of its members, it may be seen no longer to cope adequately with the exigencies of life. Or someone may innovate[8] in ways that appeal to the society as a whole as an improvement.

External change is produced by the impact of more or less radically altered physical conditions (changes in climate, reduction of the capacity of the habitat to support the population), or by the impact of outside human influences.[9] These may be benign or hostile, they may be passive, just there; or active, interfering with more or less coercion.

At this point it is appropriate to bring up the question of causation, which in turn evokes the insistence of Harris and his colleagues that historical causation must be material, not ideational. Ideas do not count as historical causes for Harris. But while conceding that material causes play a much greater role than many anthropologists or Christians have recognized, it does seem rather drastic, in a world which has been so strongly affected by ideas such as the gospel of Jesus Christ, the dark vision of the Ayatollah Khomeini, and the utopia of Karl Marx, to deny any important causative role for ideas. Granted, we must take seriously the insistence of the sociology of knowledge that these ideas themselves have sociocultural roots; but it is by no means necessary to make the relationship deterministic in the strong sense. In fact, it is quite unnecessary to see this as an either/or matter.

The process of cultural change rarely brings everyone along in approving lockstep; any change will affect people differently, some being benefited, some penalized. Some persons in every society are tempera-

---

[8]Homer G. Barnett, *Innovation: The Basis of Cultural Change* (New York: McGraw-Hill, 1953).

[9]Melville J. Herskovits, *Acculturation: The Study of Culture Contact* (Gloucester MA: P. Smith, 1958).

mentally imaginative, flexible, open to or eager for change, others are temperamentally rigid and conservative. So any period of notable change will also be a time of more or less social turmoil; the extreme examples of rapid cultural change, those in which change is brought about by overt societal conflict and violence, can be called revolutions.

But any time of crisis and incipient change is an opportunity for someone with a specific vision to make an effort to direct the process in the direction of that vision. Thus, times of social turmoil and traumatic cultural change have often been opportunities for the gospel; but a return to stability can close off the opportunity, as happened in Japan in the 1950s. In a kind of reductio ad absurdum of this insight, Mao Dzedong attempted in China to make the revolution a permanent, ongoing process, with the disastrous results we all know about. The literature also brings us examples of much less drastic purposeful change, as in the work of Paliau in Manus, off the New Guinea Coast, as documented by Margaret Mead and Theodore Schwartz.[10]

In this instance, the situation of the people was experienced as painful. Traditional culture was acknowledged to be inadequate to help people cope with the impact of modernity, and institutions were disintegrating. At this point a man named Paliau, not himself from Manus but from a neighboring area, arrived with a proposal. He had not had formal Western education, but he had traveled and worked in Western contexts. He proposed a quite revolutionary alteration of the culture to meet the demands of modern times; his proposal was widely accepted, and as a result Mead in 1953 found a much happier situation than she had seen in 1928.

The question for Christian missiology in relation to any planned change, it seems to me, is who is in charge of the change, who makes the decisions, who benefits, and who is hurt. Change engineered by a dominant minority to favor its own interests at the expense of the majority is surely unethical and unchristian. Change imposed without open and free discussion and consensus is likewise unacceptable. So is change brought about by an outsider's fiat, however well-intentioned he or she may be. The gospel is a liberating power, it expands people's range of choice; it is not a coercive or manipulative force which restricts people's freedom of choice. But a

---

[10]Margaret Mead, *New Lives for Old: Cultural Transformations, Manus, 1928–1953* (New York: William Morrow, 1966); Theodore Schwartz, *The Paliau Movement in the Admiralty Islands, 1946–1954*, Anthropological Papers of the American Museum of Natural History, part 2 (1962) 211–421.

missionary may, like Paliau, be a source of ideas which may help people choose a direction for their society.

## Ethical Relativity and Ideology

Is culture essentially good, ethically neutral, bad, or a mixture? It seems increasingly clear that it is a mixture of good and bad; but the relationship of good and bad is not simple; one cannot, for instance, characterize some traits as good and others as bad, as was commonly done by missionaries in the past; some missionaries and missiologists continue to think in these terms. It turns out that few if any cultural traits are either wholly good or wholly bad, especially if their functional interconnections are recognized.

It is here that we must consider the important question of cultural relativity in its ethical dimension. Cultural relativity, especially as espoused by Boas and Herskovits,[11] is the idea that there are no absolute criteria for making value judgments, especially ethical judgments. For judgments presuppose standards and criteria, and it turns out that each culture has its own criteria for making judgments, which are not reducible to one another. Each culture comprises certain goals which society has posited for itself and which it considers good and proper, and it strives through its members to achieve these goals; insofar as they succeed, they approve of their own performance; insofar as they fail, they disapprove.

But different cultures propose different goals, and it is inappropriate to judge one culture by the goals and criteria of another; after all, if a culture is not trying to elaborate high technology, it is unfair to condemn it because it has not achieved high technology. In other words, it's all a matter of culture, everything is relative to a given culture.

As I said in an earlier chapter, this can be carried as far as one wants to go; the only limit is the strength of one's stomach. Is headhunting "just culture," or is infanticide, or is cannibalism? Was Hitler's "final solution" just "German culture"? Was Hiroshima a perfectly understandable expression of American culture? How far do we go? Some, as we saw in chapter 5, have tried, in the absence of genuine absolutes, to substitute universals: putatively, these would be values about which all human beings

---

[11]Melville J. Herskovits, *Cultural Relativity,* ed. Frances Herskovits (New York: Vintage Books, 1973); David Bidney, "Cultural Relativism," in *International Encyclopedia of the Social Sciences,* ed. David L. Sills (New York: Macmillan, 1968) 3:543-47.

can agree and which they can apply in making judgments.[12] But two questions obtrude: are there such universals? This is an empirical question. The second is more fundamental: is it legitimate to move directly from an *is*, however widespread, to an *ought*? I have my doubts.

Nevertheless, a special kind of ethical cultural relativity, with appropriate limits, is a very important insight for Christians: it helps us to relativize and subject to God's judgment *all* human arrangements and ideas, including our own, as they must be relativized and subjected if we are not to lapse into idolatry. For ethnocentrism, like covetousness, is at least potentially idolatrous: we tend to absolutize the very imperfect human arrangement which is our culture, and to judge other people by it.

It is important to distinguish, as Herskovits and Bidney have, between *cultural* relativity and total individual relativity. For it is a universal trait of all cultures that they do have ethical positions which they inculcate into their members and which they enforce.

Theologically speaking, each human culture is a collective expression of the creativity inherent in the image of God in human beings, and as such is not only good, but indispensable; it is not possible to conceive of a true human being without placing him or her in a particular cultural matrix. It is the culture that gives determinate shape to the open-ended potentials which constitute our genetic heredity and thus enables us to be truly human.[13] This was evident in that paradigmatic expression of quintessential humanity, Jesus of Nazareth: he did not become a general "essence of humanity," but a first-century lower-middle-class Galilean Jew.

On the other hand, the fall has fatally infected every aspect and detail of culture, no matter how much good it expresses, so that nothing fully escapes the perversion of sin. A particularly striking example is found in the destructive effects of loyalty to family, kin, or nation taken to extremes. To love one's own and one's own kind is good; to love one's own and *therefore* to hate the stranger is bad, but extremely common. Similar ruinous effects have touched all aspects of culture, so that it is crucial that all cultures, our own included—or perhaps our own especially, since it is

---

[12]Alison Dundes Renteln, "Relativism and the Search for Human Rights," *American Anthropologist* 90/1 (March 1988): 56-72.

[13]Goldschmidt, *Comparative Functionalism*; see also Elvin Hatch, *Culture and Morality: The Relativity of Values in Anthropology* (New York: Columbia University Press, 1983).

the one we are prone to absolutize— must be seen to be under the judgment of God. One important dimension of not being "conformed to this age" (Romans 12:2) is that our minds are transformed, with the result that it is the will of God rather than the (cultural) patterns of this world that are seen to be good, and acceptable, and perfect.

One pervasive effect of the fall in cultures is the creation of ideologies; by "ideology," I mean a set of ideas whose chief purpose is to rationalize and justify a sociocultural situation which is fundamentally unjust and damaging to some of its participants.[14] Ideologies are devised by those who benefit from the unjust situation for two purposes: to enable them to feel good about themselves, and to disarm any potential protest and rejection by the victims of the situation. It is in this sense that what Marx said about religion in his time was a recognition that European Christianity itself had degenerated into an ideology: it had become an "opiate for the people."

A fundamentally just society and culture would have no need of an ideology, since an ideology is a mystification, a wilfull misrepresentation of what is the case in order to perpetuate injustice.

### Epistemological Relativity

Toward the end of chapter 5 I discussed the current hot debate in anthropology about epistemological relativity, the idea that knowledge like morality is relative to a given culture or a given social position.[15] Many anthropologists, and it goes without saying many Christians, are very nervous about the implications of this position. Both anthropologists and Christian thinkers try very hard to maintain an area, small as it may be, in which what they know is not subject to the common conditions of human knowledge. They seek for some knowledge, and some formulation of knowledge, which is absolutely "there" and "true" no matter where they are standing.[16]

One ploy among theologians is to appeal to divine revelation, and especially to a divinely inspired Scripture. It is diagnostic, for instance, that

---

[14]Charles R. Taber, "Culture, Ideology, and Mission," in *Unto the Uttermost*, ed. Doug Priest, Jr. (Pasadena: William Carey Library, 1984) 155-75.

[15]Clifford Geertz, *The Interpretation of Cultures* (New York: Basic Books, 1973).

[16]E.g., Max L. Stackhouse, *Apologia: Contextualization, Globalization, and Mission in Theological Education* (Grand Rapids: Eerdmans, 1988); also Carl F. H. Henry, "Comment on 'Is There More than One Way to Do Theology?' " *Gospel in Context* 1/1 (January 1978): 22-23.

nowhere in the six volumes of Carl F. H. Henry's magnum opus, *God, Revelation, and Authority*,[17] is there what I would consider a minimally adequate treatment of the hermeneutical process. But one does not have to be a "liberal" to see that whatever may be the properties of the Bible as a collection of divinely inspired texts, the very human process by which we try to determine what those writings mean is a hermeneutical process, one in which cultural relativity plays an unavoidable role through and through. I am not here concerned with the Bible as such, but with the ways in which human beings interpret the Bible.

But it is quite true that total relativism destroys the possibility of meaning. Einstein's theory itself can make sense of the material universe only because it does posit one unchanging constant: the velocity of light. In connection with that, everything else can be both meaningful and relative; without it, nothing could be meaningful, and Einsteinian physics would be impossible.

It is the same, it seems to me, with epistemology in general: if in cultural relativity there is no unchanging constant, nothing means anything. Realizing this, the Enlightenment proposed various grounds for absolute certainty. Locke and the American Founding Fathers, for instance, proposed "Natural Law," and the latter appealed to it explicitly in the Declaration of Independence. But the wider experience of the contemporary period makes a shambles of that.

Another Enlightenment candidate for an absolute is Humanity or Human Nature. This superficially resembles my discussion of universal human requirements for survival; but in fact it is much more akin to the earlier emphasis on the universality of Reason, and more recently to the suggestion of Lévi-Strauss that all human beings think alike. The trouble with this is that knowledge does not derive only from the universal mental operations of persons— processual realities—but also from the specific culturally-given contents of human minds—substantive realities. Exactly the same logical processes—syllogisms, for instance—lead to totally different conclusions if the premises are different.

I do not think it is possible to escape this irreducible relativity of *all* human endeavors, including philosophy, science, and theology, which

---

[17]Carl F. H. Henry, *God, Revelation, and Authority*, 6 vols. (Waco TX: Word Books, 1976–1983).

make use of human languages and cultural systems of meaning. So where is the Absolute?

I think only God is Absolute, as Barney suggested in his discussion of the supracultural.[18] I do not mean our ideas about God or our statements about God, but God as God. God has revealed the divine nature primarily in the eternal Son, Jesus of Nazareth. Our knowledge of God is *primarily* personal knowledge, and only secondarily is it to be found in the useful but culturally relative verbal formulations which we use. Accepting this fact allows us to see that what is universal in human nature is the divine image; and what is universal in natural law is the creative design of God for good.

I think it is on foundations such as these, even though they are often not acknowledged, that human beings are painfully groping toward an embryonic "law of nations," as embodied for instance in the United Nations Declaration of Human Rights.

### Cultural Determinism and Human Freedom

Does culture totally determine the individual, or does the individual have a measure of freedom within which to make deliberate and responsible—or irresponsible!—choices? There is no doubt that the preponderance of anthropologists are, as we have seen, basically determinists; especially, it seems, with respect to the nonliterate cultures which have been their traditional field of concentration. No doubt this is the case in part because of the ambition of many of them to be "scientific" after the example of the physical sciences; in part because of their desire to formulate exceptionless descriptions and explanations; and no doubt in part because of their hope that a description based on the testimony of a handful of informants can be legitimately generalized as a description of "the culture of community X."

There are, however, minority voices, notably that of David Bidney,[19] which argue that it is not possible to describe the human scene in a rigor-

---

[18]G. Linwood Barney, "The Supracultural and the Cultural: Implications for Frontier Missions," in *The Gospel and Frontier Peoples*, ed. R. Pierce Beaver (South Pasadena: William Carey Library, 1973) 48-57; "The Challenge of Anthropology to Current Missiology," *International Bulletin of Missionary Research* 5 (October 1981): 172-77.

[19]David Bidney, *Theoretical Anthropology* (New York: Columbia University Press, 1953).

ously deterministic manner because human beings always have a significant measure of freedom with regard to their cultures.

With respect to the debate about the supposed difference in this regard between "primitive" and modern societies, I make only three observations. First, it seems to me that modern Westerners tend to exaggerate greatly the freedom they enjoy, because they are unaware of the extent to which their views and choices are in fact shaped by social forces such as class affiliation. Second, under the influence of anthropologists, we have tended to think that "primitives" are strongly determined by their cultures, and are therefore not free. We also often think the same thing about persons under socialism. Third, the sense of wide choice we subjectively experience in the West is often spurious. When at the supermarket I face the array of breakfast cereals, I can be almost paralyzed by the variety; but the options are in reality virtually indistinguishable, and my freedom to choose outside of the array to obtain genuinely economical and nutritious cereals is very limited.

## Indigenization, Inculturation, Contextualization

I have already discussed the classical notion of "indigeneity" in previous chapters: the "three-self" formula of Venn and Anderson, and the expansion of the concept under the influence of anthropology to include significant areas of cultural expression.

This is as good a place as any to mention briefly the concept of "inculturation," which is also currently in use. This is mainly a Roman Catholic usage. The term was first used in French as a verb in the 1930s, in specific relation to Roman Catholic missionary work in Japan, but it was not generalized until the 1960s and especially the 1970s; though the practice is much older in Catholic missiology, as Shorter has described it with great insight.[20]

In essence, inculturation is based on the analogy of the incarnation: just as the Eternal Son was incarnated, that is became a human being, not in general, but in the specific culture of lower-middle-class Galilean Jewry in the early first century, so the gospel today, and its human messengers, needs to become humanly incarnate in all of the specific cultures of the peoples to whom mission is addressed. Though the explicit theological and

---

[20]Aylward Shorter, W.F., *Toward a Theology of Inculturation* (Maryknoll NY: Orbis Books, 1988).

biblical foundations of "inculturation" were not identical with those of "indigenization," the outward manifestations were often not unlike.

More recently, and clearly quite independently of its earlier Catholic usage of which he was unaware, the American Protestant missiologist G. Linwood Barney has also used "inculturation."[21] For him, the analogy was not theological but anthropological: starting from the existing concepts of "enculturation" (education in the comprehensive sense) and "acculturation" (the results of the mutual influence of cultures on each other), he devised a way of speaking about the way in which the "supracultural" gospel could be effectively and appropriately expressed in the enormous diversity of human cultures, and came up with "inculturation."

But among Protestant missiologists, indigenization continued to be the normal term used for the general subject matter of what missions were trying to accomplish.

But this idea itself has come under attack in the last couple of decades, especially by a number of Christian thinkers and leaders in the non-Western world. They have proposed both a new term and a new definition: "contextualization."[22] The idea was not simply to replace a term arbitrarily, but to represent significant differences in emphasis between the classical concept of indigenization as I have described it above, and a more adequate approach.

I will list briefly six differences between the two concepts, though no one of course suggests that all of these were totally original; most of them had been at least partially anticipated by theorists of indigenization.[23]

1. Indigenization, at least since the influence of anthropology began to be felt, placed the emphasis on culture, in the narrow sense of socially rooted ideas people hold about a certain set of questions, and almost always excluding consideration of concrete ecological, social, political, or economic conditions. Contextualization argues forcefully that *all* aspects of the human context are areas in which human sin and evil are expressed,

[21]Barney, "The Supracultural."

[22]Theological Education Fund, *Ministry in Context: The Third Mandate Programme of the Theological Education Fund 1971–1977* (Bromley, England: Theological Education Fund, 1972).

[23]Charles R. Taber, "Contextualization, Indigenization, and/or Transformation," in *The Gospel and Islam: A 1978 Compendium*, ed. Don M. McCurry (Monrovia CA: Missions Advanced Research and Communication Center, 1979) 143-54.

and therefore areas to which the gospel of the coming kingdom of God needs to be explicitly addressed. This includes matters of wealth and poverty, obesity and starvation, power and powerlessness, privilege and oppression. Similarly, contextualization rejects the limiting of interest to what happens internally within a single social group, but demands that relations between groups, including nations, also be considered.

2. Indigenization, as we have seen, tended toward a static, even backward-looking view of culture. Contextualization insists on a flexible view, often a present-and-future-oriented view, and an acceptance of the reality and often the desirability of sociocultural change. The gospel should have an impact on the *trajectory* of ongoing change.

3. Indigenization generally held to the view, as we have seen, of culture as closed and self-contained. Contextualization insists on considering relations between cultures and social groups, right up to the global scale.

4. Indigenization tended to focus on what was going on "out there" on the "foreign mission field," and was concerned, for instance, with the ever-present danger of syncretism out there. Contextualization demands that what goes on in the sending countries and churches also be scrutinized critically; it points out, for instance, the numerous instances of syncretism that pervade Western churches.

5. Indigenization tended to assume that the gospel and its theological elaboration would be "the same" in all cultures, barring necessary but superficial adjustments in the form of presentation. Contextualization insists that the gospel is in a sense not even known until a proper analysis and critique of the context has been done, because to be good news it must address the specifics of each context; the example of Jesus is cited, who did not repeat any conversations, but made each human encounter one of a kind because of the uniqueness of each interlocutor. Theology also must explicitly and intentionally address the critical spiritual issues of each context, and not attempt to be universal and timeless.[24] In fact, theology cannot help but be conditioned by context; the point is to make that conditioning prophetic and redemptive rather than accidental and syncretistic.

6. Despite loud protests to the contrary, indigenization tended to assume a fairly critical and even definitive role for the missionary in shaping the entire process. The literature sounded as though the missionary really

---

[24]Robert J. Schreiter, C.PP.S., *Constructing Local Theologies* (Maryknoll NY: Orbis Books, 1984).

knew and could really decide what would happen, could at will initiate or arrest any part of it. Contextualization places the burden of initiative and authority squarely on Christians of the local context.

In some cases, in a manner parallel to that described in chapter 6 for moratorium, it is suggested that foreigners have no role to play in contextualization; but this, it seems to me, is an understandable overreaction. I maintain that the initiative and authority should be firmly in local hands; but outsiders can play a crucial role by posing questions, by offering alternatives, and so on. Schreiter, cited just above, suggests such an approach, which is important in order for a sense of the church universal to be preserved.

It is into this picture that I want now to inject two questions borrowed from a paper by Max Stackhouse.[25] In my paraphrase, "How big is a 'here'? How long is a 'now'?" As can be seen, these questions raise critically the questions of scale and scope, both in space and in time.

Is "Africa" a context? Is "West Africa"? Is "Ghana"? Is "Ashanti"? Is "Kumasi"? *Yes,* in each instance. For that matter, for some purposes the whole world, or some apparently arbitrary set of places in the world, can be a context that needs to be taken into consideration in missiology. For example, the improbable combination Kimberley-Cape Town-Amsterdam-New York is a context, if you are talking about the diamond trade. Saudi Arabia-Yemen-Indonesia-Nigeria-et cetera are a context if you are talking about petroleum. More accurately, the complex including producer nations and customers is a single context. At the other end of the spectrum, a single household in a shanty town in Kumasi is a context for some purposes. In other words, how big the context is and exactly what it includes all depends on what issue you are talking about. In particular, in studying any asymmetrical relation (debtor-creditor, oppressor-oppressed), enormous distortions occur if one examines only one end of the pole involved.

With respect to missions, for instance, sending churches and receiving churches constitute *together* a context that needs to be examined as such.[26]

---

[25]Max L. Stackhouse, "Contextualization in Theological Education," *Theological Education* 23/1 (Autumn 1986): 79-84.

[26]Charles R. Taber, "Structures and Strategies for Interdependence in World Mission," in *Mission Focus: Current Issues,* ed. Wilbert R. Shenk (Scottdale PA: Herald Press, 1980).

For some purposes one can look at only one end, but not for many. The reason for this is that a good many of the problems and difficulties experienced at one end, especially the less powerful end, tend to arise from the other end.

Stackhouse's chief concern in the article I am citing has to do with the relation of the local church to the church universal. This is also a chief focus of many theorists of contextual theology, such as Robert Schreiter.[27] Missiologically, it is crucial that one not neglect the organic relation of a newly founded church, however isolated and local, to the church universal; and of its emerging theology to the body of theologies coming from the rest of the Body. Only in this way can the inevitable tendencies to syncretism be escaped—in all parts of the Body. This does *not* mean that one church has tutelage over any other, but that all mutually submit to each other's scrutiny for the good of all and the glory of their one Lord.

With respect to the time dimension, all human groups, and consequently all human cultures, are, as we have seen, presently engaged in a trajectory of change, in which they influence each other for good or ill. Sometimes some cultures change slowly, others fast. Sometimes within a culture some domains change slowly, others fast. And in all cultures, some people deplore and resist change, others welcome and promote it, while many don't have any idea what is happening.

If in this flux one wants to practise contextually appropriate missionary principles and plant contextually authentic churches—or encourage toolong-dependent imitation churches to become contextually authentic—how does one go about it?

Chiefly, one needs to encourage local Christians to dreams dreams, to take initiatives and risks, to face and understand their particular reality, to enter into a dialogue between their reality and the Scriptures, to develop a profound sense of *who* they are and of *where* they are, and of what Christ wants them to become and where he wants them to go.

Negatively, quit trying to return to the past, to put things into neat, unchanging boxes, to control or determine the process. Have faith in God, in the Holy Spirit, in the Scriptures, in the young church.

Positively, place at the disposal of the young church what resources you have that they don't yet. Operate on the Pauline principle that the one Lord of the one church has given an assortment of gifts and resources to

---

[27]Schreiter, *Constructing Local Theologies.*

that one church, but that the initial distribution may be very unequal (2 Corinthians 8,9 and Romans 15). Specifically—and here I borrow heavily from Loewen,[28] though not verbatim— you, the outsider, have in many cases an awareness of the broader world, Christian as well as non-Christian, from which you can offer a range of options to stimulate their thinking. You may place at their service your skills with critical analytical tools, both biblical and social scientific. You may serve as a sounding board for their ideas. However, do not be surprised if you find that at some points they are already ahead of you in sophistication about some things! I would assume, for instance, that a Latin American congregation which included a few graduate students could well be better versed in the relevant social sciences than the foreign missionary. Do not do for them what they can do for themselves.

## Religion and Culture

Finally, what is the relationship of culture to religion, and religion to culture?

Before the rise of functionalism, that is before there was any serious acknowledgement of the integration of culture, religion was typically viewed as more or less isolated and sui generis, and it was good, bad, or indifferent as such according to the predilections of the investigator or the missionary. We have already seen the negative views which missionaries of the nineteenth almost universally held with regard to the religions of the peoples among whom they worked. Sometimes, especially among nonliterate peoples—"savages," "primitives"—they refused to acknowledge that what was practised merited the name "religion" at all. Religions which had scriptures—Hinduism, Buddhism, and Islam being the chief ones— were recognized to be more sophisticated, but that in no way decreased the animus of most missionaries against them. The religions, "primitive" or "high," were alike "heathen," "pagan," "demonic," and productive of every sort of social abuse and moral vice.

Missionaries of the earliest period disagreed about whether it was necessary to know anything about the "heathen" religions, though most of those working among adherents of the literate religions held that it was,

---

[28]Jacob A. Loewen and Anne Loewen, "The 'Missionary' Role," in Jacob A. Loewen, *Culture and Human Values,* ed. William A. Smalley (Pasadena: William Carey Library, 1975) 428-43.

and this view gradually became almost universal. But one learned about the religions exclusively to make one's attack on them more effective. Confrontational apologetics were often the order of the day, though as the decades passed the tone became gradually less shrill. But even those who gained a measure of respect and appreciation for the religions—and they were a growing number— never doubted that in order to experience God's salvation people had to forsake their religions and become Christians.

Ironically, as we have seen, missionaries seldom hesitated to use for *Elohim/Theos,* and even for *Yahweh,* the local name of the Sky God or the High God. But, as we saw in chapter 4, they did not understand the implications of this nearly as well as their hearers and converts.

One of the best-documented facts about the modern Protestant missionary movement is that by and large its outstanding successes have taken place in the "primitive" parts of the world, among nonliterate peoples. So-called animists in many regions have responded in great numbers to the missionary message and have thronged into the church. Meanwhile, members of literate societies and enscripturated religions have responded meagerly, and often have offered determined resistance. Various explanations have been suggested to account for these different responses.

Some think that the greater sophistication of the literate cultures enabled their members to resist being made to feel inferior, whereas "primitives" readily accepted the missionaries' assessment of their cultural "backwardness." This explanation stands or falls with the validity of the notion of "primitivity," which is not rock-solid, as we saw in chapter 5. Others suggest that the experience of conquest and colonization at the hands of the West led people to accept the religion of their conquerors. But this will not do, since countries of literate civilizations were also conquered or at least vanquished and humiliated, and their resistance to the gospel of their conquerors only became the more determined.

A hypothesis which seems to me more plausible, though it has not been rigorously tested, is this: nonliterate peoples did often accept Christianity wholesale, but they did so within their own frame of reference and for their own reasons. As pragmatists concerned with coping with "the powers" in relation to everyday life, they often adopted Jesus as an additional power, one of great utility, to help them deal with life, especially the new situation created by the presence and power of Westerners. In many cases, I suggest, this happened with no change in worldview at all.[29] Christianity fitted neatly into the slot occupied by traditional religion, sometimes supplanting it, sometimes supplementing it. One can, of course, wonder whether this is good or bad. But it seems to me that that is what probably happened. Those aspects of traditional religion that most shocked missionaries often did not disappear, they simply went underground. Could it be that the "primitives" found a very effective way to resist spiritual conquest by bending?

Early anthropologists, for their part, were also usually dismissive of the religions they studied, but for different reasons; they tended to dismiss religion as such, including the "high" religions, and especially including Christianity and Judaism, which were the religions of which many of them had had existential experience. This rejection was motivated—as with Comte—by the notion that religion as such represented a prescientific way of dealing with reality. At bottom, said Freud, it was projection and illusion. It did not refer to any transcendent Reality or Truth, but it was useful (Comte, Spencer) to mystify and pacify the populace and to legitimate the social order.

When Durkheim launched the functionalist perspective, he did not rehabilitate religion as religion in the classical sense, that is as having to do with the Ultimate and the Transcendent. But he "explained" it on a totally new basis: religion served a "function," it contributed significantly to the well-being, effective working, and stability of society by invoking legitimation and sanctions from the Beyond.[30] But, he argued, when one got behind the curtain, one learned that what the social group *really* worshiped was itself, as a divinized entity.

Since Durkheim had himself studied the "elementary forms of the religious life," that is, the religion of "primitives," functionalists in anthropology could follow him more directly than in some other areas of culture. Functionalism made religion simply one aspect of culture and nothing more. It embodied beliefs, rituals, specialists, and so on, and like every other aspect of culture it served a variety of social and personal purposes for its adherents. One did not raise the question of truth or falsity in

[29]Donald R. Jacobs, "Culture and the Phenomena of Conversion," *Gospel in Context* 1/2 (April 1978): 4-14.

[30]Emile Durkheim, *The Elementary Forms of the Religious Life*, trans. John Ward Swain (Repr. New York: Collins, 1961; orig. 1912).

any metaphysical way—such questions would be meaningless, said logical positivism—one simply noted that it turned out to be socially useful that people believed that certain things were so.

In this vein, anthropologists did a great number of studies of cultures which included a chapter on "the religion." A few, including Malinowski and Evans-Pritchard, did more extended studies focused on religion itself, though Malinowski concentrated more on magic and sorcery.[31] A number also wrote theoretical works proposing overall "explanations" of "primitive" religion.[32] It will be noted that, in keeping with the division of labor described in chapter 5, anthropologists rarely if ever studied the enscripturated religions.

More recently, anthropologists have studied modern societies, mostly at the level of narrowly defined subcultures. But it is my impression that such studies of religion as have been appearing recently have been sharply focused, as in descriptions of the "cargo cults" of Melanesia and other "religions of the oppressed" and "revitalization movements," or in descriptions of what happened to Christianity as it was adopted by particular peoples. Some of these studies are of excellent quality.[33]

Meanwhile missionaries and missiologists had begun to diverge, separating and eventually polarizing into two camps with regard to religion and the religions. A large number, encouraged by the works of Barth and especially Kraemer,[34] maintained essentially unchanged the classical negative stance, that the other religions are bad and must be radically dis-

[31]Bronislaw Malinowski, *Coral Gardens and Their Magic,* 2 vols. (New York: American Book Co., 1935); E. E. Evans-Pritchard, *Witchcraft, Oracles and Magic Among the Azande* (Oxford: Clarendon Press, 1965).

[32]Robert H. Lowie, *Primitive Religion* (New York: Boni and Liveright, 1924); Paul Radin, *Primitive Religion: Its Nature and Origin* (New York: Viking, 1937); E. E. Evans-Pritchard, *Theories of Primitive Religion* (Oxford: Clarendon Press, 1965); Anthony F. C. Wallace, *Religion: An Anthropological View* (New York: Random House, 1966).

[33]Anthony F. C. Wallace, "Revitalization Movements: Some Theoretical Considerations for Their Comparative Study," *American Anthropologist* 58 (1956): 264-81; Peter Worsley, *The Trumpet Shall Sound: A Study of Cargo Cults in Melanesia,* 2nd ed. (New York: Schocken Books, 1968); George R. Sanders, ed., *Culture and Christianity: The Dialectics of Transformation* (New York: Greenwood Press, 1988).

[34]Karl Barth, *Church Dogmatics, vol. 1, pt. 2,* trans. G. T. Thomson and Harold Knight (Edinburgh: T.&T. Clark, 1956; orig. 1932) 280-361; Hendrik Kraemer, *The Christian Message in a Non-Christian World* (New York: Harper and Row, for the International Missionary Council, 1938).

placed by Christianity; many had not noticed the negative stance of Barth with respect to Christianity as a religion. Others took increasingly flexible and even relativistic positions. An early proponent of this latter view was Hocking.[35] This view is most vigorously espoused today by Hick, Knitter, Wilfred Cantwell Smith,[36] as well as by some of the proponents of inter-religious dialogue.[37]

But it seems to me that both extremes in this polarization take far too many unexamined a prioris for granted, so that their ability to assess empirical evidence is severely impaired. And they tend to think of each religion—or even "the religions" en masse—as monolithically susceptible to generalized evaluation. But a good many questions need to be asked and answered before one can conclude that the devotees of any particular religion—some or all of them—are either *thereby* going to heaven or *thereby* going to hell. Though this topic will be the central concern of another book not yet written, I offer the following preliminary propositions:

1. All human beings and groups have available to them sources for some knowledge of the existence and character of God. I am using "knowledge" here in the barest sense of "awareness of information"; failure to distinguish this from genuinely saving, existential knowledge of God bedevils the literature. These universally available sources are chiefly creation (Romans 1:19-23; Psalm 19:1-6) and human conscience (Romans 2). Some peoples also have prophets who have encountered God and brought back reports of the encounter. Finally, some peoples have also heard of the decisive entrance of God into the human predicament in the Person of the Eternal Son incarnate in Jesus of Nazareth (Hebrews 1:1-4). These sources of knowledge about God are successive and cumulative, though the last is final, complete, and definitive. The lesser sources provide incomplete but authentic information about God.

2. Just as God in the pre-Christian era accepted people who responded in *faith* to the limited information known to them, so that they truly moved

[35]Laymen's Foreign Mission Inquiry, Commission of Appraisal, William E. Hocking, chair., *Re-Thinking Missions* (New York: Harper, 1932).

[36]John Hick, ed., *The Myth of God Incarnate* (London: SCM Press, 1977); Paul Knitter, *No Other Name?* (Maryknoll NY: Orbis Books, 1985); John Hick and Paul Knitter, eds., *The Myth of Christian Uniqueness* (Maryknoll NY: Orbis Books, 1985).

[37]Stanley Samartha, *Courage for Dialogue* (Geneva: World Council of Churches, 1981); Raimundo Panikkar, *The Interreligious Dialogue* (New York: Paulist Press, 1978).

from knowing about God to knowing God, so I see no reason to suppose that God rejects people today who similarly respond in *faith* to what information they have. God surely does not reject people because they have not responded to information which, through no fault of their own, they did not have. People who, in Kraft's phrase, are "informationally B.C."[38] have the same opportunity to believe and obey as Abraham had.

3. This is not to say that all do so respond, or that all will ultimately be "saved" regardless of the reponse they have made to God's overtures to them. Rather, it is to say that the question of whether or not a given person knows God in the salvific sense is *not* automatically answered by discovering whether or not he or she has heard of Jesus, or whether he or she has joined a Christian church or belongs to another religion. Religious censuses, however accurate they might ideally become, can never in any serious sense answer the question of salvation or damnation. How many Christians are "saved," and how many "lost"? How many Muslims are "saved," and how many "lost"? God only knows, and we must be content with that.

4. This is because no religion, not even Christianity, saves anyone; only God saves, through Jesus Christ. But if God could save Abraham and Melchizedek through Jesus Christ, why should he not be able to save others who, like them, have never heard of Jesus, but have responded in faith to what information they had?

5. This in no way undercuts the imperative for world mission, since we are commanded to be witnesses and promised that we will be witnesses. It only undercuts the triumphalistic notion that unless we go, no one can be saved. What kind of obedience would it be that operated only if the ultimate destiny of others depended absolutely on it?

Furthermore, I suspect that in every society, there may well be very few who are spiritually sensitive, and who therefore may be supposed to respond in faith to a mere glimmer of divine light; these, the history of mission ever since Cornelius shows, eagerly welcome any additional light from God.[39] But there may well be many more who are less spiritually sensitive

---

[38]Charles H. Kraft, *Christianity in Culture* (Maryknoll NY: Orbis Books, 1979) 126, 239, 253-57.

[39]Vincent J. Donovan, *Christianity Rediscovered: An Epistle from the Masai* (Maryknoll NY: Orbis Books, 1982).

and who require a good bit of light before they take note of it and respond
in faith. For these, it is important to make that additional light available.

6. Each religion, including empirical Christianity, is an institutional-
ized response to whatever light of divine self-disclosure is available. But
the quality of the response varies: it may, hypothetically, be *yes, no,* or
*yes, but.* Moreover, there is no rule that says that every individual devotee
of a religion has personally made the same response as has been made by
the institutional religion. It is quite conceivable that, within a religion which
has chosen to turn away from divine light and worship idols, individual
members may have chosen to say *yes* to God. Thus, of two persons participating in a given religion side by side, one may be "saved" and the
other "lost."

An important variable regarding religion, it seems to me, relates to what
I said in an earlier section about different types of society. It seems clear
that, structurally, religion relates to the rest of culture in quite different ways
in (a) a small-scale, nonliterate society; (b) a differentiated, literate, urban
society; and (c) a modern secular society. The diagrams below illustrate
the differences.

I should explain one feature of these diagrams: by using the term "Ultimate" to refer to what people address through their religion, I am leaving
open whether they are addressing the true God, or whether they are addressing idols. This depends on the quality of their response: *yes, no,* or
*yes, but.*

In a "primitive" society, as we saw in an earlier section, religion is
not separately embodied in a distinct institution, but constitutes a powerful
intrinsic part of everything. However, in the absence of alternatives, it may
well be taken for granted and observed in a quite relaxed, unreflective way
by many devotees.

In a complex, urban society, religion is embodied in a distinct institution and has important full-time functionaries, most often priests who are
charged with custody of temple and ritual. It often at least aspires to supreme control through its monopoly on access to the Ultimate; but it also
often finds itself challenged by or even subservient to the political institution. Moreover, because it at least potentially has a true sense of transcendence, it can give rise to prophets who may in the name of the Ultimate
challenge the status quo. This was, of course, what happened in ancient

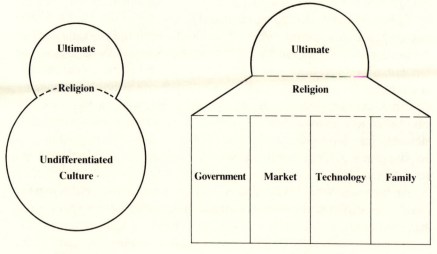

MODEL 1                                         MODEL 2

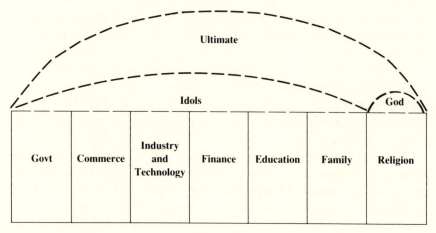

MODEL 3

Israel. But it also happened with the work of Gautama Siddharta and with Muhammad.

In a secularized modern society, where the religious institution is only one among many quite distinct, specialized, and autonomous institutions—the state, the economy, and the academy being three others—and rarely the most important, there is plenty of room for religion to be nominal, and for the ultimate allegiance of people to be elsewhere, in quite other domains. But since "ultimate" is another designation for "god," whatever is ultimate for people—money, national security, scientific progress, personal self-realization—is their idol.[40]

It is in just such a society that Luther's doctrine of the two kingdoms can be most dangerous: one where the overarching societal commitment to a dominant religious perspective is lost, and the other institutions have achieved virtually total autonomy, so that they project their own idols for the worship of the people.

But I must conclude this section. Religion as the organized *human response* to whatever information is available about the Ultimate—what I would theologically call "revelation"—is indeed a part of culture: it comprises beliefs formulated in verbal and symbolic forms provided by a language and culture and consonant with a cultural worldview. It comprises rituals which are nothing if not cultural. It comprises specialists and experts. It comprises human membership and concomitant ideas of group dynamics. In all of these ways, religion is cultural and culturally relative and contingent. Revelation itself is not a part of culture; it is the initiative of God, the only Absolute, the only Ultimate. But the human response to revelation, religion, is a part of culture.

## Conclusions

Culture, I have said, is a very complex but very human reality. Indeed, it comprises everything that human beings think, feel, say, and do as human beings, as persons who have realized their God-given potential by means of social processes. It binds social groups together and guides their corporate life and activity. It enables human groups to relate usefully and creatively to the environment in which they dwell. It is, consequently, impossible to understand the human condition without understanding cul-

---

[40]Charles R. Taber, "God vs Idols: A Model of Conversion," *Journal of the Academy for Evangelism in Theological Education* 3 (1987–1988): 20-32.

ture. Christians who are seriously committed to sharing the gospel of Jesus Christ with other human beings must understand the cultures of those beings in order to make authentic contact with them, so that the gospel is truly good news for them and not mere propaganda.

Anthropology, and especially its central concept, "culture," offers important tools for understanding the cultures which missionaries encounter. But anthropology is also a particular cultural endeavor, limited and limiting. Its philosophical underpinnings are not fully, and sometimes not at all, compatible with a Christian view of things.

So what should Christians do with anthropology and its assistance? Should they reject it because of its flaws? Should they adopt it wholesale because of its utility? Or should they not, as Origen advised Gregory Thaumaturgus in the third century, "despoil the Egyptians" with careful discrimination, using what gold they offer to build a tabernacle among human beings for God? The question, it seems to me, answers itself.

# Bibliography

Adeney, Miriam. *God's Foreign Policy*. Grand Rapids: William B. Eerdmans Pub. Co., 1984.

Allen, Roland. *Missionary Methods: St Paul's or Ours?* Repr. Grand Rapids: William B. Eerdmans Pub. Co., 1962. ¹1912.

_____. *The Spontaneous Expansion of the Church and the Causes that Hinder It*. Repr. Grand Rapids: William B. Eerdmans Pub. Co., 1962. ¹1927.

Anderson, Rufus. *To Advance the Gospel*. Ed. R. Pierce Beaver. Grand Rapids: William B. Eerdmans Pub. Co., 1971.

*Assembly Record, The*. 1899–1920.

Baëta, C. G., ed. *Christianity in Tropical Africa*. London: Oxford University Press, 1968.

Barnett, Homer G. *Innovation. The Basis of Cultural Change*. New York: McGraw-Hill, 1953.

Barney, G. Linwood. "The Supracultural and the Cultural: Implications for Frontier Missions." In *The Gospel and Frontier Missions*, ed. R. Pierce Beaver, 48-57. South Pasadena CA: William Carey Library, 1973.

_____. "The Challenge of Anthropology to Current Missiology." *International Bulletin of Missionary Research* 5 (October 1981): 172-77.

Barth, Karl. *Church Dogmatics*. Vol. 1, part 2. Trans. G. T. Thomson and Harold Knight. Repr. Edinburgh: T. & T. Clark, 1956. ¹1932.

Beaver, R. Pierce. *Ecumenical Beginnings in Protestant World Mission*. New York: Thomas Nelson & Sons, 1962.

_____. *Church, State, and the American Indians*. St. Louis: Concordia Pub. House, 1966.

_____. *American Protestant Women in World Mission*. Rev. ed. Grand Rapids: William B. Eerdmans Pub. Co., 1980.

Bede, Saint, the Venerable. *Ecclesiastical History of the English Nation*. Ca. C.E. 731-32.

Beekman, John, and John Callow. *Translating the Word of God*. Grand Rapids: Zondervan Pub. Co., 1974.

Benedict, Ruth. *Patterns of Culture*. Boston: Houghton Mifflin Co., 1934.

_____. *The Chrysanthemum and the Sword*. Boston: Houghton Mifflin, 1946.

Besier, Gerhard. "Mission and Colonialism in Friedrich Fabris." In *Missionary Ideologies in the Imperialist Era: 1880–1920*, ed. Torbin Christensen and William R. Hutchison. Aarhus, Denmark: Aros, 1982.

Bidney, David. *Theoretical Anthropology*. New York: Columbia University Press, 1953.

_____. "Cultural Relativism." In *International Encyclopedia of the Social Sciences*, ed. David L. Sills, 3:543-47. New York: The Macmillan Co., 1968.

Block-Hoell, Nils E. "Norwegian Mission to South Africa 1880–1920: Colonialistic Confrontation or Apostolic Approach?" In *Missionary Ideologies in the Imperialist Era: 1880–1920*, ed. Torbin Christensen and William R. Hutchison, 13-22. Aarhus, Denmark: Aros, 1982.

Boas, Franz. *Contribution to the Ethnography of the Kwakiutl*. New York: Columbia University Press, 1923.

_____. *General Anthropology*. Boston: D. C. Heath, 1935.

_____. *Race, Language and Culture*. New York: The Macmillan Co., 1940.

Bosch, David J. "The Structure of Mission: An Exposition of Matthew 28:16-20." In *Exploring Church Growth*, ed. Wilbert R. Shenk, 218-48. Grand Rapids: William B. Eerdmans Pub. Co., 1983.

Brown, Ina Corinne. "The Anthropological Approach." In *Christian World Mission*, ed. William K. Anderson. Nashville: Commission on Ministerial Training, The Methodist Church, 1946.

Buell, Raymond Leslie. *The Native Problem in Africa*. 2 vols. New York: The Macmillan Co., 1928.

Buxton, T. F. *The African Slave Trade and Its Remedy*. Repr. London: Pall Mall, 1968. ¹1838.

Carpenter, Joel A., and Wilbert R. Shenk, eds. *Earthen Vessels: American Evangelicals and Foreign Missions, 1880–1980*. Grand Rapids: William B. Eerdmans Pub. Co., 1990.

Childe, V. Gordon. *What Happened in History?* New York: Pelican Books, 1946.

Chomsky, Noam. *Language and Mind*. New York: Harcourt, Brace & World, 1968.

Christensen, Torbin, and William R. Hutchison, eds. *Missionary Ideologies in the Imperialist Era: 1880–1920*. Aarhus, Denmark: Aros, 1982.

*Church at Home and Abroad, The*. 1887–1898.

Clooney, Francis X. "Roberto de Nobili: Adaptation and Reasonable Interpretation of Religion." *Missiology* 18 (January 1990): 25-36.

Codrington, R. H. *The Melanesians*. Repr. New Haven CT: HRAF (Human Relations Area Files) Press, 1957; Oxford: The Clarendon Press, 1891.

Conklin, Harold. "Hanunoó Color Categories." *Southwestern Journal of Anthropology* 11 (1955): 339-44.

Conn, Harvie M. *Eternal Word and Changing Worlds*. Grand Rapids: Zondervan Pub. Co., Academie Books, 1984.

Corwin, Charles. "Cultural Diversity as a Dynamic for Church Growth." *Evangelical Missions Quarterly* 17 (1981): 15-21.

Cove, A. Cleveland, ed. *Fathers of the Third Century*. Vol. 6 of *The Ante-Nicene Fathers*. Repr. Grand Rapids: William B. Eerdmans Pub. Co., 1951.

Curtin, Philip D. " 'Scientific' Racism and the British Theory of Empire." *Journal of the Historical Society of Nigeria* 2 (1960).

Dawson, Christopher. *Religion and the Rise of Western Civilization*. Garden City NJ: Image Books, 1958.

Deloria, Vine, Jr., *Custer Died for Your Sins. An Indian Manifesto*. New York: Avon Books, 1971.

Dennis, James S. *Christian Missions and Social Progress*. 3 vols. New York: Fleming H. Revell Co., 1897, 1899, 1906.

Donovan, Vincent J. *Christianity Rediscovered: An Epistle from the Masai*. Maryknoll NY: Orbis Books, 1982.

Douglas, Mary. *Natural Symbols: Explorations in Cosmology*. New York: Vintage Books, 1973.

_____, ed. *Rules and Meanings: The Anthropology of Everyday Knowledge*. Harmondsworth, England: Penguin Books, 1973.

Drahan, Michael. "Christianity, Culture and the Meaning of Mission." *International Review of Mission* 75 (July 1986): 285-303.

Durkheim, Emile. *The Elementary Forms of the Religious Life*. Trans. John Ward Swain. Repr. New York: Collins Books, 1961. [1]1915.

Eggan, Fred. "Ethnology and Social Anthropology." In *One Hundred Years of Anthropology*, ed. J. O. Brew. Cambridge MA: Harvard University Press, 1968.

Ellul, Jacques. *The Technological Society*. Trans. John Wilkinson. New York: Alfred A. Knopf, 1970.

Evans-Pritchard, E. E. *Witchcraft, Oracles and Magic Among the Azande*. Oxford: The Clarendon Press, 1965.

——————. *Theories of Primitive Religion*. Oxford: The Clarendon Press, 1965.

Filbeck, David. *Social Context and Proclamation*. Pasadena: William Carey Library, 1985.

Fischer, John L. *The Eastern Carolines*. New Haven CT: HRAF (Human Relations Area Files) Press, 1970.

Forman, Charles W. "Missions in Papua New Guinea." In *Missionary Ideologies in the Imperialist Era: 1880–1920*, ed. Torbin Christensen and William R. Hutchison, 23-33. Aarhus, Denmark: Aros, 1982.

"For the Liberation of the Indians (Barbados Declaration)." *International Review of Mission* 60 (1971): 277-84.

Fox, Charles E. *The Threshold of the Pacific: An Account of the Social Organization Magic and Religion of the People of San Cristoval in the Solomon Islands*. London: Kegan Paul, Trench, Trubner, and Co., 1924.

Frazer, James G. *The Golden Bough: A Study in Magic and Religion*. 12 vols. 3rd ed. New York: The Macmillan Co., 1935. ¹1890.

Freedman, Jonathan. "An Interview with Eric Wolf." *Current Anthropology* 28/1 (February 1987): 107-18.

Freeman, Derek. *Margaret Mead and Samoa: The Making and Unmaking of an Anthropological Myth*. Cambridge MA: Harvard University Press, 1983.

Freud, Sigmund. *Totem and Taboo*. Trans. James Strachey. New York: Norton, 1952.

——————. *The Future of an Illusion*. Trans. W. D. Robson-Scott. New York: Norton, 1957; orig. 1927.

Geertz, Clifford. *The Interpretation of Cultures*. New York: Basic Books, 1973.

——————. *Local Knowledge*. New York: Basic Books, 1983.

——————. *Islam Observed: Religious Development in Morocco and Indonesia*. New Haven CT: Yale University Press, 1968.

Glüer, Winfrid. "German Protestant Missions in China." In *Missionary Ideologies in the Imperialist Era: 1880–1920*, ed. Torbin Christensen and William R. Hutchison. Aarhus, Denmark: Aros, 1982.

Goldschmidt, Walter. *Comparative Functionalism: An Essay in Anthropological Theory*. Berkeley and Los Angeles: University of California Press, 1966.

Goodenough, Ward H. "Componential Analysis and the Study of Meaning." *Language* 32 (1956): 195-216.

_____. *Property, Kin, and Community on Truk.* 2nd ed. Hamden CT: Archon Books, 1978.

Gordon, Robert. "On the Myth of the Savage Other." *Current Anthropology* 30 (April 1989): 205.

_____. "Radcliffe-Brown in South Africa and the Origins of the Intellectual Critique of Apartheid." Unpublished paper, n.d.

Graebner, Fritz. *Methode der Ethnologie.* Heidelberg: C. Winter, 1911.

Grunlan, Stephen A., and Marvin K. Mayers, *Cultural Anthropology: A Christian Perspective.* Grand Rapids: Zondervan Pub. Co., 1978.

Hallencreutz, Carl F. "Church-Centered Evangelism and Modernization-Emphasis in Swedish Missions 1880–1920." In *Missionary Ideologies in the Imperialist Era: 1880–1920,* ed. Torbin Christensen and William R. Hutchison, 62-74. Aarhus, Denmark: Aros, 1982.

Hamilton, Kenneth. *To Turn from Idols.* Grand Rapids: William B. Eerdmans Pub. Co., 1973.

Harris, George. "On Foreign Missions in Connection with Civilization and Anthropology." London: Bell & Daldy, 1868.

Harris, Marvin. *The Rise of Anthropological Theory.* New York: Thomas Y. Crowell Co., 1968.

Hatch, Elvin. *Culture and Morality: The Relativity of Values in Anthropology.* New York: Columbia University Press, 1983.

Hay, Alexander Rattray. *Saints and Savages: Brazil's Indian Problem.* London: Hodder & Stoughton, (?)1924.

Headland, Isaac Taylor. *Some By-Products of Missions.* New York: The Methodist Book Concern, 1912.

Henry, Carl F. H. "Comment on 'Is There More than One Way to Do Theology.' " *Gospel in Context* 1/1 (January 1978): 22-23.

_____. *God, Revelation, and Authority.* 6 vols. Waco TX: Word Books, 1976–1983.

Herskovits, Melville J. *Man and His Works: The Science of Cultural Anthropology.* New York: Alfred A. Knopf, 1948.

_____. *Acculturation: The Study of Culture Contact.* Gloucester MA: P. Smith, 1958.

_____. *Cultural Relativism.* Ed. Frances Herskovits. New York: Vintage Books, 1973.

Hick, John, ed. *The Myth of God Incarnate*. London: SCM Press, 1977.

Hick, John, and Paul Knitter, eds. *The Myth of Christian Uniqueness*. Maryknoll NY: Orbis Books, 1985.

Hiebert, Paul G. *Cultural Anthropology*. Philadelphia: J. B. Lippincott, 1976.

—————. *Anthropological Insights for Missionaries*. Grand Rapids: Baker Book House, 1985.

Hoekendijk, J. C. "A Perspective on Indonesia." In *Christopaganism or Indigenous Christianity?*, ed. Tetsunao Yamamori and Charles R. Taber, 75. South Pasadena: William Carey Library, 1975.

*Home and Foreign Record of the Presbyterian Church, The*. 1850–1870.

Horne, Melville. *Letters on Missions, Addressed to the Protestant Ministers of the British Churches*. Andover: Flagg and Gould, 1815.

Hunter, Jane. *The Gospel of Gentility: American Women Missionaries in Turn-of-the-Century China*. New Haven CT: Yale University Press, 1984.

Hutchison, William R. "Modernism in Missions: the Liberal Search for an Exportable Christianity." In *Christianity in China*, ed. John K. Fairbank. Cambridge MA: Harvard University Press, 1974.

International Missionary Council. *Report of the Jerusalem Conference*. Vol. 4. *The Christian Mission in Light of Race Conflict*. Vol. 5. *The Christian Mission in Relation to Industrial Problems*. Vol. 6. *The Christian Mission in Relation to Rural Problems*. New York and London: International Missionary Council, 1928.

Jacobs, Donald R. "Culture and the Phenomena of Conversion." *Gospel in Context* 1/2 (April 1978): 4-14.

—————. *Pilgrimage in Mission*. Scottdale PA: Herald Press, 1983.

Jäschke, Ernst. "Bruno Guttmann's Legacy." *International Bulletin of Missionary Research* 4/4 (October 1980): 165-69.

Johnston, James, ed. *Report of the Centenary Conference on the Protestant Missions in the World*. 2 vols. London: James Nesbit & Co., 1888.

Junod, Henri A. *The Life of a South African Tribe*. 2nd ed. London: The Macmillan Co., 1927.

Keysser, Christian. *A People Reborn*. Trans. Alfred Allin and John Kuder. Pasadena: William Carey Library, 1980.

Knitter, Paul. *No Other Name?* Maryknoll NY: Orbis Books, 1985.

Koop, Allen V. *American Evangelical Missionaries in France 1945–1975*. Lanham MD: University Press of America, 1986.

_____. "American Evangelical Missionaries in France 1945–1975." In *Earthen Vessels: American Evangelicals and Foreign Missions, 1880–1980*, ed. Joel A. Carpenter and Wilbert R. Shenk, 180-202. Grand Rapids: William B. Eerdmans Pub. Co., 1990.

Kraemer, Hendrik. *The Christian Message in a Non-Christian World*. New York: Harper & Row, for the International Missionary Council, 1938.

Kraft, Charles H. "An Anthropological Apologetic for the Homogeneous Unit Principle in Missiology." *Occasional Bulletin of Missionary Research* 2 (1978): 120-26.

_____. *Christianity in Culture*. Maryknoll NY: Orbis Books, 1979.

Krass, Alfred C. *Five Lanterns at Sundown: Evangelism in a Chastened Mood*. Grand Rapids: William B. Eerdmans Pub. Co., 1978.

_____. "Mission as Inter-Cultural Encounter—A Sociological Perspective." In *Down to Earth*, ed. Robert T. Coote and John Stott, 231-45. Grand Rapids: William B. Eerdmans Pub. Co., 1980.

Kroeber, Alfred L. *Anthropology*. New York: Harcourt, Brace & Co., 1923.

_____. *Configurations of Culture Growth*. Berkeley CA: University of California Press, 1944.

_____. *The Nature of Culture*. Chicago: University of Chicago Press, 1952.

Kroeber, Alfred L., and Clyde Kluckhohn. *Culture: A Critical Review of Concepts and Definitions*. Anthropological Papers 47/1. Cambridge MA: Peabody Museum, 1952.

Küng, Hans. *Theology for the Third Millenium*. New York: Doubleday, 1988.

Kuper, Adam. *The Invention of Primitive Society: The Making and Unmaking of an Illusion*. London and New York: Routledge, 1988.

Latourette, Kenneth Scott. *The Great Century*. Vols. 5 and 6 of *A History of the Expansion of Christianity*. Repr. Grand Rapids: William B. Eerdmans Pub. Co., 1970. ¹1943, 1944.

Laurie, Thomas. *The Ely Volume: Or, the Contributions of Our Foreign Missions to Science and Human Well-Being*. Boston: American Board of Commissioners for Foreign Missions, 1881.

Laymen's Foreign Mission Inquiry, Commission of Appraisal, William E. Hocking, chair. *Re-Thinking Missions*. New York: Harper & Bros., 1932.

Leenhardt, Maurice. *Do Kamo: Person and Myth in Melanesia*. Trans. Basia Miller Gulati. Chicago: University of Chicago Press, 1979; 1947.

Lévi-Strauss, Claude. *Structural Anthropology*. Trans. Claire Jacobson and Brooke Grunfest Schoepf. New York: Basic Books, 1963.

——————. *The Elementary Structures of Kinship*. Trans. James Harle Bell and Richard von Sturmer. Ed. Rodney Needham. Boston: Beacon Books, 1969.

——————. *The Raw and the Cooked*. Trans. John and Doreen Weightman. New York: Harper & Row, 1969.

Lévy-Bruhl, Lucien. *How Natives Think*. Trans. Lilian A. Clare. New York: Washington Square Press, 1966; orig. 1910.

——————. *Primitive Mentality*. Trans. Lilian A. Clare. New York: The Macmillan Co., 1923; orig. 1922.

Lewis, Oscar. "The Culture of Poverty." *Scientific American* 215 (1966): 19-25.

——————. *Life in a Mexican Village: Tepoztlán Restudied*. Urbana: University of Illinois Press, 1963.

Lindsell, Harold. *Missionary Principles and Practice*. Old Tappan NJ: Fleming H. Revell Co., 1955.

Lingenfelter, Sherwood G., and Marvin K. Mayers. *Ministering Cross-Culturally*. Grand Rapids: Baker Book House, 1986.

Lipner, Julius. " 'Being One, Let Me Be Many': Facets of the Relationship between the Gospel and Culture." *International Review of Mission* 74 (April 1985): 158-68.

Loewen, Jacob A. *Culture and Human Values*. Ed. William A. Smalley. Pasadena: William Carey Library, 1975.

Loewen, Jacob A., and Anne Loewen. "The 'Missionary' Role." In Jacob A. Loewen, *Culture and Human Values*, ed. William A. Smalley, 428-43. Pasadena: William Carey Library, 1975.

Lounsbury, Floyd G. "A Semantic Analysis of the Pawnee Kinship Usage." *Language* 32 (1956): 158-94.

Lowie, Robert H. *Primitive Religion*. New York: Boni and Liveright, 1924.

Luzbetak, Louis J., S.V.D. *The Church and Cultures: New Perspectives in Missiological Anthropology*. Maryknoll NY: Orbis Books, 1988.

——————. "Prospects for Better Understanding and Closer Cooperation between Anthropologists and Missionaries." In *Missionaries, Anthropologists, and Culture Change*, vol. 1., ed. Darrell L. Whiteman, 1-53. Williamsburg VA: Department of Anthropology, College of William and Mary, 1985.

McGavran, Donald A. *Understanding Church Growth*. Rev. ed. Grand Rapids: William B. Eerdmans Pub. Co., 1980.

——————. "The Priority of Ethnicity." *Evangelical Missions Quarterly* 19 (1983): 14-23.

Malina, Bruce J. *The New Testament World: Insights from Cultural Anthropology.* Atlanta: John Knox Press, 1981.

Malinowski, Bronislaw. *Argonauts of the Western Pacific.* London: Routledge, 1922.

_____. *Coral Gardens and Their Magic.* 2 vols. New York: American Book Co., 1935.

Mead, Margaret. *Coming of Age in Samoa.* New York: William Morrow, 1928.

_____. *New Lives for Old: Cultural Transformation, Manus, 1928–1953.* New York: William Morrow, 1966.

Miller, Elmer. "The Christian Missionary: Agent of Secularization." *Missiology* 1/1 (January 1973): 99–107.

Miller, Stuart Creighton. *Benevolent Association.* New Haven and London: Yale University Press, 1982.

*Ministry in Context: The Third Mandate Programme of the Theological Education Fund 1971–1977.* Bromley, England: Theological Education Fund, 1972.

*Missionary Chronicle, The.* 1833–1849.

Mobley, Harris W. "The Ghanaian's Image of the Missionary: An Analysis of the Published Critiques of Christian Missionaries by Ghanaians, 1867–1965." Ph.D. diss., Hartford Seminary Foundation (Hartford CT), 1966.

Morgan, Lewis Henry. *Ancient Society.* New York: Henry Holt and Co., 1877.

Nacpil, Emerito P. "Mission But Not Missionaries." *International Review of Mission* 60/239 (July 1971): 356–62.

Neill, Stephen. *A History of Christian Missions.* Harmondsworth, England: Penguin Books, 1964.

Nida, Eugene A. *Bible Translating.* New York: American Bible Society, 1947.

_____. *God's Word in Man's Language.* New York: Harper & Bros., 1952.

_____. *Customs and Cultures.* Repr. Pasadena: William Carey Library, 1975. New York: Harper & Bros., 1954.

_____. *Message and Mission.* New York: Harper & Row, 1960.

_____. *Toward a Science of Translating.* Leiden: E. J. Brill, 1964.

_____. *Componential Analysis of Meaning.* The Hague: Mouton, 1975.

Nida, Eugene A., and Charles R. Taber. *Theory and Practice of Translation.* Leiden: E. J. Brill, 1969.

Niebuhr, H. Richard. *Christ and Culture.* New York: Harper & Row Colophon Books, 1951.

_____. *The Social Sources of Denominationalism*. Repr. Cleveland: World/ Meridian Books, 1962; New York: Henry Holt, 1929.

Norris, Frederick W. "Strategy for Mission in the New Testament." In *Exploring Church Growth*, ed. Wilbert R. Shenk, 260-76. Grand Rapids: William B. Eerdmans Pub. Co., 1983.

Nottingham, Elizabeth K. *Religion: A Sociological View*. New York: Random House, 1971.

Oberg, Kalervo. "Cultural Shock: Adjustment to New Cultural Environments." *Practical Anthropology* 7/4 (July-August 1960): 177-82.

Oldham, J. H. *Christianity and the Race Problem*. London: SCM Press, 1924.

Padilla, C. René. "The Unity of the Church and the Homogeneous Unit Principle." In *Exploring Church Growth*, ed. Wilbert R. Shenk, 285-303. Grand Rapids: William B. Eerdmans Pub. Co., 1983.

Panikkar, Raimundo. *The Interreligious Dialogue*. New York: Paulist Press, 1978.

Parshall, Phil. *Bridges to Islam*. Grand Rapids: Baker Book House, 1983.

Penniman, T. K. *One Hundred Years of Anthropology*. New York: William Morrow and Co., 1974; 1935.

Pierard, Richard V. "*Pax Americana* and the Evangelical Missionary." In *Earthen Vessels: American Evangelicals and Foreign Missions, 1880–1980*, ed. Joel A. Carpenter and Wilbert R. Shenk. Grand Rapids: William B. Eerdmans Pub. Co., 1990.

Piggin, Stuart. *Making Evangelical Missionaries 1789–1858*. N.p.: The Sutton Courtenay Press, 1984.

Pike, Kenneth L. *Language in Relation to a Unified Theory of the Structure of Human Behavior*. Vol. 1. Glendale CA: Summer Institute of Linguistics, 1954.

Platt, Donald C. "An Anthropological Approach to Mission: Bruno Guttmann in Kilimanjaro." In *The Gospel and Frontier Peoples*, ed. R. Pierce Beaver, 137-53. South Pasadena: William Carey Library, 1973.

Pobee, John S. "The People of God and the Peoples." In *Exploring Church Growth*, ed. Wilbert R. Shenk, 181-90. Grand Rapids: William B. Eerdmans Pub. Co., 1983.

*Preparation of Missionaries, The. See* World Missionary Conference.

*Presbyterian Monthly Record, The*. 1871–1886.

Radcliffe-Brown, A. A. *The Andaman Islanders*. Cambridge: Cambridge University Press, 1922.

Radin, Paul. *Primitive Religion: Its Nature and Origin*. New York: Viking Press, 1937.

Redfield, Robert. *The Folk Culture of Yucatan*. Chicago: University of Chicago Press, 1941.

_____. *The Primitive World and Its Transformations*. Ithaca NY: Cornell University Press, 1953.

_____. *The Little Community and Peasant Society*. Chicago: University of Chicago Press, 1960.

_____. *Tepoztlán, a Mexican Village: A Study of Folk Life*. Chicago: University of Chicago Press, 1946.

Renteln, Alison Dundes. "Relativism and the Search for Human Rights." *American Anthropologist* 90/1 (March 1988): 56-72.

*Re-Thinking Missions*. See Laymen's Foreign Mission Inquiry.

Reyburn, William D. "Identification in the Missionary Task." In *Readings in Missionary Anthropology II*, ed. William A. Smalley, 746-56. South Pasadena: William Carey Library, 1978.

_____. "Identification—Symptom or Sublimation?" In *Readings in Missionary Anthropology II*, ed. William A. Smalley, 757-67. South Pasadena: William Carey Library, 1978.

Richardson, Don. *Peace Child*. Glendale CA: Regal Books Division, G/L Publications, 1974.

_____. *Eternity in Their Hearts*. Ventura CA: Regal Books, 1984.

Robert, Dana L. " 'The Crisis of Missions': Premillenial Mission Theory and the Origins of Independent Evangelical Missions." In *Earthen Vessels: American Evangelicals and Foreign Missions, 1880–1980*, ed. Joel A. Carpenter and Wilbert R. Shenk, 29-46. Grand Rapids: William B. Eerdmans Pub. Co., 1990.

Roseberry, R. S. *The Soul of West Africa*. Harrisburg PA: Christian Publications, Inc., 1947.

Ross, Edwin B., ed. *Beyond the Myths of Culture: Essays in Cultural Materialism*. New York: Academic Press, 1980.

Salamone, Frank A. "Missionaries and Anthropologists: An Inquiry into the Ambivalent Relationship." *Missiology* 14/1 (January 1986): 55-70.

Samartha, Stanley. *Courage for Dialogue*. Geneva: World Council of Churches, 1977.

Sanders, George R., ed. *Culture and Christianity: The Dialectics of Transformation*. New York: The Greenwood Press, 1988.

Sanneh, Lamin. *Translating the Message*. Maryknoll NY: Orbis Books, 1989.

Schlunk, Martin. "Missions and Culture." *International Review of Missions* 13 (1924): 532-44.

Schott, Joseph. *The Ordeal of Samar.* New York and Indianapolis: Bobbs-Merrill, 1964.

Schmidt, Wilhelm. *The Culture Historical Method of Ethnology.* Trans. S. A. Seeker. New York: Fortuny, 1939.

Schreiter, Robert J. *Constructing Local Theologies.* Maryknoll NY: Orbis Books, 1984.

Schwartz, Theodore. *The Paliau Movement in the Admiralty Islands, 1946–1954.* Anthropological Papers of the American Museum of Natural History. Part 2. 1962.

Sharp, J. Lauriston. "Steel Axes for Stone-Age Australians." *Practical Anthropology* 7/2 (March-April 1960): 62-73.

Shenk, Wilbert R., ed. *Exploring Church Growth.* Grand Rapids: William B. Eerdmans Pub. Co., 1983.

──────. *Henry Venn—Missionary Statesman.* Maryknoll NY: Orbis Books, 1983.

Shorter, Aylward, W.F. *Toward a Theology of Inculturation.* Maryknoll NY: Orbis Books, 1988.

Singer, Milton. "Culture: The Concept of Culture." In *International Encyclopedia of the Social Sciences,* ed. David L. Sills, vol. 3. New York: The Macmillan Co., 1968.

Smalley, William A. "Culture Shock, Language Shock, and the Shock of Self-Discovery." *Practical Anthropology* 10/1 (January-February 1963): 49-56.

──────, ed. *Readings in Missionary Anthropology II.* South Pasadena: William Carey Library, 1978.

Smalley, William A., and Marie Fetzer. "A Christian View of Anthropology." In *Modern Science and Christian Faith,* ed. F. Alton Everest, 98-195. Wheaton IL: Van Kampen Press, for the American Scientific Affiliation, 1950.

Smith, Edwin W. "Social Anthropology and Mission Work." *International Review of Missions* 13 (1924): 518-31.

──────. *The Golden Stool: Some Aspects of the Conflict of Cultures in Africa.* London: Holborn Pub. House, 1927.

Smith, Gordon H. *The Missionary and Anthropology.* Chicago: Moody Press, 1945.

Soper, Edmund. *The Philosophy of the Christian World Mission.* New York: Abingdon-Cokesbury, 1943.

Stackhouse, Max L. "Contextualization and Theological Education." *Theological Education* 23/1 (Autumn 1986): 79-84.

_____. *Apologia: Contextualization, Globalization, and Mission in Theological Education.* Grand Rapids: William B. Eerdmans Pub. Co., 1988.

Stanley, Sam. "The Panajachel Symposium." *Current Anthropology* 16/4 (December 1975): 518-24.

Steward, Julian A. *Theory of Culture Change.* Urbana: University of Illinois Press, 1955.

Stipe, Claude E. "Anthropologists versus Missionaries: The Influence of Presuppositions." *Current Anthropology* 21 (April 1980): 165-79.

Sundermeier, Theo. "Missiology Yesterday and Tomorrow." *Missionalia* 18/1 (April 1990): 259-69.

Sutlive, Vinson H., Jr. "The Anthropologist and the Missionary: Irreconcilable Enemies or Colleagues in Disguise?" In *Missionaries, Anthropologists, and Culture Change,* vol. 1, ed. Darrell L. Whiteman, 55-87. Williamsburg VA: Department of Anthropology, College of William and Mary, 1985.

Sundkler, Bengt. *The World of Mission.* Grand Rapids: William B. Eerdmans Pub. Co., 1965.

Taber, Charles R. "Contextualization, Indigenization, and/or Transformation." In *The Gospel and Islam: A 1978 Compendium,* ed. Don M. McCurry. Monrovia CA: Missions Advanced Research and Communication Center, 1979.

_____. "Structures and Strategies for Interdependence in World Mission." In *Mission Focus: Current Issues,* ed. Wilbert R. Shenk. Scottdale PA: Herald Press, 1980

_____. "Culture, Ideology, and Christian Mission." In *Unto the Uttermost,* ed. Doug Priest, Jr., 155-75. Pasadena: William Carey Library, 1984.

_____. "God vs Idols: A Model of Conversion." *Journal of the Academy for Evangelism in Theological Education* 3 (1987–1988): 20-32.

Tawney, R. H. *Religion and the Rise of Capitalism.* New York: Harcourt, Brace and Co., 1926.

Tax, Sol. "Action Anthropology." *Current Anthropology* 16/4 (December 1975): 514-17.

Tempels, Placide. *La phiolosophie bantoue.* 3rd ed. Paris: Présence Africaine, 1949.

Tillich, Paul. *Theology of Culture.* Ed. Robert C. Kimball. New York: Oxford University Press, 1959.

Tippett, Alan R. *Solomon Islands Christianity.* London: Lutterworth Press, 1967.

Turner, Victor W. *The Forest of Symbols: Aspects of Ndembu Ritual.* Ithaca NY and London: Cornell University Press, 1967.

_____. *The Ritual Process*. Chicago: Aldine Pub. Co., 1969.

Tylor, Edward B. *Primitive Culture*. 2 vols. New York: Henry Holt & Co., 1889; 1871.

Venn, Henry. *To Apply the Gospel*. Ed. Max Warren. Grand Rapids: William B. Eerdmans Pub. Co., 1967.

Villa-Vicencio, Charles. *Trapped in Apartheid*. Maryknoll NY: Orbis Books, 1988.

Waard, Jan de, and Eugene A. Nida. *From One Language to Another*. Nashville: Thomas Nelson and Sons, 1986.

Wagner, C. Peter. *Our Kind of People*. Atlanta: John Knox Press, 1979.

Wallace, Anthony F. C. "Revitalization Movements: Some Theoretical Considerations for Their Comparative Study." *American Anthropologist* 58 (1956): 264-81.

_____. *Religion: An Anthropological View*. New York: Random House, 1966.

Wallerstein, Immanuel. *The Modern World-System: Capitalist Agriculture and the Origin of the European World-Economy in the Sixteenth Century*. New York: Academic Press, 1974.

_____. *The Capitalist World-Economy*. Cambridge: Cambridge University Press, 1979.

Walls, Andrew F. "British Missions." In *Missionary Ideologies in the Imperialist Era: 1880–1920*, ed. Torbin Christensen and William R. Hutchison, 159-66. Aarhus, Denmark: Aros, 1982.

_____. " 'The Best Thinking of the Best Heathen': Human Learning and the Missionary Movement." In *Religion and Humanism*, ed. Keith Robbins,. Oxford: Basil Blackwell, for the Ecclesiastical Historical Society, 1981.

_____. "The American Dimension in the History of the Missionary Movement." In *Earthen Vessels: American Evangelicals and Foreign Missions, 1880–1980*, ed. Joel A. Carpenter and Wilbert R. Shenk, 1-25. Grand Rapids: William B. Eerdmans Pub. Co., 1990.

Warneck, Gustav. *Outline of a History of Protestant Missions from the Reformation to the Present Time*. Trans. and ed. George Robson. New York: Fleming H. Revell, (?)1901.

Westermarck, Edward. *A History of Marriage*. 3 vols. London: The Macmillan Co., 1891.

White, Leslie A. *The Evolution of Culture*. New York: McGraw-Hill, 1959.

Whiteman, Darrell L. *An Introduction to Melanesian Cultures*. Goroka, Papua New Guinea: The Melanesian Institute, 1984.

_____, guest ed. *Missionaries, Anthropologists, and Culture Change*. Vol. 1. Williamsburg VA: Department of Anthropology, College of William and Mary, 1985.

Williams, F. E. *The Blending of Cultures: An Essay on the Aims of Native Education*. Anthropological Reports no. 16. Territory of Papua, 1935.

Wolterstorff, Nicholas. *Until Justice and Peace Embrace*. Grand Rapids: William B. Eerdmans Pub. Co., 1983.

World Missionary Conference. *The Preparation of Missionaries*. Report of Commission 5. Edinburgh: Oliphant, Anderson and Ferrier; New York: Fleming H. Revell Co., 1910.

Worsley, Peter. *The Trumpet Shall Sound: A Study of Cargo Cults in Melanesia*. 2nd ed. New York: Schocken Books, 1968.

# INDEX